$ELLEBRITY
MY ANGLING AND TANGLING
WITH FAMOUS PEOPLE
GEORGE LOIS

GEORGE LOIS DIRECTING JOE NAMATH
TYPING A LETTER ON AN OLIVETTI,
BEING DICTATED BY HIS FLIRTATIOUS
FEMALE BOSS.

$ELLEBRITY

1. **FLOYD PATTERSON** LEFT FOR DEAD IN THE RING (ESQUIRE)
2. **BROOKLYN DODGERS** THINKING OF GOING TO LOS ANGELES? (AMERICAN AIRLINES)
3. **YOGI BERRA** TALKS TO A CAT WITH A LONG ISLAND ACCENT: **WHITEY FORD** (PUSS 'N BOOTS)
4. **ANDY WARHOL** DROWNING IN A GIANT CAN OF CAMPBELL'S SOUP (ESQUIRE)
5. **MUHAMMAD ALI** PALM READING OF ALI'S HAND IN ALI/FRAZIER III FIGHT PROGRAM (CUTTY SARK)
6. **PAT BENATAR, DAVID BOWIE, BOY GEORGE, DIRE STRAITS, EURYTHMICS, HALL & OATES, HUEY LEWIS AND THE NEWS, BILLY IDOL, MICHAEL JACKSON, MICK JAGGER, CYNDI LAUPER, MADONNA, GEORGE MICHAEL, STEVIE NICKS, POLICE, LIONEL RICHIE, TEARS FOR FEARS, THUNDERBIRDS, PETE TOWNSHEND, VAN HALEN, ZZ TOP** "I WANT MY MTV" (MTV)
7. **JOE NAMATH** "MY OLD PAL OVALTINE!" (OVALTINE)
8. **NAUGA** THE BIRTH OF AN UGLY CELEBRITY SPOKESMAN (UNIROYAL)
9. **ADOLF HITLER** SEARCHING FOR HITLER IN GERMANTOWN (ESQUIRE)
10. **NEW YORK YANKEES** OPENING DAY LINEUP WITH AN ITALIAN ACCENT (TRATTORIA)
11. **ALEXANDER HAMILTON** OUR PLEDGE TO THE FOUNDER OF THE POST (NEW YORK POST)
12. **SUSAN BLAKELY** BECOMES A STAR BY MILKING A COW (REVLON)
13. **JIMMY BRESLIN** "HELLO? EDWARDS & H-H-HANLY?" (EDWARDS & HANLY)
14. **MICKEY MANTLE** "I'M LEARNIN'. I'M LEARNIN.'" (EDWARDS & HANLY)
15. **BOBBY RIGGS, MARGARET COURT SMITH, BILLIE JEAN KING** MEN VS. WOMEN (CUTTY SARK)
16. **FLOYD PATTERSON** DEFENDS **"CASSIUS CLAY"** (ESQUIRE)
17. **GARRY KASPAROV VS. ANATOLY KARPOV** NOSE TO NOSE (1990 WORLD CHESS CHAMPIONSHIP)
18. **ROBERT BENCHLEY** IMMEDIATE AMBIANCE (CHARLEY O'S)
19. **ALGER HISS** PRESENTS A TYPEWRITER TO SPORTSWRITER **RED SMITH** (SPORT MAGAZINE)
20. **MONA LISA, PINOCCHIO, JAWS** WHY IS THIS SHARK LAUGHING? (ORTHODONTIST CENTERS OF AMERICA)
21. **SONNY LISTON** THE FIRST BLACK SANTA (ESQUIRE)
22. **JACK NICHOLSON, PETER FONDA, DENNIS HOPPER** ST. PATRICK'S EASY RIDER MARQUEE (ESQUIRE)
23. **PAUL REVERE** THE SHOT HEARD 'ROUND THE WORLD (RONRICO RUM)
24. **ROBERT MOSES, MOSES & GOD** "MOSES–THOU SHALT NOT BUILD A ROAD" (COMMITTEE TO SAVE FIRE ISLAND)
25. **CHIEF JOHNNY BIG TREE** THE MAN WHO POSED FOR THE INDIAN NICKEL (ESQUIRE)
26. **BOB DYLAN** JOKERMAN, MTV BEST VIDEO OF THE YEAR (COLUMBIA RECORDS)
27. **SUSAN ANTON, MARVIN HAGLER, TELLY SAVALAS** "I'M JUST WILD ABOUT HARRAH'S!" (HARRAH'S)
28. **SENATOR JACOB JAVITS** THE MISSING CAMPAIGN PORTRAIT (1962 RE-ELECTION CAMPAIGN)
29. **PRIEST ON $64,000 QUESTION** 15 MINUTES OF FAME (CBS TELEVISION)

79. **MARILYN MONROE** INVITATION TO SEVEN YEAR ANNIVERSARY (LHC)

80. **LEEZA GIBBONS, CHRIS EVERT, RITA MORENO, SUSAN LUCCI, KATHY MATTEA, HEATHER WHITESTONE**
MYSTERY CELEBS: WHOSE LEGS ARE THESE? (NO NONSENSE LEGWEAR)

81. **MAYOR JOHN LINDSAY** AWOL AT THE HARLEM ICE HOUSE (ESQUIRE)

82. **SUSAN SARANDON** ON TV AS A "YOUNG MAMA" IN 1967 (REDBOOK MAGAZINE)

83. **SANDY DUNCAN** SINGS "I'M YOUR MOTHER" (LESTOIL)

84. **AUNT JEMIMA** CREATING AUNT JEMIMA SYRUP (QUAKER)

85. **ROBERT KENNEDY** RUTHLESS BOBBY TAKES ON THE SILVER-HAIRED GRANDPA (1964 SENATE CAMPAIGN)

86. **DR. SPOCK** "WHAT KIND OF BABY WAS DR. SPOCK?" (LADIES' HOME JOURNAL)

87. **LT. WILLIAM CALLEY** A KILLER CELEBRITY COVER (ESQUIRE)

88. **MICHAEL JACKSON, SHIRLEY TEMPLE, E.T., MOZART, KELSO, CATS, RIN TIN TIN**
5TH ANNIVERSARY: FAMOUS 5-YEAR-OLDS (USA TODAY)

89. **HUBERT HUMPHREY** THE DUMMY ON THE LAP OF **LBJ** (ESQUIRE)

90. **WALT CLYDE FRAZIER** A COOL DUDE SUPERSTAR MODELING CLOTHES (ESQUIRE)

91. **CHARLIE CHAPLIN** THE BODYBUILDER IS A TRAMP (BOTANY '500')

92. **CARLOS SANTANA, CALVIN KLEIN, TOMMY HILFIGER, RALPH LAUREN**
THE FIRST-NAME FAME GAME (CARLOS BY CARLOS SANTANA)

93. **BOB COUSY, WHITEY FORD, BOOMER ESIASON, MRS. ALAN KING**
HOMETOWN LONG ISLAND CELEBS (CENTRAL FEDERAL SAVINGS)

94. **PHYLLIS DILLER, RICHARD (JAWS) KIEL** "I LOVE MY MUG...ROOT BEER" (PEPSI)

95. **THIRTEEN WOMEN SENATORS** THE SISTER POWER DREAM TEAM (TALK MAGAZINE)

96. **THE UNKNOWN CELEB** WHOSE EAR IS THIS? (KERID EAR DROPS)

97. **PATRICK EWING** PHOENIX SIGNS EWING (PHOENIX BASKETBALL SHOES)

98. **DUSTIN HOFFMAN** "LITTLE BIG MAN" IN NEW YORK CITY (ESQUIRE)

99. **MARCUS ALLEN, BOBBY BONILLA, DENNIS BYRD, RAY CHILDRES, ROGER CLEMENS, JOHN ELWAY, LEONARD MARSHALL, ERIC DAVIS, RICHARD DENT, MIKE DITKA, BOOMER ESIASON, JUMBO ELLIOT, DENNIS CONNER, ERNEST GIVENS, BOB GOLIC, JIM HARBAUGH, JEFF HOSTETLER, JIM KELLY, HOWIE LONG, RONNIE LOTT, DAN MARINO, WARREN MOON, GREG NORMAN, DARRYL STRAWBERRY, JOE PATERNO, RICK PITINO, ANDRE REED, LAWRENCE TAYLOR, GABRIELA SABATINI, MIKE SINGLETARY, BRUCE SMITH, THURMAN THOMAS**
"IN YOUR FACE" MAKES ESPN NO.1 (ESPN)

100. **MUSSOLINI, JIMMY CAGNEY, LYNDON JOHNSON, BURT LANCASTER, ROSALIND RUSSELL**
X-RATED CELEBRITY QUOTES ON WALLS OF MA BELL'S (RESTAURANT ASSOCIATES)

120. **BO SVENSON** "HANG OVER THIS CLIFF OR I'LL THROW YOU OFF IT!" (PUSS 'N BOOTS)

121. **KIRK DOUGLAS** IMITATES HIMSELF FOR **HOLYFIELD/TYSON** FIGHT (TVKO)

122. **RICHARD BENJAMIN, THEODORE BIKEL, TRUMAN CAPOTE, HOWARD COSELL,**
ERNEST GRUENING, MICHAEL HARRINGTON, JAMES EARL JONES, ROY LICHTENSTEIN,
SIDNEY LUMET, GEORGE PLIMPTON, BUDD SCHULBERG, JOSE TORRES
12 ANGRY MEN STAND UP FOR ALI (ESQUIRE)

123. **ELVIS PRESLEY, LESLIE UGGAMS** ELVIS LIVES! (AMERICAN CANCER SOCIETY)

124. **JACK DEMPSEY, CASEY STENGEL, BETTY GRABLE, JANE RUSSELL**
TWO MACHO MEN AND TWO HOLLYWOOD SEX SYMBOLS WHO LOVE PUSSYCATS (TABBY CAT FOOD)

125. **ED KOCH, MAYOR JOHN F. HYLAN** THE MAYOR IN 1924 ANNOUNCES THE BIRTH OF LITTLE EDDIE KOCH
(ED KOCH 60TH BIRTHDAY PARTY)

126. **NEW YORK POST REPORTERS** "WE'RE KEEPING THE SIZZLE BUT ADDING THE STEAK!" (NEW YORK POST)

127. **NORMAN JEWISON, ANDREA DROMM** A STAR IS SCORNED (NATIONAL AIRLINES)

128. **JACK LEMMON, TYNE DALY, EDWARD JAMES OLMOS** UNION, YES! (AFL-CIO)

129. **PHANTOM OF THE OPERA, AZANIA OF THE JUNGLE, ROBIN HOOD** SELLING CONDOMS ON TV (LIFESTYLES)

130. **BILL WENNINGTON** SUBSTITUTES FOR **MICHAEL JORDAN** (RITZ CAMERAS)

131. **BEARDED CELEBS** WELCOME BEARDED **DAVE MARASH** BACK TO NEW YORK (CBS-TV)

132. **REGGIE JACKSON, TOMMY TUNE, CAROL CHANNING, EARTHA KITT,**
DONALD O'CONNOR, ADAM WEST, DOWNTOWN JULIE BROWN,
HECTOR CAMACHO, NANCY SINATRA, WILT CHAMBERLAIN, GENE SHALIT,
LESLEY ANN WARREN, RITA MORENO, THE POINTER SISTERS
15 MASKED CELEBS MAKE RIO THE BIG WINNER IN VEGAS (RIO HOTEL & CASINO)

133. **ERNIE KOVACS** A DREAM DAY WITH ERNIE KOVACS TURNS INTO A NIGHTMARE (DUTCH MASTERS)

134. **GROUCHO MARX** THE LAST OF THE MARX BROTHERS LEAVES US LAUGHING (ESQUIRE)

135. **PUSS 'N BOOTS** MY CAT FOLLOWS IN THE FOOTSTEPS OF THE MOST FAMOUS CAT EVER (PUSS 'N BOOTS)

136. **TARZAN** & **JANE** SHOW UP FOR PORTRAIT, 300 LB. **BOY** STAYS HOME (ESQUIRE)

137. **SENATOR HOWARD BAKER, BILL MARRIOTT JR., JOE & DEBORAH NAMATH, JOAN COLLINS,**
WILT CHAMBERLAIN, MAYOR JANE BYRNE, CHARLES SCHWAB, DIAHANN CARROLL,
MICKEY MANTLE, WILLIE MAYS, WILLARD SCOTT SINGING FOR USA TODAY (USA TODAY)

138. **JEAN GENET, WILLIAM BURROUGHS, TERRY SOUTHERN, JOHN SACK**
AN UNDERGROUND INTELLECTUAL DREAM TEAM COVERS THE 1968 DEMOCRATIC CONVENTION (ESQUIRE)

139. **JOHN F. KENNEDY, ROBERT F. KENNEDY, DR. KING** AT ARLINGTON CEMETERY (ESQUIRE)

OBNOXIOUS CELEBS

1. **LAUREN BACALL**
   CELEBRITY FROM HELL.

2. **MICHAEL JACKSON**
   "MAKE MY NOSE THINNER, SLIM DOWN
   MY NOSTRILS, AND LIGHTEN MY SKIN."

3. **ROY COHN**
   JOE McCARTHY'S FAVORITE TERRORIST
   DURING THE '50s.

4. **ROBIN GIVENS**
   EXTRA! EXTRA! EX SLUGS IT OUT
   WITH ADMAN.

5. **RUBIN HURRICANE CARTER**
   NO GOOD DEED GOES UNPUNISHED.

6. **CALVIN KLEIN**
   DEFINITELY NOT A GOOD SPORT.

7. **WILLIE MAYS**
   "WILLIE DON'T CRY."

8. **LISA LING**
   80% OF LIFE IS SHOWING UP.

9. **ROSEANNE BARR**
   WE'RE TALKIN' SERIOUS OBNOXIOUS HERE!

10. **JACKIE ROBINSON**
    THIS ONE HURTS!

11. **RUDOLF NUREYEV**
    WHO SAYS A GENIUS CAN'T BE A JERK?

12. **IVANA TRUMP**
    ALL THAT GLITTERS IS NOT GOLD.

MY ALL-TIME FAVORITE CELEBS

1. **JOE FRAZIER**
   THE "GORILLA" SHOWS HIS CLASS.

2. **JAMES BEARD**
   THE MONUMENTAL DEAN OF CUISINE.

3. **ANDY WARHOL**
   THE INAUDIBLE VOICE OF THE AVANT-GARDE.

4. **JOE NAMATH**
   THE BABE RUTH OF HIS TIME.

5. **SALLY RAND**
   FAN-TASTIC STRIPPER.

6. **VIRNA LISI**
   SEARCHING FOR A WOMAN WITH BALLS.

7. **YOGI BERRA**
   90% OF SHOOTING A COMMERCIAL
   WITH YOGI WAS HALF MENTAL.

8. **JACQUELINE KENNEDY**
   "GEORGE, MAY I HAVE THE PLEASURE
   OF THIS DANCE?"

9. **FRANCO COLUMBU**
   THE SARDINIAN SUPERMAN.

10. **JOHN F. KENNEDY JR.**
    THE PUBLISHING PRINCE OF CAMELOT.

11. **ELLEN BURSTYN**
    "I LOVE MARCHING WITH ALI,
    BUT HE KEEPS GRABBING MY ASS."

12. **MELBA MOORE**
    MELBA MOORE GOES TO PRISON.

BONUS OBNOXIOUS LIST

JACK NICHOLSON

ROGER CLEMENS

LESLIE ANN WARREN

PETER GRAVES

PAT RILEY

ERICA JONG

RAQUEL WELCH

HEROES

1. **MUHAMMAD ALI**
   HE WAS A SELF-FULFILLING PROPHECY.
   HE *WAS* THE GREATEST.
2. **MICKEY MANTLE**
   AMERICA'S HEERO!
3. **HUGH SCOTT**
   "THE ONLY THING THAT SEPARATED
   RICHARD NIXON FROM FASCISM...
   WAS HUGH SCOTT."
4. **BOB DYLAN**
   THE COMPOSER OF "HURRICANE" VISITS
   RUBIN CARTER BEHIND BARS.
   (BEHIND BARS?)
5. **ROBERT REDFORD**
   MY HERO (AND NO.1 FAN).
6. **JOE LOUIS**
   THE ICON IN MY SON'S BEDROOM.
7. **ROBERT KENNEDY**
   "GIVE ME A LEVER
   AND I CAN MOVE THE WORLD."
8. **AL NEUHARTH**
   "GODDAMMIT, LOIS...THERE IS NO AMERICA!"
9. **PAUL ROBESON**
   OUR MOST BELOVED, PERSECUTED HERO.
10. **DR. SPOCK**
    THE GOOD DOCTOR SAVES THE WORLD.
11. **MICK JAGGER**
    THE PATRON SAINT OF MTV.
12. **GARRY KASPAROV**
    THE KING AND EYE.

MY MOST MEMORABLE CLIENTS

1. **JOE BAUM**
   "RUN THE SHIT!"
2. **CHARLES REVSON**
   "I KNOW IT'S CHRISTMAS EVE, BUT WHEN
   MR. REVSON CALLS A MEETING, HE CALLS A MEETING!"
3. **SAM BRONFMAN**
   MASSA SAM AND HIS PIG-FUCKING AGENCY.
4. **NATHANIEL GOODMAN**
   "YOU MAKE THE MATZOS, I'LL MAKE THE ADS!"
5. **ED HORRIGAN**
   BARBARIAN AT THE GATE.
6. **WARREN G. MAGNUSON**
   THE FINGER–POINTING SENATOR.
7. **J. DAN BROCK**
   MY $4,000,000 PHONE CALL.
8. **THE REISE BROTHERS**
   THE BIGGEST GONIFFS IN TOWN.
9. **ALAN MacDONALD**
   HOW STOUFFER'S GOT FAT ON LEAN CUISINE.
10. **JIM HINDMAN**
    THE KNUTE ROCKNE OF THE CAR CARE INDUSTRY.
11. **HARDING LAWRENCE**
    THE HAWAIIAN ROUTE FOR BRANIFF WAS IN THE BAG.
12. **DR. HANS NORDHOFF**
    SELLING A NAZI CAR IN A JEWISH TOWN.

MY (NEW YORK ART DIRECTORS CLUB) HALL OF FAME BOSSES:

1. **REBA SOCHIS**
2. **BILL GOLDEN**
3. **HERB LUBALIN**
4. **BILL BERNBACH**
5. **BOB GAGE**

GEORGE LOIS, 1964

INTRODUCTION
$ELLEBRITY (THE ART OF CHOOSING CELEBRITIES TO SELL A PRODUCT)

Enlisting a celebrity to sell cat food, an airline, off-track betting, an analgesic or a lube job would seem to be a delusionary strategy, fraught with irrationality (and seeming suspiciously to be motivated by a starfucker mentality). But let's face it, it's a starstruck world. We're all suckers for a famous face. A celebrity can add almost *instant* style, atmosphere, feeling, and/or meaning to any place, product or situation–unlike any other advertising "symbol." Unfortunately, celebs are too often used in belittling and demeaning ways (belittling to them, demeaning to the product). Too often they end up looking like mercenaries, doing the spot *only* for money. Moreover, the traditional idea of having celebrities say they use products insults our intelligence. (I call it Star-dumb-dumb.) You can be victorious playing the Fame Game only if your choice of celebrity is inspired. I use celebrities for the pleasant shock of their seeming irrelevance to the product, for unexpected juxtapositions, for certain connotations and implications, for a marriage between myth and marketplace, for a subtle but deep credibility. I have blatantly, and very often, used celebrities as a tool to express a startling and outrageous *selling* idea. A broke Joe Louis asked maverick stockbrokers *Edwards & Hanly: Where were you when I needed you?* (Fan dancer Sally Rand called the same stockbrokers *fan-tastic brokers!*) Rocky Marciano served up Piel's Beer and Rocky Graziano, sporting a Rex Harrison accent, sold Breakstone, the more *cultured* yogurt. Sinatra, Gleason, Hope and Dangerfield touted Off-Track Betting as a new team in town, *The New York Bets.* For Revlon's Milk Plus 6 shampoo, Susan Blakely preened and mooed, *Like my hair? Meet my hairdresser!* as a pull-back revealed a cow. Teary-eyed heroes Mantle, Wilt, Oscar, Unitas and Dandy Don cried, *I want my Maypo!* For Olivetti, a fast-typing Joe Namath fought off the advances of his female boss. In one star-studded day, odd couples Salvador Dali & Whitey Ford, George Raft & Hermione Gingold, Sonny Liston & Andy Warhol, Satchel Paige & Dean Martin Jr., Marianne Moore & Mickey Spillane and Ethel Merman & Bennett Cerf paired up for Braniff's battle cry, *When you got it–flaunt it!* Dorothy Lamour sang in sarong, *I'm off on the road to Morocco* for Royal Air Maroc. Spoofing instant glamour, homely Alice Pearce used Coty lipstick to transform into a sexy Joey Heatherton. For *USA Today*, Willard Scott, Joan Collins, Diahann Carroll, Mays and Mantle, Chicago Mayor Jane Byrne and Senator Howard Baker sang out: *I read it every day.* Non-Greeks E.G. Marshall, Ralph Bellamy, Zsa Zsa, Neil Sedaka, Roddy McDowell, Patty Duke and 33 other celebrities announced, oddly enough, *I'm going home...to Greece* for the Greek National Tourist Organization. When MTV was a programming disaster, Mick Jagger ordered Rock fans to deluge cable operators with *I want my MTV* phone calls. (Every rocker alive, including Madonna, begged us to be in subsequent spots.) To transform ESPN from a mickey-mouse sports network to one with "attitude," John Elway, Jim Kelly, Howie Long, Dan Marino, Greg Norman and Bruce Smith performed their *In Your Face* antics. I've featured enough athletes in my work to fill a small stadium (and a book)! Along the way, I conceived senatorial campaigns for gentlemanly Jacob Javits, crabby Warren Magnuson, avuncular Hugh Scott and charismatic Robert Kennedy. Using celebrities can be a daunting experience because everything is magnified: money problems, image concerns, schedules, shoots, credits, legalities, directing them, egos, ambitions, fears. (I happen to like working with people who ain't entirely normal.) It's worth all these magnified problems if the results are fresh, exciting, memorable and truly effective, on the tube, in the streets, in the marketplace. When a *Big Idea* celeb campaign has the power to become new language and startling imagery that enters the popular culture, advertising communication takes on a dimension that leaves competitive products in the dust. When celebrity... is transformed into *$ellebrity*. This book is a 50-year trove of ideas and memories, crowded with unrepentant namedropping.

1. FLOYD PATTERSON, LEFT FOR DEAD, ALONE IN THE RING.
(CALLING A TITLE FIGHT ON MY FIRST MAGAZINE COVER.)

The bout between heavyweight champ Floyd Patterson and monster challenger Sonny Liston was scheduled a week after the October 1962 issue of Esquire would hit the newsstands.
To bring a new attitude and excitement to the magazine, I created a surrealistic image on defeat (using a Floyd Patterson look-alike), on how the world treats a loser in the ring, in business, in life. I admired Patterson, but *knew* Liston would demolish him (even though Floyd was a 5 to 1 favorite).
The press went to town writing about the chutzpah of calling a fight on a magazine cover (mostly ridiculing the prediction) and the issue was a sellout. Liston KO'd Patterson in the first round.
The cover poignantly said that nobody loves a loser, but Esquire went on to legendary fame and fortune, climbing in circulation from a half million to nearly two million during that golden age of journalism.

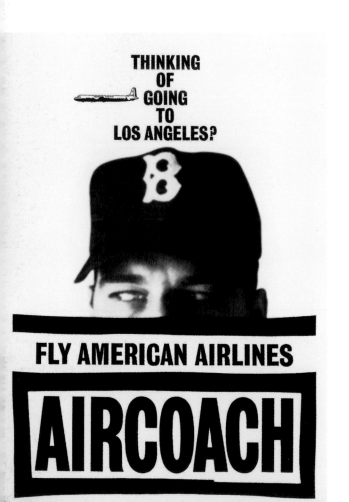

2. MY FIRST AD WAS ALSO MY FIRST SHOT USING A CELEBRITY. OUR BELOVED BUMS WERE HEADED WEST, BUT NO DODGER HAD THE BALLS TO POSE FOR THIS AMERICAN AIRLINES AD.
(SO, WHO IS THIS JOCK?)

In 1955, New York was traumatized by rumors that Brooklyn Dodgers owner Walter O'Malley would soon move the franchise to La-La land. It's always an eye-opener when you can tie something hot happening in the news with an advertisement, so for an American Airlines destination ad I showed a Dodger peering west with the headline *Thinking of going to Los Angeles?*.
I tried to get one of the players to pose for the ad, but everyone chickened out. So yours truly posed for it, casting my baby blues westward. I slammed an airline logo over my puss to keep the message authentic. Bookings on American to Los Angeles took off the next day–and alas, the treacherous O'Malley did, indeed, take flight with Jackie, Pee Wee, Campy and the Duke.

"Yogi, you know I was once a five-pound weakling. Then I started eating Puss 'n Boots. Now look at me!"

3.
**MY FIRST $ELLEBRITY COMMERCIAL.
VIEWERS LAPPED UP YOGI TALKING
TO THE ONLY CAT WHO COULD
PITCH WITH A LONG ISLAND ACCENT.**

"Who knows more about cats than Puss 'n Boots?!"

In 1962, Yankee catching great Yogi Berra, a pussycat of a man,
starred in a beautifully photographed TV spot talking to a cat doing fantastic exercises
on a trampoline, to show how fit he was. Then, shot from behind, the
cat talked up a blue streak, bobbing and weaving, as the Yog listened patiently.
I work out every day. Gym, roadwork, you know. When Yogi questions the
source of the cat's energy, he gets a tome from the cat on Puss 'n Boots, winding
up with *Yogi, you know I was once a five-pound weakling.*
Then I started eating Puss 'n Boots. Now look at me! — followed by a Yogi punchline:
Who knows more about cats than Puss 'n Boots?! The charming juxtaposition of
the bearish Yogi Berra engaged in a dialogue with a pussycat was a visual tour de force
as the cat's verbal wisdom convinced viewers that a real discussion was taking
place. The voice of the cat, as any real baseball fan knew, was Yogi's famous
batterymate Whitey Ford. (The young actor I used in a test commercial to prove
to my client that the visual concept of a TV interview with a cat would be convincing was
the then aspiring actor Alan Alda, who was a riot. But as tempting as it was
to use the unknown Alda, I knew that the totally fresh use of an *unlikely* celebrity...sells.)

4. THE IMAGE OF A CAMPBELL'S SOUP CAN WAS BECOMING THE SYMBOL OF THE POP ART MOVEMENT. SO I DECIDED TO DROWN ANDY WARHOL IN HIS OWN SOUP.

This cover has become the supreme statement of Esquire's juxtaposition of the celebration of pop culture in the '60s...as their great editor Harold Hayes deconstructed celebrity. The pervading image of the whole Pop Art movement of that era was Andy Warhol's Campbell's soup can. Maybe Andy was an innovator and an original thinker, but he was most certainly a major-league showman. Any guy who can parlay a soup can (not to mention that mundane Brillo box) into personal stardom may not fit my definition of an artist, but Andy Warhol certainly was hot stuff. When I asked him to pose in his finest drowning position, he knew it was a friendly spoof of his original claim to fame, and he enjoyed that fame enough to welcome his bewigged puss on one of those Esquire covers that were getting so much attention. We photographed Warhol and the open can of soup separately. When I put Andy in the soup, I almost lost him.

5. THE HAND OF A KING IN THE MUHAMMAD RELIGION.

A hands-on touch when I created a fight program (see 116, Favorite Celebs 1)
for the Ali/Frazier III Thrilla in Manila was to make contact with Madame Phyllis Woodbury,
a seer and palmist who did a thriving business in Harlem. I handed her two life-size
photos of men's hands (Muhammad Ali and Joe Frazier) without telling her who
they were. After her uncanny analysis (she said that
the hand of the unnamed Ali revealed him to have been
a king in the Muhammad religion!) I disclosed
the identity of her subjects.
Then, I asked for her prediction.
She, alas, said *Frazier* would win.
Palmist yes, seer no.

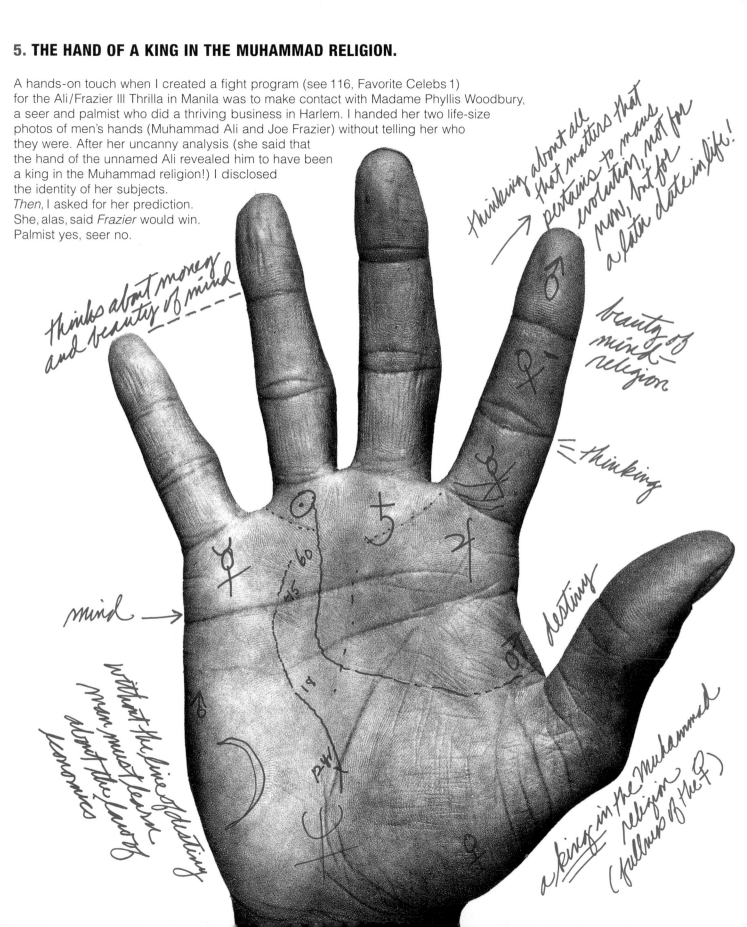

thinking about all that matters that pertains to mans evolution, not for now, but for a later date in life!

thinks about money and beauty of mind

beauty of mind - religion

= thinking

mind →

destiny

without the line of destiny man must learn about the laws economics

a king in the muhammad religion (fullness of the ♀)

6. OH YES, MTV WAS A FLOP.
UNTIL I CONNED THE SAME KIDS WHO IN THE LATE '60s
CRIED "I WANT MY MAYPO".
TO TAKE MICK JAGGER'S ADVICE IN THE EARLY '80s
AND BELLOW "I WANT MY MTV" INTO A PHONE.

Hard to believe today, but after its first year of operations, MTV was an abject failure. A 24-hour rock 'n' roll channel? The two thousand people at the cable convention that announced MTV literally laughed the Warner Amex honchos off the stage. Music publishers insisted the MTV concept could kill their business. Record companies swore they would never produce music videos. Advertisers considered it a joke. Ad agency experts snickered. Cable operators scoffed. A fledgling concept faced crib death. Despite an introductory period of advertising, MTV was a total wipeout. After a zero year, the whiz kids at MTV asked me to do an emergency "trade" campaign, to change the minds of the cable operators of America, most of whom believed kids who rocked were into sex and drugs. But I had a better idea, the Big Idea: to go right to the rock-loving audience and shove MTV down the rock-hating cable operators' throats. Guerrilla warfare at its nastiest. Along with my introduction of "living" MTV logos, the upstart MTV, led by the post-pubescent Bob Pittman, thought I was a wily old fox for bridging the years with my updated *I Want My Maypo* slogan, and I produced an audacious campaign, delivered by rock superstars Mick Jagger, Peter Townshend and Pat Benatar. *I want my MTV* ignited a firestorm of popular demand for MTV within minutes after the commercials ran in each market. The clincher in each commercial was this windup sequence as a voice-over proclaims: *If you don't get MTV where you live, call your cable operator and say...* (we then cut to Mick Jagger, who bellows into a telephone:) *I want my MTV!* In each city, thousands called moments after viewing the commercial and screamed for their MTV! Within months, MTV was in 80% of all households; record companies *begged* to have their videos on the channel; advertisers looked at MTV as a must-buy for viewers 14 to 28; and every Rock star in the world pleaded with us to mimic Mick Jagger's plea in our follow-up commercials. They flew to New York and lined up to go on film: David Bowie, Stevie Nicks, Lionel Richie, Madonna, Sting, Hall & Oates, Dire Straits, Tears for Fears, Cyndi Lauper, ZZ Top, Eurythmics, Billy Idol, Boy George, George Michael, Thunderbirds, Van Halen, Huey Lewis and the News, The Cars, Michael Jackson and every Rock star who wanted to explode their record sales. Six months after the start of the campaign, *Time* magazine called MTV "the most spectacular pop culture phenomenon since the advent of cable television– and, arguably, since the invention of the tube itself." Now owned by Viacom, MTV Networks is a financial powerhouse, among the most profitable companies in the world.

A MAJOR CONTRIBUTION TO THE IMAGERY OF MTV WAS MY "CHANGEABLE LOGO" CONCEPT: TRANSFORMING THEIR STATIC LOGO INTO AN ACTION SYMBOL, CONSTANTLY CHANGING WITH CONCEPTUAL GRAPHICS. WHEN I SHOWED THE YOUNG MARKETING GUNS THE ROLLING STONES LOGO LEAPING OUT OF THEIR MTV LOGO, THEIR LAWYER PATRONIZINGLY INSISTED MTV WOULD HAVE TO RE-REGISTER THE LOGO WITH EACH VISUAL CHANGE. BUT TOP GUN BOB PITTMAN, THE MISSISSIPPI METHODIST MINISTER'S SON, BELIEVED! PITTMAN STUCK HIS TONGUE OUT AT HIS LAWYER, AND ROCK FANS ALL OVER AMERICA LAPPED IT UP.

Lois Pitts Gershon
(the "I want my MTV"
ad agency) thanks
the terrific artists
who graciously appear in
our TV campaigns.

7. WHEN JOE NAMATH WAS IN HOT WATER WITH THE NFL OVER HIS BACHELORS III JOINT, I USED THE SCOTCH-DRINKING SUPERSTAR TO SELL OVALTINE TO KIDS.

Dick Schaap (then at NBC) caught Broadway Joe Namath, still in his prime, at the filming of commercials for Ovaltine and his eyes popped. "Do you think this will hurt your image?" he asked the New York Jets superstar. "Well as long as I drink Ovaltine in the right places I think I'll be able to keep my bad-boy reputation," said Joe. The National Football League had forced Namath to cut all ties to Bachelors III, his hot Lexington Avenue bar, fearing "mob influence." Namath was known as a Johnny Walker guzzler, but I knew him as a barfly who would nurse one scotch & water all night long. With this ill-deserved reputation, showing him talking about Ovaltine's nutritional value for kids made this campaign a showstopper! Joe introduced young kids to his teammates Gerry Philbin, Emerson Boozer and John Dockery. *My o-o-o-old pal Gerry Philbin*, he said, and then introduced the kids to *My o-o-o-old pal Ovaltine*, with the kids playing back that mnemonic line to Namath and the TV audience. (Johnny Carson launched into an unforgettable parody of the commercials, playing Joe as he held booze instead of Ovaltine.) While the commercials addressed to kids ran during the day, Joe talked to parents at night in a commercial in which he straightforwardly told them he was selling their kids during the day. It was a kid/parents trap play. My old pal Joe Namath had actually been an Ovaltine fan when he was a kid in Pennsylvania. Ovaltine, the household name of a generation before, became famous again (with sales that more than doubled) by riding a heavy Johnnie Walker Scotch drinker. P.S. The image below is from a sales film I created for Cutty Sark. When the booze trade saw Namath doing a "testimonial" for Johnny Walker, a hated competitor, they couldn't believe their eyes. Hugging the monumental bottle of Cutty, Joe said, *Y'know why I'm switching to Cutty Sark? Because their bottles are bigger!*

MY AGENCY AD THAT APPEARED IN THE FIRST ANNUAL MTV MUSIC VIDEO AWARDS PROGRAM IN 1985.

ACROSS: PETE TOWNSHEND, MICK JAGGER, CYNDI LAUPER
PAT BENATAR, JOHN COUGAR-MELLENCAMP, STEVIE NICKS
JOE ELLIOT (DEF LEPPARD), MADONNA, BILLY IDOL
ADAM ANT, LIONEL RICHIE, HALL & OATES
DAVID BOWIE, PETER WOLF (J. GEILS BAND), RIC OCASEK (THE CARS)
BOY GEORGE (CULTURE CLUB), POLICE

8.
THE BIRTH
(AND NEAR DEATH)
OF AN UGLY
CELEBRITY SPOKESMAN:
THE NAUGA!

First, UniRoyal created Naugahyde, a superb leathery vinyl. An instant winner in the
furniture market, it begat many ripoffs. Soon the world was surfeited with fake leathers and
bewildered decorators who couldn't tell which was which. To separate Naugahyde from
the copycats, designer Kurt Weihs and I spawned the ugly Nauga, a mythical species who shed
their hide once a year for the good of mankind (and UniRoyal). The Nauga, taller than
a basketball center, became a spokesman for Naugahyde on TV and in national magazines.
(Inside the Naugahyde costume was the sweating comedian Chuck McCann.)
The Nauga became a hangtag, and a 12-inch doll for kids. But before our first ad ran
(the Nauga is ugly, but his vinyl hide is beautiful) legal objections were raised. Too many people,
it was claimed by the Federal Trade Commission, might look upon the ugly
Nauga as a for-real living species. *Huh?!* Its hide might be considered genuine leather,
they contended, and that could be deemed deceptive advertising. "Kill the Nauga,"
they said. "Over my dead body," I said. Research to the rescue! A bunch of us from my
ad agency hit Fifth Avenue and showed tourists and New Yorkers our Nauga ads
and asked, "Is this a real animal?" "What, are you nuts?" they answered. "That's just a big,
fat, ugly, snarling, make-believe creature with a cute tush." The ugly Nauga was spared.
He went into the marketplace and UniRoyal overwhelmed their competitors.
Today, the 12-inch Nauga doll is a collector's item (Jenette Kahn, the high-voltage president of
DC Comics, sleeps with 31 of the sexy beasts in her bedroom). The ugly Nauga lives on.
That's my boy!

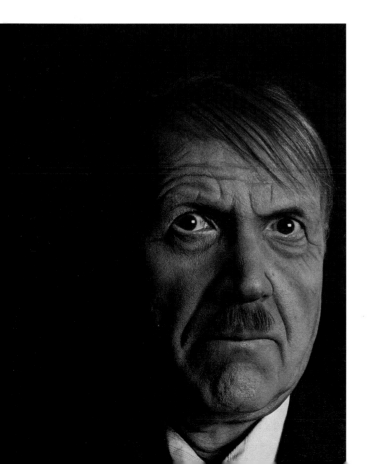

9. SEARCHING FOR HITLER IN "GERMANTOWN."

1965 was the 20th anniversary of the day the 56-year-old
Adolph Hitler blew his maniacal brains out.
Yet a pollster had found that almost half of all Americans
believed he had bamboozled the avenging Russian Army.
They were convinced that he spirited himself out
of his Berlin bunker into the arms of a loving, loyal Argentina.
By the '60s, neo-Nazism was rearing its appalling head
in Germany and even in America. Resigned to the brutal
fact that Fascism and anti-Semitism had never died,
I reincarnated the leader of the Third Reich, emerging
from the shadows of exile, pleading for redemption
on the cover of Esquire magazine:
This month I will be 76 years old. Can I come home now?
Photographer Harold Kreiger and I searched...vainly...
for exactly the unfortunate face that could double as
Der Führer. Eerily, we encountered him in a German beer hall
in Manhattan's Yorkville. Before WWII, Yorkville crawled
with pro-Nazi brownshirts of the German-American Bund.
As he sat there, beckoning for another stein of beer
with a flawless Nazi salute, we knew we found our Hitler.

10. HOLY COW! AFTER THIS AD RAN, YANKEE GREAT PHIL "RIZZUTO" RECOMMENDED TRATTORIA FOR THE BEST "RISOTTO" IN TOWN.

Opening day in 1964 for the
New York Yankees
was ushered in by this baseball lineup
with a *molto* Italian accent.
Nostalgic baseball fans who loved
to eat, ate it up.

	ACTUAL NAMES:
1B	JOE PEPITONE
2B	JOHNNY PESKY
SS	PHIL RIZZUTO
3B	TY COBB
LF	MICKEY MANTLE
CF	JOE DIMAGGIO
RF	BABE RUTH
P	BOB LEMON
C	YOGI BERRA
MGR	CASEY STENGEL

11. OUR PLEDGE TO ALEXANDER HAMILTON.

When real estate mogul Peter Kalikow purchased the New York Post from Rupert Murdoch in 1988, it was widely assumed that he was interested solely in the newspaper's real estate assets, without any ambitions for its journalistic potential. This ailing newspaper was beset by dwindling circulation, advertiser resistance, and a Murdoch-inherited shlock image. ("Mr. Murdoch", went the apocryphal remark attributed to a prominent retailer in response to Murdoch's pitch for ads in the Post, "your *readers*...are our *shoplifters*!") Such was the scuttlebutt in the Big Apple when Kalikow took over, following an impressive line of previous owners before Murdoch that included Dorothy Schiff, Franklin D. Roosevelt (one of a consortium of owners in the 1920s), Oswald G. Villard, William Cullen Bryant...and its founder Alexander Hamilton. To lay to rest this damaging rumor and to convince New Yorkers that the Post was headed for renewed prominence in the city, I established at the outset a strong sense of commitment to the newspaper's heritage. (To me, New Yorkers' understanding that the Post was founded by Alexander Hamilton, a Revolutionary War hero, a founding father of the nation, and the icon on our $10 bill, would bring new meaning to the imagery of their New York Post.) We redesigned Kalikow's newspaper, beginning with a fast-paced masthead, and on the new masthead I slapped an oval engraving of Alexander Hamilton, overlooking the newspaper he had founded in 1803. Simultaneously we created a jumbo bus shelter poster that was seen throughout the city, boldly delivering this message: *A reassuring word to Alexander Hamilton, the founder of the Post... Don't worry, your paper is in good hands!* This poster, hanging proudly behind Kalikow in his office whenever he was interviewed on TV, may well have prodded him to commit himself to the new Post. Indeed, I believe our "Hamilton pledge" helped keep the Post alive – it was a breath of fresh air, it shored up morale, it was a meaningful message to the world that Kalikow was serious...and probably stiffened his resolve. New owners of the Post removed the countenance of the journalist Alexander Hamilton from the masthead. They just don't get it.

A reassuring word to Alexander Hamilton, the founder of the Post.
Don't worry, your newspaper is in good hands!
NEW YORK POST

12. SUSAN BLAKELY BECOMES A STAR BY ASKING "LIKE MY HAIR? MEET MY HAIRDRESSER."

The great tycoons of American business invariably understand two things:
Power and *Concepts*. In 1974 we launched a new shampoo
for the legendary Charles Revson, whose brilliant career proved he understood
women (in his *advertising*). Revlon branded their product Milk Plus Six,
a name designed to dramatize to women that health-giving milk was a dominant
ingredient. Our concept for Milk Plus Six was *Like my hair? Meet my hairdresser.*
That may sound bland, but when model Susan Blakely, standing in a lovely
meadow, uttered, *Meet my hairdresser*, the camera pulled back to reveal a *cow*
as she delivered a mellifluous *Moooooooo!* While the commercial was still in storyboard
form, the brass at Revlon wanted no part of showing it to their boss.
Instead, they reluctantly agreed to allow me to show it to him, but only with the clear
understanding that we would all pretend that nobody knew what I was going
to present. If Charles chewed me out, nobody else would be blamed.
When I laid it on Revson, he frowned at me incredulously, a look of admiring
exasperation I have come to recognize among the many benevolent
tyrants for whom I have worked, and said, without affectation or qualification:
"I like it, Lois. Let's milk it." I heard an audible exhaling of tension
from his staff, followed by a robust "We knew you'd love it, Charles!"
The campaign ran in a crowded field, but the product took off, remaining
a healthy brand for over a decade.

"MOOOOOOOO!"

In 1967, to make an unknown stockbroker famous and sell the hoi polloi in town, the tough-talking New Journalist Jimmy Breslin, in a 10-second TV spot, confidently states: *The stock market used to intimidate me. But these days I've got no compunction about picking up the phone and calling Edwards & Hanly.* Then the literary celeb from Queens brings the phone to his ear, looks dead into it, and stammers out his hidden fears: *Hello? Edwards & H-H-Hanly?* We cut to a logo and a voiceover announcer says: *Edwards & Hanly, the brokers you've waited for.*

13. "HELLO? EDWARDS & H-H-HANLY?"

14. A DOWN-HOME MESSAGE FOR A STOCKBROKER FROM THE MICK.

Like Joe Louis (see 48) the great Mickey Mantle's fame was no guarantee of financial security; he was known to have lost a bundle investing in lousy business deals. So in 1967, we shot the Mick for Edwards & Hanly, in glorious black and white, looking square in the camera as he bared his soul: *Boy, I'm telling you when I came up to the big leagues, I was a shufflin,' grinnin,' head-duckin' country boy. Well, I'm still a country boy, but I know a man down at Edwards & Hanly. I'm learnin.' I'm learnin.'* A few nights after the spot hit the airwaves, Johnny Carson had a field day with *I'm learnin. I'm learnin,'* and the line became an au courant phrase among talk show denizens and stand-up comics all over America.

15. BILLIE JEAN KING MUST HAVE SEEN THIS AD.

Cutty Sark had been thrashing about for a creative breakthrough and were considering whether they should scuttle Cutty's famous logo of a tall sailing ship. My answer (and slogan): *Don't give up the ship!* That call to non-action became one of the best-known and talked about campaigns in the booze business, and Cutty's sailing ship sailed profitably into the sunset. Each of the color magazine spreads and dozens of small-space newspaper ads had its own salty headline. For *New York* magazine: *I gave up my favorite restaurant because Gael Greene said to, but...I won't give up the ship!*
For magazines in Chicago: *If you hate Picasso and you work at the Civic Center...Don't give up the ship!*
Posters for New York subways: *If you've had it up to here with graffiti...Don't give up the ship!*
And almost daily, I created newspaper ads that reacted to the news of the day. For instance...the morning after Bobby Riggs humiliated Margaret Court Smith in their $50,000 winner-take-all tennis match, I served up this ad in papers all over America. Less than a year later, the ad proved prophetic when Billie Jean King ran Riggs ragged, and became an heroic and iconic symbol of the feminist movement.

16. THE FIRST OF THREE ESQUIRE COVERS IN DEFENSE OF "CASSIUS CLAY."

Before a November 1965 championship bout, Floyd Patterson foolishly taunted
Muhammad Ali by continually referring to him as Cassius Clay, his Kentucky slave name.
To avenge this disrespect for his religion, Ali vowed he would not only beat Patterson,
he would "whup" him. And so he did. Holding up the near-unconscious Patterson,
punctuating blow after crippling blow with the mantra "What's my name! What's my name!,"
until, in the 12th round, Floyd fell to the canvas–not merely beaten, but humiliated.
Eight months later, Harold Hayes and I, knowing Floyd was a fair man and a good Christian,
convinced him to speak out in defense of the Muslim preacher, a convicted "draft dodger,"
stripped of his title and not allowed to fight for a living, waiting for his appeal to
reach the Supreme Court. When I called Floyd to make a date for a cover photo shoot with
his tormenter, he agreed. But the ex-champion (who skulked around Brooklyn's
Bed-Stuy streets wearing a beard as a disguise after losing face by blowing a title bout
to "foreigner" Ingemar Johanson) insisted on a *midnight* shoot. No problem.
I explained the cover idea to a seemingly grateful Ali (a preaching Patterson and a mute Ali),
begging him to receive Floyd with grace. Ali was the first trash-talker in sports,
and Floyd Patterson was the last gentleman in boxing. Ali was a sweetheart, but his biting
tongue could turn off the sensitive Patterson. At the stroke of midnight, almost
cowering in a longshoreman's cap and heavy overcoat (on a sweltering day in June),
Floyd slipped into photographer Carl Fischer's studio. He saw Ali and froze in his tracks.
Muhammad lovingly spread his arms, almost trotted up to Patterson, whispered
"Hiya, Champ," and the two champions hugged...and wept.

17. "DON'T SHOW KASPAROV HOW PUTTING HIS AND KARPOV'S PROFILE NOSE TO NOSE MADE A CHESS PIECE MIRACULOUSLY APPEAR BETWEEN THEM. HE'LL NEVER SPOT IT!"

For the World Chess Championship series between Garry Kasparov and his brilliant challenger, Anatoly Karpov, that began at the Hudson Theater in Manhattan in 1990, I created the ultimate confrontation in the fierce combat of chess. Kasparov's business managers insisted that the eagle-eyed Kasparov, arguably the greatest chess player in history, would be oblivious to it. When the Russian chess genius saw the poster, the white chess piece between his profile and Karpov's hit him like an emotional illumination, and he gasped in astonishment. "Na Zdorovye, tovarich!" he said, "Kasparov and Karpov, nose to nose, and betveen them...ah vite kveen!"

18. IMMEDIATE AMBIANCE, INVOKING THE NAME OF THE PERFECT CELEBRITY.

Dropping Robert Benchley's name gave the Manhattan watering hole Charley O's instant ambiance. The copy is right on the nose, but try reading it with a different name: Try it with Robert Goulet. Okay, now try *Peter* Benchley. Now go back to the ghost of Robert Benchley, perhaps the wittiest raconteur of Algonquin Round Table fame (along with the likes of Dorothy Parker, Alexander Wolcott, George S. Kaufman, Harold Ross, Helen Hayes, Raoul Fleischmann, Jane Grant, Irving Berlin and George Gershwin). When the mythical Charley O longed for the legendary Benchley the restaurant's atmosphere came to life. It happened on Day One. (If only Robert Benchley was there!)

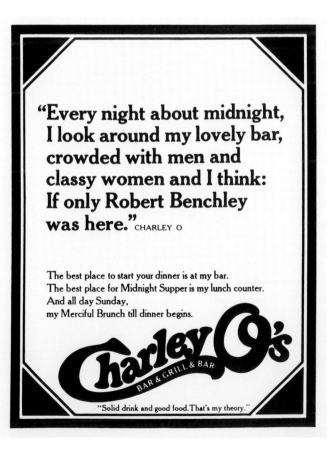

"Every night about midnight, I look around my lovely bar, crowded with men and classy women and I think: If only Robert Benchley was here." CHARLEY O

The best place to start your dinner is at my bar.
The best place for Midnight Supper is my lunch counter.
And all day Sunday,
my Merciful Brunch till dinner begins.

Charley O's
BAR & GRILL & BAR

"Solid drink and good food. That's my theory."

GARRY KASPAROV VS. ANATOLY KARPOV 1990 WORLD CHESS CHAMPIONSHIP

OCTOBER 8 – NOVEMBER 10, 1990
NEW YORK CITY

19. WHY IS THIS MAN LAUGHING?

I got my client Olivetti to contribute one of their dandy Lexicon electric typewriters to give to legendary *New York Times* columnist Red Smith at a sports award ceremony. While I was at it, I also arranged for a presenter. Was it Ted Williams? Joe DiMaggio? Jackie Robinson? Naah. I came up with none other than a bona fide historical figure, Alger Hiss, the former State Department official who was convicted of perjury in a celebrated 1950 case that eventually hinged on a disputed typewriter.

After a whammo introduction at the ceremony by Dick Schaap, then the editor of *Sport* magazine, Mr. Hiss, a self-described Red Smith fan, said, "I was told that my sole purpose was to be a sight gag." A few stiffs stalked out, but he got a standing ovation, while Johnny Bench, the 1976 World Series MVP recipient, wondered who the hell Hiss was. (Since then, evidence has been uncovered showing that the "smoking pistol" typewriter at the two Hiss trials was an FBI fake. In the Congressional hearings that led to his indictment, the arch pursuer of Hiss was a young crewcut congressman from California, one Richard Milhous Nixon. The famous Alger Hiss conviction, based on a phony typewriter, became the springboard for Nixon's career, which came to an infamous end, based on *real* tapes.)

20. WHY IS THIS SHARK LAUGHING?

OCA (Orthodontic Centers of America) manages hundreds of orthodontic practices in the U.S.
They were hurting because they needed more cavities to fill. My campaign was designed
to charm moms and their youngsters with the memorable imagery of Pinocchio, Mona Lisa, and Jaws
(of *Jaws* movie fame) with straight, gleaming, superstar smiles, created by one of the skilled,
professional OCA orthodontists. (And it didn't cost us a dime to get them to flash their magical smiles.)
Each spot was created to seemingly be a unique message from orthodontic groups in their specific vicinity:
If Phoenix's Dr. Gerta can transform Pinocchio's wooden grin into this real life one
(Geppetto's puppet gives us a dazzling smile)...*If our Dr. Glovsky can reshape Jaws' mouth into this
friendly one* (the Great White shows us his lovely human choppers)...*If Dr. Wickson can make
Mona Lisa's smirk a work of art* (Da Vinci's masterpiece comes to life with a picture perfect smile)...
*imagine how the same artful skill can change your youngster's problem teeth into a
lifelong, knock'em dead smile!* Call volume shot up 150%, new patients' starts and revenue
soared dramatically, and the orthodontists grinned all the way to the bank.

21. THE FIRST BLACK SANTA.

Sonny Liston was perfect for the part. By 1963 he was known by everyone
as the meanest man in the world. He was a sullen and surly champion, a badass.
He had served time for armed robbery, was a labor goon and a hit man for the mob,
and didn't give a damn about his image. This newest heavyweight champion
of the world flaunted a menacing image at a time when rising racial fever dominated
the headlines. The early '60s were the years of Freedom Rides, of Dr. Martin Luther King,
of black revolution, of rising racial tensions. I was looking into the eyes of a changing
America, and I wanted to put it on the cover of Esquire magazine.
I explained the idea of a black Santa to Liston's idol, Joe Louis. "That'll be the day,"
said Joe skeptically, but he went ahead and twisted Sonny's arm. For the shoot,
photographer Carl Fischer and I went to Las Vegas, a place Liston called home because
he was a notorious dice freak. We set up in a hotel room with our photo gear,
ready to capture the Western world's newest Santa, and snapped the first shot.
But Sonny wouldn't stay put. He couldn't resist the crap tables in the lounge.
I snitched to Joe Louis. He lumbered over to Liston's table, grabbed his ear, wrenched
him around and led him back to the elevator. "Git," he whispered in Sonny's ear. "Git!"
Bent over like a puppy on a leash, Liston returned to the room and we photographed
the first black Santa to our hearts' content. All hell broke loose when the image
appeared on the newsstands, smack in the middle of the Christmas season. Esquire lost
advertisers and received threatening phone calls and hate mail. Subscribers
demanded refunds and Esquire's ad sales honcho chastised me in the press. Editor
Harold Hayes said that Sonny Liston created more trouble than any cover since
the invention of movable type. But it set the spirit for the magazine for years to come
(with a circulation leap from half a million to almost two million). In a recollection
of the Liston cover eighteen years later, *Sports Illustrated* recalled the event, calling it
a chillingly accurate anticipation of the black revolution: "Four months after
Liston won the title, Esquire thumbed its nose at its white readers with
an unforgettable cover. On the front of its December 1963 issue, there was Liston
glowering out from under a tasseled red-and-white Santa Claus hat, looking like the last
man on earth America wanted to see coming down its chimney."
And *Time* magazine described the cover as "one of the greatest social statements
of the plastic arts since Picasso's *Guernica*." Ho, ho, ho.

PETER FONDA   DENNIS HOPPER
JACK NICHOLSON
IN EASY RIDER

22. THE RKO ST. PATRICK'S MARQUEE, STARRING THE CULT FILM OF THE HIP GENERATION.

A good magazine cover, like a strong package design, usually explains what's inside.
A good issue of Esquire enabled me to make a personal comment about what I thought the magazine was trying to say. And in the '60s, this wildly inventive, deadly serious publication was magazine journalism at its peak of achievement. The August 1970 issue featured a sheaf of articles on the spreading youth culture, but it seemed to lack a definitive point of view. To my mind, American postwar films basically remained white-bread until a stoned Jack Nicholson, Peter Fonda, Dennis Hopper and crew brought the biggie Hollywood studios to their knees with the cheapo, culture-crashing *Easy Rider*. So I gave it one. I focused on the new movies and called them the *Faith of our Children.* Then I superimposed the marquee of that low-budget runaway hit over the majestic doors of St. Patrick's Cathedral. To American kids, *Easy Rider* had become a cult film. The Catholic Archdiocese of New York was not pleased. (To this day, whenever I stroll past St. Paddy's, I always pull out $10.50 if I feel like going in.)

23. PASSING THE WORD THAT PAUL REVERE WAS LOADED.

For 200 years American kids have revered Paul Revere for warning the countryside that the British were coming, the British were coming, when actually he was trotting around tipsy on rum. Sometimes the best ads come from good spadework. In 1962, when we dug into the history of rum, we came upon this historical nugget. Paul Revere, the distinguished Boston silversmith, whose legendary ride of April 1775 made him a hero of the creation of our nation, had been guzzling Puerto Rican rum at Isaac Hall's distillery on the night of his revolutionary call to arms. *This* was the shot heard 'round the world. When we said that this was *The true story of Paul Revere* we were absolutely serious. What a coup! What a discovery! What a winner! What an outrage, screamed The Daughters of the American Revolution! They bombarded Ronrico Puerto Rican Rum with telegrams, letters, calls and threats. Which proves that nothing, but nothing, is more shocking than the absolute truth.

The shot heard 'round the world

(the true story of Paul Revere)

It was the eighteenth of April, 1775, the sweet night air anticipated Summer, and Paul Revere did not ride out to rouse the countryside.

No, he just wanted to warn Hancock and Adams of impending arrest. On the way he stopped in on his friend, Isaac Hall, captain of the Medford Minutemen. Captain Hall owned a rum distillery. One shot led to another. And another. And another.

PUERTO RICAN RUM. 80 PROOF. WHITE OR GOLD LABEL.

Paul Revere bounded into his saddle, shouted "The British are coming," and you know the rest.

In those sensible days every town by law *had to* have a tavern. And Puerto Rican rum was the best a man could drink. It still is.

Have you tried the light, clear, ineffably fragrant rum that is now called Ronrico? Have you tasted the uncannily clever Bloody María? No?   But you will

GENERAL WINE AND SPIRITS COMPANY, NEW YORK 22

Ronrico from Puerto Rico

24. STOPPING ROBERT MOSES IN HIS TRACKS WITH MY ELEVENTH COMMANDMENT.

In 1962, Robert Moses (the omnipotent master broker who built highways in, out, under and through New York with little concern for mass transit needs) decided to bulldoze the length of Fire Island, a string of small beach communities off Long Island, and turn an idyllic community into a California freeway. It was decreed by New York's imperious Highway Commissioner that a four-lane highway was needed to carry cars across the 20-mile length of Fire Island, linking at either end the two bridges from the Long Island mainland. Plans were drawn to construct the highway right over the length of sandbar and through the skinny line of summer homes, forever destroying Fire Island as a magical vacation wonderland, where the only vehicles allowed were fire trucks, police jeeps and kiddie wagons. Moses' scheme seemed like a fait accompli. Then my wife Rosie got mad and organized the Tenants Committee to Save Fire Island to prevent the Moses road. To win the battle against City Hall, they needed a Big Idea. So I invoked the name of God (and the art of Michelangelo) and did this poster. Rosie and her committee plastered them all over Long Island, and carried them as picket signs. And boy did they picket! New York newspapers and TV stations took up the cause, and finally, Rosie's gang of protesters put the fear of God into Robert Moses at a raucous public hearing, chanting "Moses–Thou shalt not build a road, Moses–Thou shalt not build a road." Moses gave up, and the road was never built.

25. MAKING THE MAN WHO POSED FOR THE INDIAN NICKEL FAMOUS.

I spotted an article on the American Indian in the advanced draft of the March '64 Esquire. On a lark, I phoned the Bureau of Indian Affairs in Washington to inquire whether they had the remotest notion as to what Native American posed for the Indian/Buffalo nickel and if he might still be alive! I felt that I was on the verge of a historical find, especially when the Washington paleface called back and stammered on the phone in shock, "His name is Chief John Big Tree...he m-m-may still be alive...if so, he should be on the Onondaga Reservation." My father-in-law, Joe "Big Feet" Lewandowski, a Syracusan, completed my research. He drove out to the reservation, where he found Chief John Big Tree in the flesh, toting twigs to light a fire in his primitive, dirt-floor cabin. He was a vigorous 87-year-old, and stood six-feet-two. I couldn't wait to catch the first plane up there, but Chief John loved to fly. He showed up at Carl Fischer's studio in a business suit, sporting a crewcut. In 1912, the sculptor James Earl Fraser had eyed the chief in a Coney Island Wild West show and asked him to pose for his Indian-head nickel, destined to become the greatest coin since ancient Greece. The chief was a Seneca, a descendant of the Iroquois Confederacy, which dates back to the 1500s. At the shoot we dressed him in a black wig and built up his toothless mouth with cotton wads. He looked awesome. We shot his historic profile and he flew back to Syracuse on Mohawk Airlines. It was vintage Americana–the now legendary Chief John Big Tree a half-century after he posed for the Indian nickel! After his noble profile hit the newsstands, he was recruited on a TV talk-show circuit, and the unknown chief became an heroic, iconic celebrity.

Chief John Big Tree

"Moses—
Thou shalt not
build a road."

26. THE CYNICAL OPTIMIST BOB DYLAN, A POET OF OUR TIME WHO CHANGED THE COURSE OF POPULAR MUSIC. (A POET SHOULD BE READ AS WELL AS HEARD.)

In 1983, Columbia Records asked Bob Dylan, an artist whose music captured the zeitgeist and imagination of the whole world, to promote his new *Infidels* album with a music video, a medium he had previously spurned. Bill Graham, the trailblazing rock promoter, asked me to create and produce a video of the iconic song *Jokerman*. In gratitude for Dylan's dynamic help in freeing the innocent Rubin Hurricane Carter, (see 69), I leapt at the chance. The Big Idea was to intercut close-ups of Dylan with images from the history of art (from a 2700 BC Sumerian idol to a "Weeping Woman" by Picasso), overlaying his lyrics so that they could be read on screen as the piercing wail of Bob Dylan's voice was heard. (A poet should be read as well as heard.) His sandpaper voice and the snarl and grit of his words chill the bones. *Rolling Stone* said, "George Lois' unique concept of Dylan's lyrics with sculpture by Michelangelo and paintings by Hieronymus Bosch spliced with close-ups of Dylan... was spectacular." And MTV voted *Jokerman* the Video of the Year.

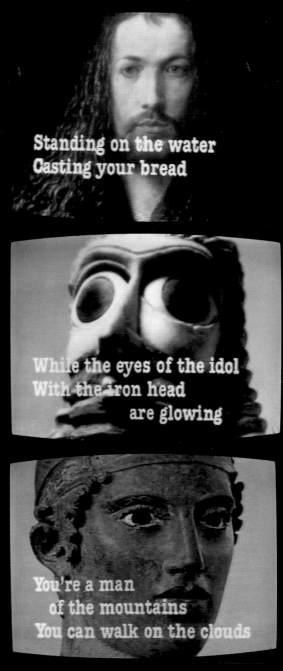

27. A SELF-FULFILLING PROPHECY: "I'M JUST WILD ABOUT HARRAH'S!"

Stuck, all alone, on the marina side of Atlantic City, far from where
a phalanx of nine casinos were packing them in,
Harrah's was a virtually unknown name among gamblers there.
(Harrah's ranking for casino awareness in Atlantic City was 1%, with
advertising and slogan awareness at zero!)
A famous, apropos song to the rescue! I created the campaign
I'm just wild about Harrah's! with long-legged Susan Anton breezing through
Harrah's glitzy gaming rooms, hotel suites and many eateries, while
delivering our instantly recognizable theme song,
I'm just wild about Harrah's...and Harrah's wild about you!–based on the
classic American song, *I'm Just Wild About Harry!*
After just three weeks of stunning Susan Anton belting it out
as she socked middleweight champ Marvelous Marvin Hagler on the jaw,
Harrah's Marina became the best-known, most talked-about casino
in Atlantic City, with gaming revenues zooming to second place.
A year later I recruited my Greek compatriot, the crooked-nosed, tux-clad,
shaven-headed Telly Savalas (who had been known to place a bet
or two in his life) to team up with Anton as we kept the campaign rolling,
maintaining Harrah's as a strong No. 2 in town. As successful as the
campaign was, we were never able to knock off the No. 1 Mirage, because
Steve Wynn had superceleb Frank Sinatra starring in his TV spots,
with the strangely appealing perception of Las Vegas Frankie being pals
with organized crime in the Sin City.

28. SENATOR JACOB JAVITS' YOUNG WIFE, MARION, WENT ON A RAMPAGE AGAINST THE REAL, YET SOMEHOW HEROIC (AND NOW MISSING) OFFICIAL PHOTO WE TOOK FOR HIS 1962 RE-ELECTION CAMPAIGN.

But Jake loved it. Finally she screamed at me,
"He looks old, he looks bald, and he looks fat!"
"Mrs. Javits," I said, "I got news for you.
Your husband is old, is bald, and he is fat!"
She hung up on me, and we ran the campaign photo.
P.S. I regret to say that after searching high and
low for the maligned photo, not one seems to exist today.
A few years after his retirement, the beloved
four-term senator from New York wrote me a lovely
letter reminiscing about the "old days"
and delighted in telling me how much Marion
hated the portrait..."She *detested* it."
So I suspect every last image was torn up,
flushed down the toilet, or burnt to
a crisp, by person or persons unknown.

Will he go for the $64,000 question?

29. 15 MINUTES OF FAME.

Fresh from the Korean War, I was cutting my teeth at CBS. The network's historic television quiz show *The $64,000 Question* (big money in 1953) drew such a massive audience that movies across America closed their doors the night of the telecast. An ad was needed to promote the appearance of a priest-contestant, trapped in the memorable isolation booth, who had reached the jackpot stage. He could pocket the $32,000 he had won thus far (over several appearances that had made him as well known as President Eisenhower) or he could go for the gold. Working late and alone that night, our production head begged me to do an ad in 10 minutes to fill a requisition he had misplaced. I did a simple ad of the celebrity priest's face, which everyone knew, with a question that everyone was asking: *Will he go for the $64,000 question?* That was the *entire* ad. I left out the by-then hallowed CBS eye – deliberately – as well as the time slot and channel number, a huge no-no for any tune-in ad. The priest was so famous, I wanted the ad to exude such confidence that by leaving out the usual nitty-gritty we were telling the world how famous the show happened to be. The next morning, when Dr. Frank Stanton, president of CBS, opened his *New York Times*, he went apoplectic at his advertising department's "screw-up." My boss Bill Golden was stunned at my audacity, telling me he had just been summoned by Dr. Stanton, but he would fall on his sword for me. I kept protesting that it was a killer ad. By the time Golden got to Frank Stanton's office to take the blame for our "production screw-up," CBS had received so many calls on the hubris and power of the ad that Dr. Stanton *congratulated* him. Bill Golden came to my office and told me how much the appreciative president of CBS admired the ad and said he had responded with "Why, thank you, Frank. I thought it would get a great reaction." As he left my room, he added, "Georgie-boy, let that be a lesson to you," winked and triumphantly strode to his corner office. The groundbreaking quiz show became a worldwide scandal a few years later when it was revealed that some of the contestants' answers were "fixed." But, thank God, our priest came out clean, and remains to this day totally unknown. (For the life of me, I can't remember his name.)

For Cuisine magazine, Christian Millau, of Gault-Millau guidebook fame, turned his Gallic perfectionism and wit to New York restaurants. Informed they would be reviewed, 19 of the chefs begged for heavenly intervention (three chickened out and never left their kitchens).
Most of the chefs pictured had their prayers answered, but it's just as well the chef from Elaine's was one of the no-shows. Millau wrote, "Elaine has the genius to know how to make a fortune serving some of the saddest food in New York," but that he "loved to go to eat Elaine's dreadful spaghetti to watch Woody Allen spend his evenings there to see him hunched over his osso bucco like an undertaker over a freshly opened tomb."

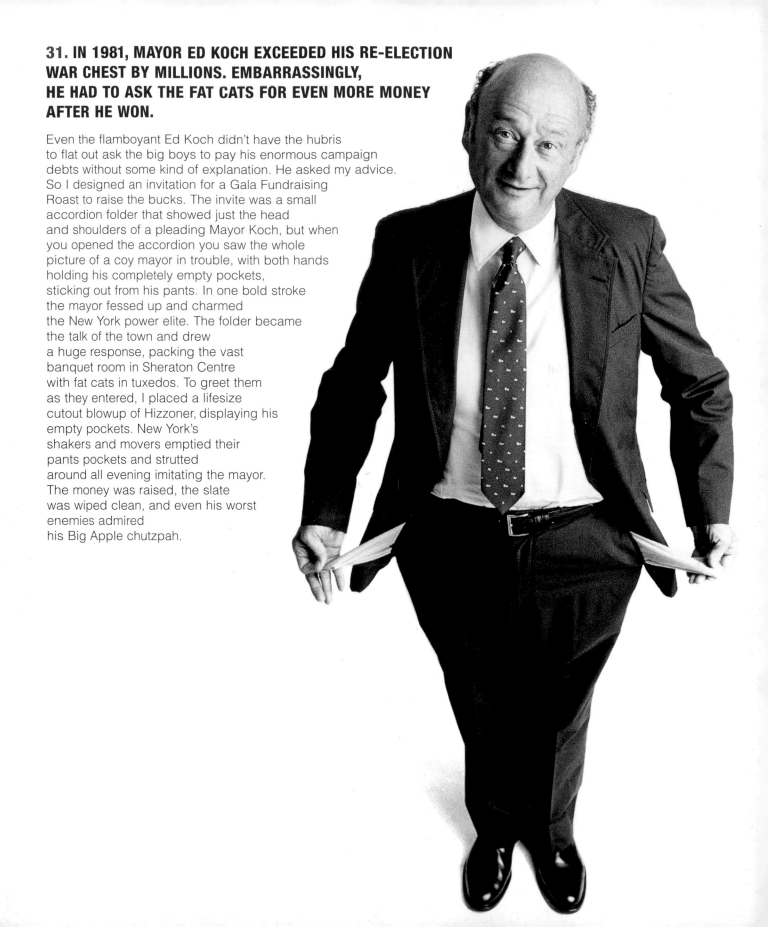

31. IN 1981, MAYOR ED KOCH EXCEEDED HIS RE-ELECTION WAR CHEST BY MILLIONS. EMBARRASSINGLY, HE HAD TO ASK THE FAT CATS FOR EVEN MORE MONEY AFTER HE WON.

Even the flamboyant Ed Koch didn't have the hubris
to flat out ask the big boys to pay his enormous campaign
debts without some kind of explanation. He asked my advice.
So I designed an invitation for a Gala Fundraising
Roast to raise the bucks. The invite was a small
accordion folder that showed just the head
and shoulders of a pleading Mayor Koch, but when
you opened the accordion you saw the whole
picture of a coy mayor in trouble, with both hands
holding his completely empty pockets,
sticking out from his pants. In one bold stroke
the mayor fessed up and charmed
the New York power elite. The folder became
the talk of the town and drew
a huge response, packing the vast
banquet room in Sheraton Centre
with fat cats in tuxedos. To greet them
as they entered, I placed a lifesize
cutout blowup of Hizzoner, displaying his
empty pockets. New York's
shakers and movers emptied their
pants pockets and strutted
around all evening imitating the mayor.
The money was raised, the slate
was wiped clean, and even his worst
enemies admired
his Big Apple chutzpah.

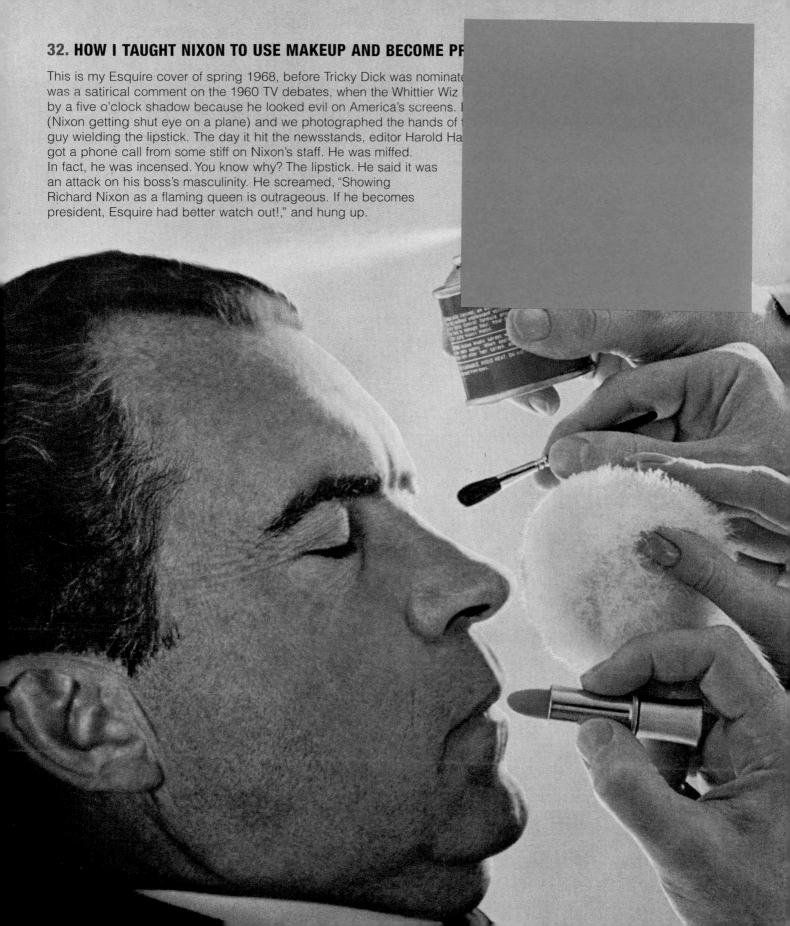

32. HOW I TAUGHT NIXON TO USE MAKEUP AND BECOME PR

This is my Esquire cover of spring 1968, before Tricky Dick was nominate
was a satirical comment on the 1960 TV debates, when the Whittier Wiz
by a five o'clock shadow because he looked evil on America's screens.
(Nixon getting shut eye on a plane) and we photographed the hands of
guy wielding the lipstick. The day it hit the newsstands, editor Harold Ha
got a phone call from some stiff on Nixon's staff. He was miffed.
In fact, he was incensed. You know why? The lipstick. He said it was
an attack on his boss's masculinity. He screamed, "Showing
Richard Nixon as a flaming queen is outrageous. If he becomes
president, Esquire had better watch out!," and hung up.

33. A STAR IS WORN!
CREATING A CELEBRITY WITH TWO OUTRAGEOUS ADS.

The young designer with a boyish grin and an unpronounceable name was totally
unknown when he was launched with a Tommy Hilfiger store on Manhattan's
Upper West Side. My opening ad (turn to next page) challenged the reader with
an audacious claim. Overnight, the burning question in town became
"Who the hell is T_ _ _ _ H_ _ _ _ _ _ _?"
Tommy Hilfiger became instantly famous and set off an avalanche
of national publicity within days. Knowing we struck gold, I then positioned him
in three successive spreads as the leader of fashion's third wave of designers:
First there was Geoffrey Beene, Bill Blass and Stanley Blacker...
Then Calvin Klein, Perry Ellis and Ralph Lauren...
followed by Tommy's impish face pissing off every inhabitant of the Seventh Avenue
schmatte business. This opening campaign outrageously put Tommy Hilfiger
on everyone's lips and millions of backs with a mere $200,000 budget.
This original 1986 Tommy campaign was a self-fulfilling prophecy, because
the young Hilfiger soon became the most famous and
successful designer brand in the world.

THE 4 GREAT AMERICAN DESIGNERS FOR MEN ARE:

R_____ L_____

P_____ E_____

C_____ K_____

T_____ H_____

THIS IS THE
LOGO OF THE
LEAST KNOWN OF
THE FOUR

In most households, the first three names
are household words. Get ready
to add another. His first name (hint) is Tommy.
The second name is not so easy.
But in a few short months everybody
in America will know there's a new look
in town and a new name at the top. Tommy's clothes
are easy-going without being too casual,
classic without being predictable.
He calls them classics with a twist.
The other three designers call them competition.

282 Columbus Avenue
at 73rd Street
New York, New York 10023
(212) 877-1270

© 1985 MURJANI

FULL PAGE MAGAZINE AD AND NEW YORK TELEPHONE KIOSK POSTER

First there was
Geoffrey Beene,
Bill Blass
and
Stanley Blacker.

Then
Calvin Klein,
Perry Ellis
and Ralph Lauren.

Today it's Tommy...

TOMMY

HILFIGER

A third wave of new American talent
is emerging in the eighties.
The brightest of the new menswear
brand names is Tommy Hilfiger.
Tommy Hilfiger's clothes are the
classics of our time.
Style marches on.

At
Tommy Hilfiger,
282 Columbus Avenue
at 73rd Street,
New York 10023
(212) 877-1270
and
Saks Fifth Avenue
Bloomingdale's
Macy's
L. S. Ayres
Neiman-Marcus
and other
fine stores.

THREE SUCCESSIVE MAGAZINE SPREADS, SPORTS ILLUSTRATED, FEBRUARY 10, 1986

34. GODS AND GLADIATORS.

This cover image kicked off an Esquire issue crammed full of exhilarating sportswriting.
Instead of a sports action cover, we photographed Darrel Dess, a pugnacious
New York Giants guard, in the mood of a Renaissance painting, praying for survival.
My headline: *Heaven help him–he's going to play 60 minutes of pro football.*
Back then, a professional athlete praying on his knees was a sight gag. My joke in 1965
has become a reality. In today's game, born-again Christians preach to teammates,
opponents, fans, the media, and anyone within earshot that the only way to heaven is
through Jesus Christ, insisting that those who aren't Christians are doomed to hell.
This bigotry towards Jews, Buddhists, Muslims and agnostics has divided many
a locker room in America. In his Second Inaugural Address, meditating on the paradoxes
of the Civil War, Abraham Lincoln, the greatest moral leader in the Western world
since Jesus Christ, intoned: *Both sides read the same Bible, pray to the same God...
and each invokes His aid against the other.* The idea of a God who is a Giants fan,
or an Eagles fan, or a Patriots fan, or a Redskins fan–is ludicrous. If there *is* a God
who watches NFL football on Sunday afternoons and Monday nights and gives a damn,
while ignoring the millions of starving children in the world, we're all in hell *now.*
(With malice toward none; with charity for all.)

35. DARRYL STRAWBERRY ON DRUGS!

In a Ritz Camera commercial,
I had Darryl Strawberry give advice
to young people:
Don't take drugs...take pictures!
A year later the Yankee slugger was nabbed
with marijuana in his pocket
and was suspended from professional
baseball, and now lives a sordid
life of drug dependency.
Another blow to truth in advertising.

36. THE NO NONSENSE AMERICAN WOMEN AWARD.

The No nonsense brand was known, all too well, as functional, utilitarian legwear.
They needed a makeover to stop declining share for a product women found so lackluster.
There wasn't a chance in hell to get any famous celeb to associate her name with
the brand. So I created *The No nonsense American Woman Award,* given each month
to a powerhouse celebrity, announced in print ads in leading women's magazines.
PR whirlwind Roberta Greene and I struggled to get a celeb to jump-start the campaign,
but the superstars we were after were used to getting a cool million to hawk a
product, and our offer was a measly $5,000 to their favorite charity.
But we hit pay dirt with Governor Ann Richards of Texas. The beautiful, white-coiffured
dynamo gave a press conference in Austin where she flashed a shapely
No nonsense-garbed leg, declaring herself to be proud to be named the very first
No nonsense American Woman. In response to a skeptical reporter, the governor belted
out in her Texas drawl: "Do I wear No nonsense pantyhose? Shoot! Check 'em out, darlin'."
The TV cameras rolled and our kickoff was shown all over America.
In short order the biggies lined up to be seen in *my* version of No nonsense "testimonial" ads:
Barbra Streisand! Tina Turner! Faye Dunaway! Jackie Joyner-Kersee!
Elizabeth Taylor! Gloria Steinem! Barbara Bush! Oprah Winfrey!
Liza Minnelli! Rosalyn Carter! and even the head of Covenant House,
Sister Mary Rose McGeady, who delicately lifted her habit
in response to a doubting reporter. (And Supreme Court justice
Susan Ginsberg wrote us, disappointed that she was not
allowed by federal law to be in an advertisement!)
No nonsense was instantly repositioned as a fresh, fashionable
brand that talked sense to the American woman of the '90s.

JANE ALEXANDER
HELEN GURLEY BROWN
BARBARA BUSH
ROSALYN CARTER
CAROL CHANNING
LEANZA CORNETT
THE DELANEY SISTERS
ELIZABETH DOLE
FAYE DUNAWAY
GLORIA ESTEFAN
ADMIRAL MARSHA EVANS
CHRIS EVERT
DAISY FUENTES
LEEZA GIBBONS
WHOOPI GOLDBERG
DR. BERNARDINE HEALY
JACKIE JOYNER-KERSEE
NAOMI JUDD
NANCY KERRIGAN
JULIE KRONE
ANGELA LANSBURY
SUSAN LUCCI
LT. REBECCA MARIER
REBA McENTIRE
SISTER MARY ROSE McGEADY
LIZA MINNELLI
RITA MORENO
ROSA PARKS
GOV. ANN RICHARDS
CHRISTINA SARALEGUI
MONICA SELES
EUNICE KENNEDY SHRIVER
SEN. OLYMPIA SNOWE
GLORIA STEINEM
MARTHA STEWART
BARBRA STREISAND
ELIZABETH TAYLOR
TINA TURNER
BARBARA WALTERS
OPRAH WINFREY
NAOMI WOLF

TO FAYE DUNAWAY

A LEGENDARY STAR
AND PERFECTIONIST WHO TAKES
NO NONSENSE FROM ANYONE,
THE OSCAR WINNER
ALSO PLAYS AN IMPORTANT ROLE
IN HELPING ABUSED
AND HOMELESS WOMEN DISCOVER
THEIR OWN STRENGTHS
AND TALENTS.

TO ELIZABETH TAYLOR

AFTER A LIFETIME OF
PASSION AND COMPASSION,
SHE REMAINS ONE OF
THE MOST BEAUTIFUL AND INSPIRING
ROLE MODELS IN THE WORLD—
THANKS IN NO SMALL PART TO HER
PIONEERING CAMPAIGN
AGAINST AIDS.

37. RUBIN CARTER. THE OPENING SALVO IN ENLISTING CELEBRITIES TO WAGE A GUERRILLA WAR TO FREE THE INNOCENT HURRICANE.

I showed this tiny ad to Rubin Hurricane Carter
the first day I visited him in the slammer.
I ran it in the news section of the national edition
of *The New York Times* a few days later.
(If it kept you from swallowing your toast too easily
as you were reading the newspaper
that morning, that was okay with me.) The whole
country was buzzing about this unprecedented
(and outrageous) ad from a convicted killer
in prison, appealing for help.
As I phoned celebrities all over the nation, many
told me how moved they were by his plea.
Among others (in two weeks time), Muhammad Ali,
Don King, Hank Aaron, Dave Anderson,
Ed Koch, Gay Talese, Jimmy Breslin, Ellen Burstyn,
Dyan Cannon, Johnny Cash, Norman Mailer,
Walt Frazier, Pete Hamill, Rev. Jesse Jackson,
Arthur Penn, George Plimpton, Bill Walton,
Harry Belafonte, Cleavon Little, Budd Schulberg,
Barry White, Ben Vereen, Burt Reynolds,
Percy Sutton, Earl Monroe, Bud Yorkin, and finally,
Bob Dylan, came to the rescue (see 69, 71).

Counting today, I have sat in prison 3,135 days for a crime I did not commit.

If I don't get a re-trial,
I have 289 years to go.
Six months ago the
'eyewitnesses' who testified
they saw me leaving
a bar in which 3 people had
been killed, admit they
gave false testimony.
Despite this, the judge
who sentenced me won't
give me a re-trial. Why?

**RUBIN HURRICANE CARTER
NO. 45475
TRENTON STATE PRISON**

38. FRANK SINATRA AND HIS SICKO-PHANTS.

In 1966 Esquire editor Harold Hayes
dispatched Gay Talese, one of
his brilliant young finds, to pursue
Frank Sinatra and write a tough piece
(now a classic) on the Chairman
of the Board's power in the
pop music world, in Hollywood,
Las Vegas and Washington.
It inspired this cover of the
brownnosing that lights up the world
of celebrities, from pesty fans
to popularity-seeking presidents.
The honor of one of the few
times I've used illustration went to a
talented pal, Ed Sorel (later of
New Yorker fame), and he nailed it.
Word got back to Esquire
that Ol' Blue Eyes was plenty burnt.
(The ubiquity of the
celebrity profile in popular
magazines since the Hayes era is
typically fawning psychobabble
based on a 15-minute interview over
caffe latte, glorified by yet
another adoring, boring, butt-kissing
magazine cover that sits unsold
on the newsstands.)

"I won't give up the ship. They can't make me. Never."

39. A PROPHETIC TAKE OF RICHARD NIXON.

A scene from my infamous 1973 sales film
(more than a year before Watergate!) that introduced Cutty Sark's
campaign, *Don't give up the ship,* to whiskey distributors.
(After spoofing FDR, Hirohito, the Duke of Windsor, Mae West,
Truman Capote, Ralph Branca & Bobby Thompson,
Neville Chamberlain, Christine Jorgensen, and other august types,
it was the president's turn.) The Nixon look-alike was
Richard *Dixon* (I swear that was his name). This outrageous scene of
our president, alone at night in the Oval Office, getting
soused (with long intervals of sipping Cutty Sark between his spiel),
fractured the whiskey crowd. At the second showing,
the FBI actually swiped the film!

ANNOUNCER VOICEOVER:
Ladies and gentlemen,
the President of the United States!
(Richard Nixon holds up Cutty bottle,
pours and drinks and drinks:)

RICHARD NIXON:

My fellow Americans.
I gave up Carswell and I gave up Haynsworth.
But I won't give up the ship.
I won't give up the ship.
Never! And Teddy can't make me either.
I am the president.
Presidents don't give up ships.
I won't give up the ship.
I won't give up the ship you understand.
They can't make me. Never.
I wouldn't give up the ship.
Not this ship. (Hugs bottle.)
No I won't give you up. (Grabs the phone:)
Henry, you get your ass over
to the Oval Office and bring some
of your broads with you.
(Impatiently waits for Kissinger
as he continues drinking.)
I won't give up the ship. Never.
Where is Henry? (On the phone:)
Henry, get in here. Now!
You could only round up four?
Well that will do. Get in here. C'mon.
I'll never give up the ship.
(Fade to black as the president continues
pouring, sipping and muttering.)

40. "DAT WAS A HELLUVA AD, GEORGE.
A JOEY ARCHER/DICK TIGER BOUT IS ALL THIS TOWN'S TALKIN' ABOUT!
BUT I STILL AIN'T GOT NO FIGHT. HOW DO WE CAGE THIS GUY TIGER?"
"NO SWEAT, JOEY," I SAID.
"LISTEN PAL, YOU GOT ANOTHER TWO HUNDRED BUCKS ON YA?"

In 1966, Joey Archer, from a neighborhood near mine in the Bronx,
was a middleweight contender, trying to get a shot at the crown. The champ then
was the Nigerian Dick Tiger, who wanted nothing to do with Archer,
a good boxer with the reputation as a spoiler. Tiger was planning a rematch with
Emile Griffith, a former champ. Archer, with a Bronx brogue equal to mine,
was a buddy of Ed Rohan, my production manager. When Rohan mentioned to me
that Archer was going nuts and he scraped up a few hundred bucks and was
looking for somebody to do PR, I figured it would be fun to use a chutzpah ad to pull it off.
I did these two one-column ads. They were minuscule but they knocked fight
fans dead. The first ad started the commotion, the second ad churned it into a furor.
The Daily News put Joey on their front page, challenging a snarling tiger
through the bars at the Bronx Zoo. Archer and his flattened beak became a hot property
on the talk-show circuit, while sportswriters attacked the surprised but complacent
Dick Tiger. Finally, the brouhaha forced an immediate elimination bout! A few months after
these tiny ads, a Griffith-Archer match was set for Madison Square Garden.
You know what happened? 1. The fight was a sellout. 2. I didn't get free tickets.
3. I had to buy them from a scalper and I paid through the nose.
4. I bet a bundle on Joey Archer. 5. He lost.

Dear Dick Tiger:

Here's why I think
I deserve
a crack at your
middleweight crown:
The last time we fought,
I beat you!

Respectfully,
Joey Archer

Dear Dick Tiger:

The Middleweight
Champion should meet
the best middleweight
(not a welterweight).
I'm a middleweight,
and I licked every man
I ever fought, including you.

Respectfully,
Joey Archer
P.S.
(How about a fight, Dick?
I'm going broke
on these ads.)

41. CLEOPATRA'S ENORMOUS CLEAVAGE.

Cleopatra was a $40 million production–
the most expensive movie made at that time.
During its filming, the affair between
Richard Burton and Elizabeth Taylor
(while hubby Eddie Fisher was growing horns)
was a worldwide scandal. Esquire did
a long, hilarious piece on the egocentric stars'
open romancing on the set. The hotter
their affair the better for *Cleopatra*'s box office.
So my Esquire cover spoof was a close-up
of a billboard in progress over the Rivoli Theatre
in Manhattan a few weeks before the
flamboyant premiere. The sign painters had
already finished Liz's breasts, so I slipped
them a twenty to raise the scaffold and get back to
the focal point of that incredible farce.

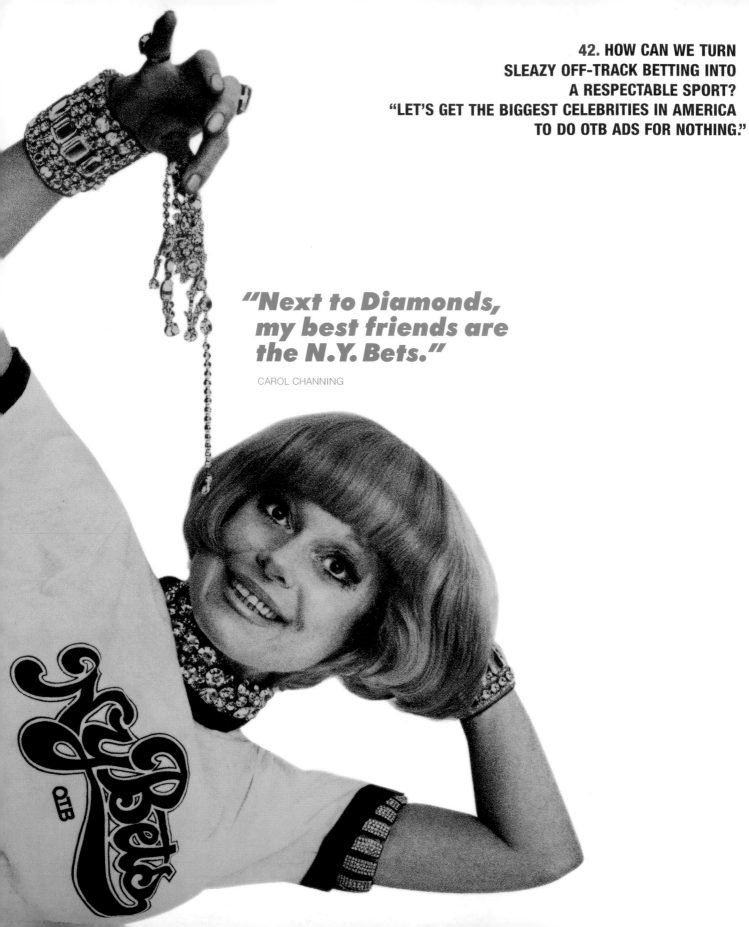

42. HOW CAN WE TURN
SLEAZY OFF-TRACK BETTING INTO
A RESPECTABLE SPORT?
"LET'S GET THE BIGGEST CELEBRITIES IN AMERICA
TO DO OTB ADS FOR NOTHING."

*"Next to Diamonds,
my best friends are
the N.Y. Bets."*

CAROL CHANNING

The chance to do legally, what so many had done outside the law! But after starting with a $700,000,000 handle the first year, OTB was left at the gate. Its macho image didn't invite female bettors...indeed, it hardly lured New York's sporting businessmen (who wouldn't want to be spotted by their bosses in a smoke-filled OTB betting parlor). So when Mayor John Lindsay put former Sanitation Commissioner Paul Screvane in charge, he gave us the job of popularizing OTB in New York. In my best Bronx accent I said to Screvane, "When celebrities come to town we'll ask them to do an ad or commercial or poster, and to show our gratitude, we'll plug their personal appearance in the Big Apple. They'll get publicity, we'll get credibility, and eliminate the 'pool hall' taint and turn every wager into a showbiz lark. And Off-Track Betting will make a bundle. (Come to think of it, it's almost like doing a public service campaign. The money goes to help out New York schools, hospitals and charities, doesn't it?) How could OTB lose?" He went for my pitch big-time. We immediately initiated every New Yorker into a new team: *You're too heavy for the Mets? You're too light for the Jets? You're too short for the Nets? You're just right for the Bets!* Our New York Bets T-shirts became the hot fashion item on the streets of New York, and we celebrated our team imagery with ads, posters and commercials, starring (gratis!) showbiz biggies Rodney Dangerfield (who showed New Yorkers how to dress better), Carol Channing, Henny Youngman, Ben Vereen, Lainie Kazan, Jack Gilford, Professor Irwin Corey, Lynn Redgrave, Imogene Coca, Bobby Short, Eddie Arcaro, Willie Shoemaker, Joey Heatherton, Joel Grey, and finally megastars Jackie Gleason, Bob Hope and Frank Sinatra. All of a sudden, betting on a horse at a betting parlor was now socially okay! After the campaign jumped OTB's handle to $1.8 billion, City Hall politics reared its ugly head and a new mayor chose a new ad agency. The "dese, dem and dose" mentality re-emerged, sales took a dive, and today, once again, you wouldn't be caught dead walking into an OTB parlor.

"And awaaay we go... to an OTB parlor." JACKIE GLEASON...WITH BOB HOPE

**"You're too heavy for the Mets?
You're too light for the Jets?
You're too short for the Nets?
You're just right for the Bets!"**

PROFESSOR IRWIN COREY

"Maybe now
I'll get some
respect."

RODNEY DANGERFIELD

"Some of my favorite performers are horses."

NYBets
OTB

43. "GEORGE, THERE'S SOME NUT ON THE PHONE WHO INSISTS HE'S FRANK SINATRA."

The coup de grace in my ongoing campaign to convince celebrities to sport *New York Bets*
T-shirts (as a public service to the city) came one day when my secretary uttered the words above.
I figured it was a call from a pal pulling my leg, but after hearing four notes of the voice
on the phone, I knew it was Frank Sinatra, calling to ask me, hell, *insisting*, that he be shown
all over town wearing our OTB sweatshirt. I gulped (not volunteering that I was responsible
for the 1966 Esquire cover that he was reported to have detested) and one week later,
the greatest name in showbiz was plastered all over town with his ringing
(I should say *singing*) endorsement.

44. "MRS. ONASSIS, WOULD YOU HONOR THE FOUR SEASONS BY GIVING US YOUR JOHN HANCOCK!"

The Four Seasons restaurant has been the marvel of the intensely competitive
restaurant business in New York City since its creation in 1959 by the
legendary Joe Baum. In 1970, its new owners, Tom Margittai and Paul Kovi,
both émigrés from their native Hungary in the aftermath of World War II,
were open to many fresh ideas about marketing to the upper crust.
Their *Power Lunch* at their spectacular Grill Room became the epitome of the
powerbroker powwow in America, and my *Spa Cuisine* moniker became
a generic name for diet gourmet food, an oxymoron when we conceived it in
the early '80s. (We had a right to sue everyone in the world for
using our registered name, but we would have been in court five days a week.)
Acknowledged as being the most beautiful restaurant in the world
(designed by Philip Johnson in Mies van der Rohe's iconic Seagram Building)
the Seasons reflected the Hungarian dynamic duo's imagination and
receptiveness to new ideas, not the least of which was a good old-fashioned
autograph book! When I showed them the idea of presenting a thick,
lush, pigskin-covered book to renowned celebrities, they recoiled at its hoi polloi
brashness. But they took a whack at it, and it soon became a signature
event among their world-famous guests. The remarkable archive of autographs
and salutations (some shown compiled on the endpapers of this book)
is a Who's Who of some of the most important people of the twentieth century.
In a stylish cookbook published in 1980 I immortalized the over one
thousand celebrities who made The Four Seasons the haute cuisine marketing
miracle of New York, by reproducing their names scribbled over the
recipes of James Beard and their master chefs.

45. JOE STALIN'S FINK DAUGHTER.

When Joe Stalin's daughter came to the U.S. in 1967, her face showed up on the cover of every magazine except *Popular Mechanics*. Newsstands from New York to California were transformed into photo galleries of a motherly Svetlana Stalin. Her old man was a despot, but I felt that anyone who told stories on her father was a lousy fink. (Call me old-fashioned.) Then Esquire ran a lead article on Stalin's little girl and I was stuck with coming up with *another* Svetlana cover. The story, written by Gary Wills, was at least a skeptical piece. It described her weird hangups with assorted religions. It analyzed how she was taken in hand by the smart boys in publishing and our Red-baiting State Department when she came to America with her red-hot manuscript about Life with Father Josef. I was so offended by her that I picked up a copy of *Newsweek*, splashed with a dreamy shot of Svetlana, grabbed a grease pencil and scribbled Stalin's moustache on her mush. Some people were offended by this cover because Svetlana had been elevated to sainthood by the time it appeared.
To those people I can only say: Your father's moustache.

46. ROBERT REDFORD PURGES HIS GUILT FOR DEPICTING JEREMIAH JOHNSON SLAUGHTERING WOLVES.

In 1968 I was having lunch with the editor of Natural History magazine. Twice a year their subscribers received two gifts, usually paperbacks, that cost the Museum of Natural History a half a buck apiece. As he was describing his gift problems, a ravishing model swept into The Four Seasons, fulsomely garbed from neck to toe in a fashionable wolf coat. My guest went ape, slamming down his Wolfschmidt vodka, and launched into a tirade against this extinction of yet another of God's species. He was a confessed wolf freak, so much so, he told me, that he owned hundreds of wolf calls on tape. Bingo! So we produced a record of wolf calls, with a commentary written by Ron Holland, another nature nut. And for the narrator, none other than Robert Redford, who was in the midst of shooting *Jeremiah Johnson* in the wilds of Utah. (I figured the great actor would welcome the chance to idealize the wolf–after killing off hundreds of them for the fur trade in his hit movie.) A month later we mailed out 250,000 records. Dogs in every neighborhood bounced off four walls when they heard the calls of their ancestors. The music critic Harold Schonberg reviewed the wolves' efforts on the *front page* of *The New York Times*! Then the rights were sold to Columbia Records, with receipts continuing to go to Natural History magazine. Robert Redford's wolf record (you should excuse the expression) was a howling success.

47. THE PONTIAC CHOIRBOYS: 87 DEALERS BECOME NEIGHBORHOOD CELEBRITIES.

An advertising committee of car dealers spells tsuris. Each Pontiac dealer had his own ad agency, each with a little advertising knowledge: 87 guys who thought they were advertising experts. You could get run over. I had to figure out (1) a campaign that would bring people to their showrooms, and (2) a campaign they could all *like*. Angelically, I called my new clients *The Pontiac Choirboys,* and showed them my idea where *each* was a star, singing parodies of five folklore melodies, pleading with car buyers. *Who* could turn down fame and fortune (and get to sing on TV)! In each commercial, the camera panned over 87 faces, each getting his spot in the limelight. Neighbors stopped into their local dealer to say they saw him singing on TV. Once inside the showroom they were fair game for a sales spiel. As the campaign hummed along and dealer traffic flowed, I filmed a sequel of three more parodies of famous songs. But instead of the Choirboys, their *wives* would be filmed, selling for their husbands. (To my chagrin, I learned several divorces were pending, while quite a few Choirboys weren't on speaking terms with their Choirgirls, or vice versa.)

THE PONTIAC CHOIRBOYS
TO THE TUNE OF *I SURRENDER DEAR*:

You ran away the other day
You said you had one price to pay
Why don't you stop around today
And we'll surrender, dear

VOICEOVER:
Your Pontiac dealer gives up!
He'll make any deal to sell you a Pontiac.

THE PONTIAC CHOIRBOYS
TO THE TUNE OF *MY BONNIE*:

Last night you walked into my showroom
We tried very hard to agree
If you really want that new Pontiac
Then bring back your money to me
Bring back, bring back
Oh bring back your money to me, to me
Bring back, bring back
Oh, bring back your money to me

VOICEOVER:
Look at all those faces.
I trust every one of those men!

THE PONTIAC CHOIRGIRLS
TO THE TUNE OF
MY DARLING CLEMENTINE:

We're the wives of
All the salesmen
And we hate
To cry the blues
But we really need your business
'Cause the kids are needin' shoes!
Oh, my darlin'
Be a darlin'
Bring us money
By the sack
Be a darlin'
Help the children
Buy a darlin' Pontiac!

48. "LOIS, WE CAN'T LET YOU KEEP RUNNING THAT JOE LOUIS SPOT FOR EDWARDS & HANLY! WE CAN'T ALLOW THE MOST FAMOUS TESTIMONIAL EVER FOR A STOCKBROKER TO BE A... BLACK MAN."

In 1967, when creating the first TV campaign ever for a stockbroker
(and for Edwards & Hanly, the least known) we needed unlikely celebs,
whose presence would swiftly suggest that here was a smart,
sharp bunch of brokers, unlike all the traditional, stuffy Wall Street houses.
Joe Louis led my list, a great man who lost all his money and ended his years
living off the kindness of friends. Using the Brown Bomber was
a powerfully subtle way of telling the world that Edwards & Hanly were not just
hip shooters–and were tuned into the real world. The spot was a mere
ten seconds long: *Edwards & Hanly–where were you when I needed you?,* he asked.
It was also a full-page *New York Times* ad with Joe's beautiful puss, sad and
deep and spectacular. The commercial was an immediate sensation as the media
exploded with articles by sportswriters, gossip columnists, financial writers,
and mass culture buffs, all clamoring to write about the almost forgotten champ.
Edwards & Hanly's business skyrocketed as they became (in a few weeks time)
as famous as Merrill Lynch. *Where were you when I needed you?* declared
that Edwards & Hanly was an honest, thoughtful broker that understood the perils
of flashy advice. Because Joe Louis was a thorn in America's conscience,
the message had the impact of Joe's first-round knockout of Hitler's favorite fighter,
Max Schmeling. But Joe's ten seconds became too famous for Wall Street
to take. Racism, once again, reared its ugly head, and the bigots
at the Exchange KO'd Joe Louis.

"I just wanna say one thing. Edwards & Hanly– where were you when I needed you?"

The New American Woman:
through at 21.

49. THE REASON THERE'S NO FILM INGENUE ON THIS ESQUIRE COVER? I COULDN'T CON ONE TO STICK HER ASS IN MY GARBAGE CAN!

From the very first cover I created for editor Harold Hayes, Esquire newsstand sales and circulation grew dramatically. Nonetheless, the ad sales gang at Esquire bitched and moaned, fearful of my "controversial" covers. Though ad pages rose through the Hayes decade, some of my covers scared some ad agencies into pulling their monthly ads. But in the sexist '60s, the ad bunch was comfortable with the traditional Esquire pinup covers and hounded Harold Hayes for Lois cheesecake. To help take some heat off Hayes,

I ended my boycott of tits-and-ass and asked firebrand Claudia Cardinale if she would mount a Triumph for a December 1966 cover. She hopped on, bellowed away in her lush Italian tongue on all cylinders and revved up a lot of engines with a big newsstand sale: more than the first black Santa (see 21), more than my anti-Vietnam War covers...pissed me off! Esquire owners, hoping for a "safe" pinup trend, pushed Hayes for yet another. So a few months later, when the great editor planned an issue on The New American Woman: Through at 21, I saw my chance. An anti-pinup pinup of a beautiful movie ingenue dumped in a trash can! (I craved the young beauty Ali MacGraw, seemingly destined for stardom.) When I told a Hollywood agent I wanted to put her client on an Esquire cover, she swooned. When I explained the visual, she swore. After more than a dozen turndowns, and presses about to roll, push came to shove so I was forced to find a willing fashion model. When Hayes pulled my cover from my monthly envelope and saw my stuffed tomato, he ate it up. (But he never asked for a "girlie" cover again.)

50. WHEN YOU GOT IT—FLAUNT IT!
A JUXTAPOSITION OF CELEBRITY ODD COUPLES, PORTRAYED AS LOVABLE SPOTLIGHT HUSTLERS, TRYING TO OUT-BULLSHIT EACH OTHER AS THEY FLY BRANIFF.

In 1967, *When you got it—flaunt it!* became an American colloquialism as well as a standard entry in the anthologies of American sayings, almost instantly. It was my slogan for Braniff—a zany, outrageous campaign that featured a smorgasbord of the world's oddest couples, exchanging the screwiest and most sophisticated chatter heard on television. Our juxtaposition of unlikely couples was unprecedented, creating the perception that when you flew Braniff International, you never knew who might be in the seat next to you. Pop guru Andy Warhol tried (but failed) to engage the sullen heavyweight champ Sonny Liston...Salvador Dali *(Wen yo godet–flawndet!)* talked baseball with Whitey Ford...black baseball legend Satchel Paige talked about youth and fame

ANDY WARHOL:
*Of course, remember there is an inherent beauty in soup cans
that Michelangelo could not have imagined existed.*

SONNY LISTON:
*(Listens to Warhol as if he's from outer space
and gives the camera a double take.)*

ANNOUNCER VO:
*Talkative Andy Warhol
and gabby Sonny Liston
always fly Braniff.
Thanks for flying Braniff, fellas.*

ANDY WARHOL:
When you got it—flaunt it!

SONNY LISTON:
*(Gives the camera another
puzzled look.)*

with neophyte Dean Martin Jr....poet Marianne Moore discussed writing with crime novelist Mickey Spillane...
Rex Reed dueled with Mickey Rooney...British comedienne Hermione Gingold trumped film legend George Raft
at his own game, whilst inundating him with pretentious palaver. Sounds wacky on the face of it, but as
we eavesdrop on these odd couples trying to outflaunt each other, we hear everything that has to be said about
Braniff. We also imply that you might bump into a celebrity or two on a Braniff flight. (Yet another spot
was produced with a Braniff stewardess welcoming an eclectic procession of business travelers: Joe Namath,
Emilio Pucci, the Italian fashion designer to the Jet Set, thespians Gina Lollobrigida, Tab Hunter and
Sandra Locke, jockey Diane Crump and the Rock group Vanilla Fudge.) They are not idealized celebrities–
they are famous people who are portrayed as lovable extroverts, combined to radiate a surreal kind of
believability. A commercial has little credibility if we think its spokespersons are hustling a buck.
Celebrities must not look like mercenaries. I make them believable by showing them in a human way,
downplaying their celebrity.

WHITEY FORD:
Now tell me the truth, don't you think a knuckleball is much harder to throw than a screwball?

SALVADOR DALI:
Oh no, no, no, no Whitey.

ANNOUNCER VO:
Whitey Ford and his new friend Salvador Dali always fly Braniff. Thanks for flying Braniff, fellas.

SALVADOR DALI:
Wen yo godet-flawndet!

WHITEY FORD:
Tell'em, Dali baby.

HERMIONE GINGOLD:
Gin! And that's four in a row, Mister Raft.

GEORGE RAFT:
I just can't get the hang of this game.

ANNOUNCER VO:
Fastfingered Hermione Gingold and innocent George Raft always fly Braniff. Thanks for flying Braniff, fellas.

HERMIONE GINGOLD:
When you got it—flaunt it!

GEORGE RAFT:
I just can't get the hang of this game.

BENNETT CERF:
We have a saying in the theater; I wonder if you ever heard it? "There's no business like show business." (Merman gives us a "what a jerk" look.)

ANNOUNCER VO:
Friendly Bennett Cerf and showstopper Ethel Merman always fly Braniff. Thanks for flying Braniff, fellas.

ETHEL MERMAN:
When you got it—flaunt it!

BENNETT CERF:
(finally recognizing her) Ethel Merman!!!!

MICKEY SPILLANE:
Well, I'll tell you frankly.
What I really wanted to be all my life was a poet.
Only I couldn't think of any of the rhymes.
You know what I mean?

MARIANNE MOORE:
I know what you mean.

ANNOUNCER VO:
Tough Mickey Spillane and
the great Marianne Moore always fly Braniff.
Thanks for flying Braniff, folks.

MARIANNE MOORE:
When you got it–flaunt it!

MICKEY SPILLANE:
You know, you got a way with words.
(Marianne giggles.)

REED: *Are you Mickey Rooney?*

ROONEY: *Aren't you Rex Reed?*

REED: *Are you really Mickey Rooney?*

ROONEY: *Aren't you really Rex Reed?*

REED: *Oh come on you gotta be kidding!*

ROONEY: *Look who's talking.*

ANNOUNCER VO: *Inquisitive Rex Reed*
and relentless Mickey Rooney always fly Braniff.
Thanks for flying Braniff, fellas.

REED & ROONEY: *(in perfect unison)*
When you got it–flaunt it!

ROONEY: *Let me tell you, Mr. Reed, the last time...*

REED: *Listen, Mickey...*

DEAN MARTIN JR.:
You've got to live fast and hard
because by the time you reach 21 it's all over.

SATCHEL PAIGE: *(with booze in hand)*
Tell me more, old-timer.

ANNOUNCER VO:
Aging Dean Martin Jr. and youthful
pitcher Satchel Paige always fly Braniff.
Thanks for flying Braniff, men.

DEAN MARTIN JR.: *(being handed a drink)*
When you got it–flaunt it!

SATCHEL PAIGE: *Drink your sarsaparilla.*

51. THE NIGHT AFTER ED SULLIVAN INTRODUCED THE BEATLES TO AMERICA, HE FLIPPED HIS WIG.

Ed Sullivan became well known as the gossipy Broadway columnist for the *Daily News* and a fierce competitor
to the almighty Walter Winchell and his nasty world as depicted in the movie and musical *Sweet Smell of Success*.
Then Sullivan became internationally famous as the stiff who introduced Elvis, and later the Beatles, to America.
Watching showman Ed Sullivan bring Beatlemania to our shores on his Sunday-night TV variety show, I knew Esquire
had to acknowledge this seemingly uncool establishment elder, with his uncanny knack for being
on the cutting edge of popular culture (even though he kept his cameras off the pelvis of Elvis a decade before).
The Liverpool Fab Four with their outrageous bowl cuts had landed, and they swiftly reached the apex of pop
music. So that Monday morning, I tried to go through channels at CBS, and ask the impresario to pose...
in a Beatles wig! My first job as a Korean vet was at CBS working for the all-powerful image-maker Bill Golden,
the creator of the CBS eye. And I knew my old boss, Bill Paley, the chairman of CBS, was a fan of my
Esquire covers. But Mr. Paley brushed me off, unsure of what effect the imagery of that "really big" showman
wearing a Beatles wig would have. So I decided to amble over to the Ed Sullivan Theater
(where David Letterman now cavorts) and camp at the entrance, like a sicko-fan, right there on Broadway.
When Sullivan finally came out, I shoved a sketch of my proposed Esquire cover in his face and talked fast.
He took a long look and grinned ear to ear, just like the photo we took the next day.
He wore his wig with unabashed gusto and smiled like Ringo.

52. AKIN TO THE EXAGGERATED THEATRICS OF WRESTLEMANIA, WE CREATED THE "MIGHTY MOUTH" OF TELEVISION. (SO YOU CAN BLAME ME FOR THE BIRTH OF NO-HOLDS-BARRED TV TABLOID JOURNALISM IN AMERICA.)

Until Morton Downey shot himself in the foot, he had the
most successful syndicated TV show in America. Bob Pittman, previously the young
daddy of MTV, wanted to create an inexpensive, popular-appeal TV talk show,
centered around one of the screwball radio personalities of the day.
We chose Morton Downey Jr. One look at his choppers and I knew he was our man.
My "Mighty Mouth" logo mirrored his striking kisser with the most dangerous
dentures in the world. To ensure that America would get his tongue-in-cheek bombast,
I produced a campaign of spots and ads that warned the world he was on the way.

53. BUSINESS AT CUISINE WAS FLAT AS A PANCAKE.
SINCE FOOD MAGAZINE COVERS WERE ALWAYS LUSCIOUS FOOD SHOTS,
I COOKED UP A SURPRISE: CELEBRITIES!

This is a sad story of how my ad campaign and covers transformed Cuisine
from a loser to a winner, only to have it gobbled up by a competitor.
To prove that epicurean magazines need not survive on recipes alone, I helped
convert Cuisine into a lifestyle magazine with the advertising theme,
Cuisine comes out of the kitchen. To send a signal to readers and the ad world that
Cuisine had, indeed, changed, I created their covers in 1984 for six explosive
months of increased circulation and hot ad sales. They included a soliloquy by the
irascible Art Buchwald, an exquisite Japanese print, a mass photo of
famous New York chefs (see 30), the Big Daddy of American cuisine, James Beard
(see Favorite Celebs 2), and on a special issue on great American sandwiches
the all-American image of Dagwood Bumstead about to dig into one of his famous
creations. Cuisine was asserting itself as a magazine of modern living,
rather than a recipe book. But when Cuisine's circulation and advertising sales took off,
their refreshing vitality frightened the leading food magazine, *Gourmet*.
The owner of Condé Nast, Sy Newhouse, bought Cuisine for big bucks to keep
readers and advertisers from comparing his lackluster publication
to the new Cuisine. "If you can't beat 'em, buy 'em!"

54. SAYONARA TO THE MOST GRANDIOSE
BASEBALL DREAM SCHEME EVER.

In 1974, when nobody knew what
a Subaru was, I persuaded the
Japanese pitching ace Masaichi Kaneda to
pitch the car. I filmed him in TV spots
with Lou Brock, Gaylord Perry,
Yogi Berra and Billy Martin–all telling their
fellow Americans of the greatness
of Kaneda. And, in sessions
with the Baseball Commissioner's office,
we plotted the first true World Series–
between America's winning team and Japan's.
But just as we were ready to spring the
campaign, a new head man took over Subaru.
He hated baseball, he hated me,
and he hated my strategy of telling America
about a star from Japan
(a baseball player or a car) and he
kamikazied my master plan.

55. SPOOFING INSTANT GLAMOUR.

On the assumption that most (intelligent) women saw lipstick ads
as the usual cosmetics con job, I created this Coty ad that ridiculed instant glamour.
Comedienne Alice Pearce, applying lipstick, proved that a little dab would not only do ya,
it would turn any wallflower into a young, sensual Joey Heatherton!
And in a TV spot, I shot Alice Ghostley, another beautifully talented non-beauty,
dissolving werewolf-style into luscious Joey. (Using unknowns as the beauty
and the beast would have been a total turn-off, but using celebrities was a total delight.)
Cremestick by Coty smeared all the other lipsticks at Bloomingdale's.

56. NOT JUST 3 PRETTY FACES.

There were seven million kids at college in 1968, and their favorite
performers included the beautiful Tiny Tim *(Tiptoe through the Tulips)*,
beautiful Michael J. Pollard *(Bonnie & Clyde)*,
and the beautiful Arlo Guthrie *(Alice's Restaurant)*.
It wasn't easy to make them look even more beautiful
than they really happened to be, but I believe
this Esquire cover succeeded beautifully.

57. "I'M LOIS." "I'M HOLLAND." "I'M CALLAWAY."
"AND WE DO THE ADVERTISING FOR EDWARDS & HANLY."

One of the spots that made the least-known Wall Street brokerage firm famous in 1967
was a commercial using three kids. The first said, *My daddy's an astronaut!*
The next said, *My daddy's a fireman!* The third said, *My daddy works for Edwards & Hanly!*
Then you hear the first two say *Woww!* Edwards & Hanly became so famous,
all the big marketing agencies began scouting for new clients in Wall Street, always
considered tombstone territory. Finally, my partners, Ron Holland,
Jim Callaway and I, decided to make *ourselves* famous. So we ran a spot where the first guy
said *I'm Lois,* the second said, *I'm Holland,* and the third said, *I'm Callaway...*
and we do the advertising for Edwards & Hanly. Then the same kids chorus went *Woww!*
We got four new accounts that week. *Woww!*

58. PROCLAIMING THE MARTYRDOM OF MUHAMMAD ALI
FOR REFUSING TO FIGHT IN A BAD WAR.

In 1967, the world heavyweight champion refused induction into the army.
He had converted to Islam, and under the tutelage of Elijah Muhammad he had become a
Black Muslim minister. When Ali refused military service as a conscientious objector
because of his new religion, a federal jury sentenced him to five years in jail for draft evasion.
Boxing commissions then stripped him of his title and denied him the right to fight, in
the prime of his fighting years. He was widely condemned as a draft dodger and even a traitor.
When Cassius Clay became Muhammad Ali, he had also become a martyr. In 1968,
while he was waiting for his appeal to reach the Supreme Court, I wanted to pose him as a modern
St. Sebastian, modeled after the fifteenth-century painting by Castagno that hangs in the
Metropolitan Museum of Art. I contacted Ali and explained my idea and he flew to New York.
At the studio, I showed him a postcard of the painting by Castagno to illustrate the stance.
Muhammad studied it with enormous concentration. Suddenly he blurted out,
"Hey, George, this cat's a Christian!" I blurted back, "Holy Moses, you're right, Champ!"
I explained to Ali that St. Sebastian was a Roman soldier who survived execution
by arrows for converting to Christianity. He was then clubbed to death, and has gone down in
history as the definitive martyr. Before we could affix any arrows to Ali, he got on the phone
with his religious leader, Elijah Muhammad. Ali explained the painting in excruciating detail. He was
concerned about the propriety of using a Christian source for the portrayal of his martyrdom.
He finally put me, a non-practicing Greek Orthodox, on the phone. After a lengthy
theological discussion and my soliloquy on symbolism, Elijah gave me his okay. I exhaled and we
shot this portrait of a deified man against the authorities. When I saw the first Polaroid as
we were posing Ali, I believe my exact words to photographer Carl Fischer were
"Jesus Christ, it's a masterpiece." Esquire had a terrifying (and very controversial) cover
that has become an iconic symbol of a period of nonviolent protest in those turbulent times.
The cover nailed down the plight of many Americans who took a principled stand against
the Vietnam War and payed a heavy price for doing the right thing. Three years after the cover ran,
the Supreme Court unanimously threw out Muhammad Ali's conviction.
Allah be praised!

"Hey, George,
this cat's a Christian!"

MUHAMMAD ALI

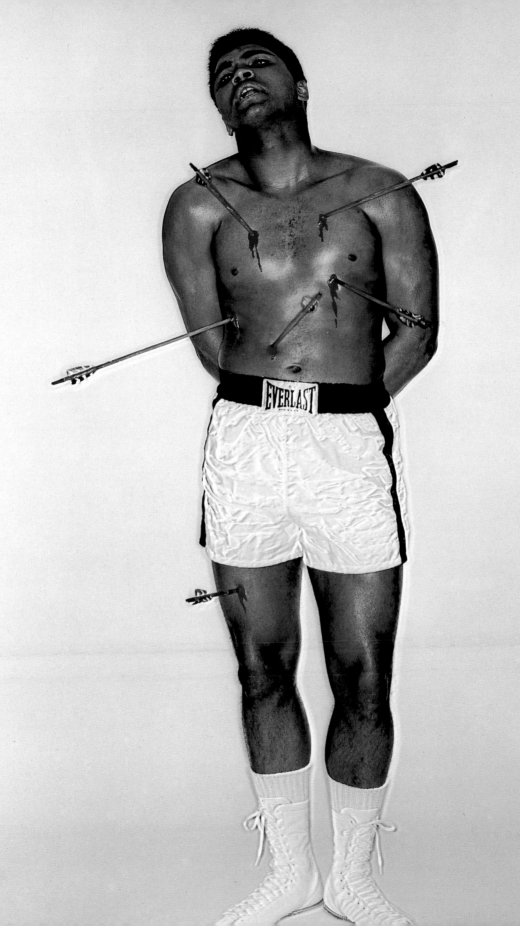

59. GETTING OLD AND FAT AND WEARING THIN AFTER 24 YEARS AS A SENATOR, AND WAY BEHIND IN THE POLLS, MAGGIE WINS IN A LANDSLIDE... BY MERELY POINTING HIS FINGER.

Republicans were licking their chops, certain that Democratic senator Warren G. Magnuson was finally a cooked goose. The polls bore them out while the press laughed at his baggy suits and the food stains on his tie, and more than implied that he was stupid, and derisively called him Maggie. The end was near and the senator and his staff felt it in their bones. He even went job hunting, lining up a federal judgeship through his old Senate drinking buddy, President Lyndon Johnson. But this was a guy America couldn't afford to lose. Magnuson had fought for Medicare, for the Atomic Test Ban Treaty, for gun control (and he was from Washington, a gun-happy state!) and was a pioneer fighter for consumer protection laws. We knew we had to begin with a memorable message that could immediately change the perception that Maggie was washed up. I stunned the senator and his troops when I proposed a seemingly self-deprecating TV spot, but with his back to the wall, he gulped, and bit the bullet. After the voters of Washington saw Maggie point a finger to his head and tap his noggin– the senator became, overnight, a folk hero, from a sure loser to a landslide winner. The image of Maggie pointing a finger to his head became an instant mnemonic throughout the State of Washington. By admitting that he may have had his faults–he was able to put across the more important truth that he had the right stuff between the ears, as people around the state mimicked our finger-pointing sign language with endearment. By underscoring his humanity, we convinced the voters in Washington State that they had a helluva man representing them in Washington, D.C.

ANNOUNCER VO:
*Senator Magnuson, there comes
a time when every young senator shows
that he's putting on years.*

SENATOR MAGNUSON:
*(Maggie's hands jut out as if to say,
"What can I do about it?")*

ANNOUNCER VO:
*Senator Magnuson,
there comes a time–sure as fate–when
slim senators assume a more "impressive" stature.*

SENATOR MAGNUSON:
*(The reference to his being overweight destroys
Maggie as he ruefully glances at his belly.)*

ANNOUNCER VO:
*So once youth is gone,
once dash is gone, what can you possibly
offer the voters of Washington?*

SENATOR MAGNUSON:
*(Maggie reels back at the zinger,
regains his poise, looks straight at the camera
and taps his head–once, twice, three times.)*

ANNOUNCER VO:
*In his rumpled suit, carrying 20 extra pounds,
and showing some signs of wear,
Warren Magnuson remains a giant in the
United States Senate.*

60. A SISSY, SUPERSTAR TOUR DE FORCE. THE GREATEST MACHO SPORTS ICONS OF THE '60s WEEPING AND MOANING ON TV.

Instead of a kid wailing at his mom for Maypo, I made a 180° turn away from the obvious. Instead of *kids* crying *I want my Maypo!*, I used the greatest superstars of professional sports to sell Maypo to small fry, five to twelve years old. Maypo had always been considered a baby cereal, and to really hit one out of the park, I had to appeal to the pre-teenagers. I showed Mickey Mantle, Johnny Unitas, Wilt Chamberlain, Ray Nitschke, Oscar Robertson and Don Meredith– all in one television spot, crying for their Maypo and shedding lifelike tears. Here was the ultimate sissification of the American macho sports hero, a twisteroo on the unconscionable hustles by jocks who manipulated kids through hero worship. Instead, the sports greats in our spot sold obliquely, displaying self-mocking wit. The words and visuals–superstars crying *I want my Maypo!*–gave the campaign extraordinary power (making it the most tearful TV spot ever made!). A single-minded merger of words and pictures had been accomplished, resulting in riveting imagery. American kids ate it up. (The word *imagery* is too often associated purely with visuals, but it is much more than that: *Imagery is the conversion of an idea into a theatrical cameo, an indelible symbol, a scene that becomes popular folklore, an iconographic image. And this imagery can be expressed in words and visuals or, ideally, both.)*

"I want my Maypo!"

MICKEY MANTLE
JOHNNY UNITAS
WILT CHAMBERLAIN
RAY NITSCHKE
OSCAR ROBERTSON
DON MEREDITH

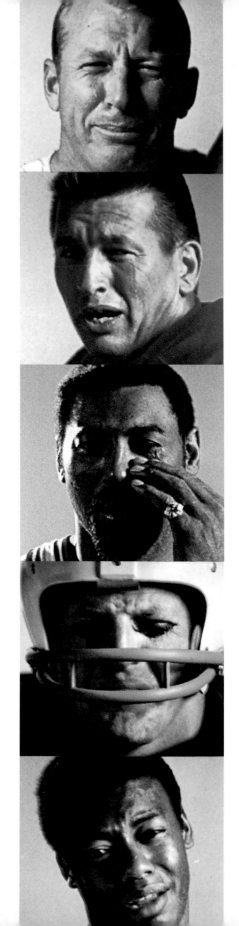

61. "I WAS SO SHOCKED— IT MADE MY HAIR STAND ON END!"

Don King, the most bombastic wheeler-dealer of our time, discovers
Circuit City offers him the lowest prices in town, *without* haggling.
With the TV camera on an extreme close-up of the flamboyant boxing promoter,
Don King belts out his message of low prices for electronic products
at Circuit City. And when he delivers his punch line, *It made my hair stand on end*,
the camera widens to reveal his signature hairdo, seemingly springing up
in front of our eyes. Another stunning example of using a celebrity for the surprise
of their *seeming* irrelevance to the product!

62. JACKIE OH!

Two vivid images, frozen in our collective memories:
the widow of our murdered 35th president, draped over her
husband's body in the fatal motorcade. Then, rigid
in a blood-splattered dress, beside Lyndon Johnson
as he is sworn in. Her elegance under fire
transformed a repulsive time of gore and national
shame, somehow elevating it to a gaunt beauty.
Then, Saint Jackie, the most public and
revered woman in America, did the
unimaginable: While still held heroic in her
grief, this strangely spacey widow of the
glorious JFK leapt into the oily embrace
of the anti-hero, Aristotle Onassis. As she
abandoned the walls of the Kennedy
compound for the blue waters of the Aegean,
she boggled the mind of even the most loyal
Jackie-lovers among us. Since, as far as we know,
Ari possessed no particular grace or attribute, we were forced
to conclude Mrs. Kennedy opted for the big bucks.
We felt betrayed, our admiration besmirched. A special
Esquire issue on "The Pursuit of Happiness" displayed our dismay.
I rather vulgarly suggested what our iconic First Lady might
want to see in her new husband and protector, grafting
his head on the body of a youthful, well-built Greek
god. Surprisingly, a business associate very close to Onassis
told me Aristotle laughed heartily when shown the cover.
(Maybe there was more to Ari than we thought.)

63. PORTRAIT OF A FAMOUS PARENT.

Before Gay Talese's *Honor Thy Father* was published, Esquire ran a lengthy excerpt from the book on the most famous wiseguy celeb of the time, Joe Bonanno, and his family, a labor of love that had taken six years to write. When I read the piece, I knew that its title was incredibly apt. Although *Honor Thy Father* was a major study of an Italian-American family enmeshed in the Mafia over two generations, it caught the deep love and loyalty between son and father, between Joe Bonanno Jr., then in federal prison, and Joe Sr., who died a ruined man. I felt the subject should be handled with a shocking reverence, rather than with Mafia-reporting sensationalism. So I got Talese to get me an entree into the Bonanno home in New Jersey, where I hoped to get a family photo of the elder Bonanno. His widow was suspicious, but Gay explained in his lush Italian what we were after and why. Mamma Bonanno dug up a few '30s-style sepia studio portraits, including this gem, and I knew I had the cover, one that would express perfectly a son's respect for his father, no matter what line of work the old man was in.

64. "I AM ALARMO, SHOUTING FROM THE ROOFTOPS. BURGLARS GET OUTTA TOWN WHEN THEY SEE THE SLOMIN'S SHIELD!"

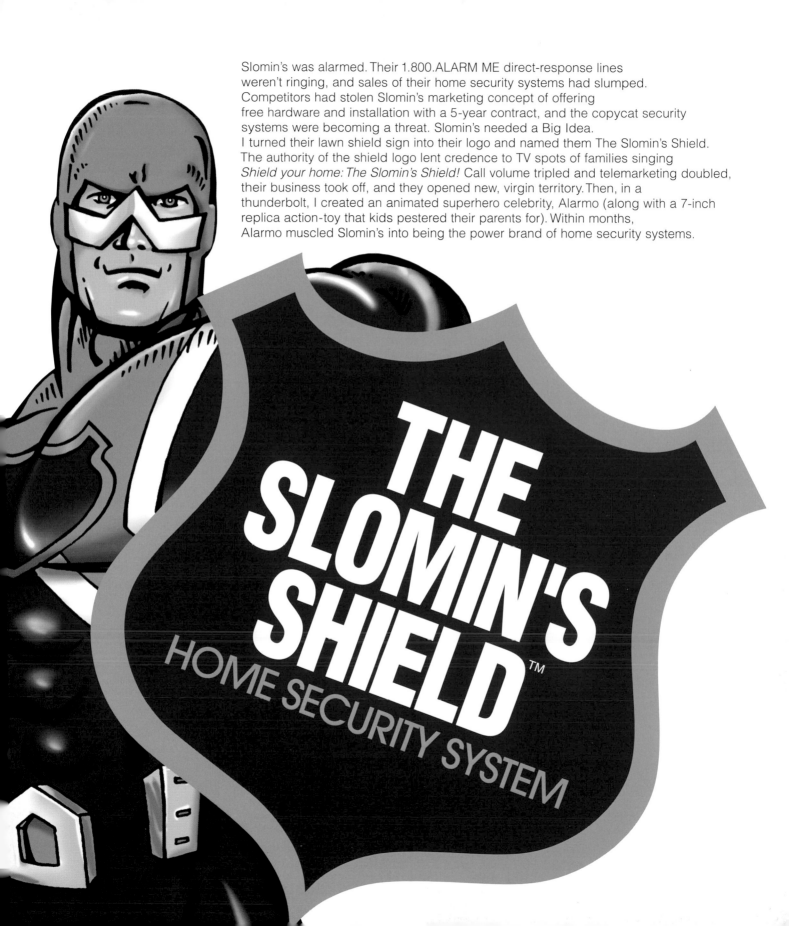

Slomin's was alarmed. Their 1.800.ALARM ME direct-response lines weren't ringing, and sales of their home security systems had slumped. Competitors had stolen Slomin's marketing concept of offering free hardware and installation with a 5-year contract, and the copycat security systems were becoming a threat. Slomin's needed a Big Idea. I turned their lawn shield sign into their logo and named them The Slomin's Shield. The authority of the shield logo lent credence to TV spots of families singing *Shield your home: The Slomin's Shield!* Call volume tripled and telemarketing doubled, their business took off, and they opened new, virgin territory. Then, in a thunderbolt, I created an animated superhero celebrity, Alarmo (along with a 7-inch replica action-toy that kids pestered their parents for). Within months, Alarmo muscled Slomin's into being the power brand of home security systems.

THE SLOMIN'S SHIELD™
HOME SECURITY SYSTEM

65. "PUMP UP AND AIR OUT!"
REEBOK'S DOMINIQUE WILKINS GOES ONE-ON-ONE
WITH NIKE'S MICHAEL JORDAN
(AND SALES JUMP FROM $100 MILLION
TO HALF A BILLION).

After two long seasons of commercials depicting superstars
toying with the Pump buttons and acting cutesy-pie,
the technologically advanced Reebok Pump shoe was perceived
as a gimmick by the fitness/athletic aficionado (or entirely
confused with Nike's Air product, which has no "air bladder" technology).
Except for the NBA players being paid to hustle them,
no serious pro or amateur athlete would be caught dead pumping up
and running in a pair of Reebok Pumps.
The Pump needed to be repositioned in the consumer's mind *and*
with the trade as a serious sports performance shoe to save the dying brand.
So I went one-on-one with Nike, telling consumers that the next time
they buy sneakers they should nix Nike and Pump up!
My in-your-face slogan: *Pump up and Air out!*
Reebok jocks talked up the Pump, explaining their built-in ankle support,
comparing it to Nike's Air products. And each ended with a jibe
at *Nike's* famous athletes. Dominique stabbed their imagery with
Michael my man, if you want to fly first-class...Pump up and Air out!
and then took a smooth 15-foot foul shot, swishing
an *Air Jordan* in a wastebasket! Boomer Esiason said: *Boomer knows
something that Bo (Jackson) don't know...Pump up and Air out!,*
winging an Air Jordan into a garbage pail. And Michael Chang took a swing
at Andre Agassi's brash "rock 'n' roll tennis" spot with:
If you want to beat those rock 'n' roll tennis guys, Pump up and Air out!,
lobbing a Nike into a trash can.
Pump sales soared, and *The Wall Street Journal* observed that
"Reebok's most recent, hard-hitting Pump ads stressing performance
are putting their company back on track. Their advertising strategy
has been in a state of disarray, and now they finally got their act together."
Reebok stock catapulted from 10 to 35.
The president of the ad agency that handled *Air Jordan* advertising
called to threaten that Michael Jordan was going to sue Dominique Wilkins!
I begged him to encourage Jordan, because the publicity would
jump the sales of the Pump to a *billion bucks!* He sheepishly hung up.

GREG NORMAN (GOLF)
DOMINIQUE WILKINS (BASKETBALL)
MICHAEL CHANG (TENNIS)
BOOMER ESIASON (FOOTBALL)
DENNIS RODMAN (BASKETBALL)
DAVE JOHNSON (DECATHLON)

The Road Runner works for Purolator Courier. We run rings around the Coyote Courier!

THE MERGER IN 2001 OF AOL AND TIME WARNER CREATED THE WORLD'S LARGEST MEDIA COMPANY. IT ALSO PRODUCED A CORPORATE CIVIL WAR, WITH NONE OF THE PROMISED "SYNERGY" DEVELOPING BETWEEN THE TWO MEDIA GIANTS. INDEED, THEY RESISTED INTERACTION: THE WARNER BROS. CARTOON DIVISION BALKED AT LICENSING THE SUPERB BRAND NAME ROAD RUNNER TO AOL'S HIGH-SPEED CABLE INTERNET SERVICE (A SYNERGISM NO-BRAINER)! ONLY AFTER A FULL YEAR OF NASTY NEGOTIATIONS WAS A DEAL FINALLY REACHED BETWEEN THE TWO CORPORATE CULTURES. FIFTEEN YEARS BEFORE, FOR PUROLATOR COURIER, MY LAWYERS AND I OBTAINED THE USE OF THE MNEMONIC ROAD RUNNER NAME, FOR A COMICALLY LOW PRICE, WITH TWO PHONE CALLS IN TWO DAYS. BEEP, BEEP!

66. A CELEBRITY BIRD TO THE RESCUE!

In 1986, when Purolator Courier's board of directors, loaded with men of awesome
pedigree and wealth, and one lady, a distinguished Margaret Thatcher type,
living caricatures of the Protestant power elite, heard my plan to enlist the services of
the Road Runner to be the spokesbird of their ailing overnight delivery business,
all I received was blank stares. My imitation of this swift desert bird and my delivery
of "Beep! Beep!" woke up a few dozers, but it was obvious I was presenting
to the only human beings in America who were not familiar with Road Runner.
But their $600 million company was being destroyed by the FedEx revolution, and
they were desperate for a miracle to get Purolator's phones to ring and boost
revenues *immediately*, or they would be out of business in the near future. So I played
them a vintage Road Runner cartoon. It was an astonishing spectacle–
America's corporate elite watching a kid's cartoon in the middle of a business day
to decide the fate of a great American corporation.
I knew we were plugged into a genuine icon of mass/pop culture. Road Runner,
the symbol of Purolator, scoots across the ground at lightning speed, leaving behind
a trail of smoke and says only two words: *Beep! Beep!* Our copy said:
The Road Runner works for Purolator Courier. We run rings around the Coyote Courier!
And our memorable, mnemonic phone number was 1-800 BEEP BEEP.
Before we premiered our campaign, a prominent story appeared in *The New York Times*,
with our toll-free number buried in Phil Dougherty's Advertising column. That morning,
15,000 phones rang off the hook! Overnight, Purolator was saved.
Only months later, Emery Freight, shaken by Purolator's eruption, bought Purolator's
investors out at a huge multiple, ridding themselves of this newly vigorous
threat to their No. 2 position behind FedEx. The wealthy board that had never heard
of Road Runner laughed, running all the way to the bank, and astoundingly,
Emery Freight never adopted the Road Runner for themselves. Go figure.

"We wouldn't have come even if you *had* invited us, Mr. Capote!"

67. MY BATTERED BEAUTY.

Wouldn't you think a 1967 cover where I dramatized violence against women would be applauded by women's groups? Not the National Organization for Women. They were plenty sore. (Beats me why.) NOW's pioneering battle against sexism and for women's rights in the late '60s was admirable, but I thought, at times, misdirected. Any "battered woman" was considered taboo and undiscussed in those days, so my visualization of it on a men's magazine cover was a shocker, and considered by them as an affront to women. I slapped a Band-Aid and a mournful look on Ursula Andress, the stunning beauty of James Bond fame. Originally, I wanted Ms. Andress to sport a shiner, but she pleaded with me not to. I could have easily retouched the photo, but I promised her I'd keep my mitts off. Stacked next to the typical women's magazine covers on the newsstands, my battered Esquire beauty was a knockout.

68. THE BALL(S) OF TRUMAN CAPOTE.

On the night of November 28, 1966, Truman Capote threw "a little masked ball" reminiscent of Versailles in 1788, in honor of *Washington Post* president Katharine Graham, inviting 540 of his closest friends. Frank Sinatra and Mia Farrow, William and Babe Paley, Harold Prince, Andy Warhol, John Kenneth Galbraith, Rose Kennedy, Tallulah Bankhead and William F. Buckley Jr. were among those anointed and summoned to the Grand Ballroom of The Plaza Hotel in New York, wearing masks and dressed in black and white. They joined "Betty" Bacall and Jerome Robbins dancing the night away. Capote was a great writer, but consumed by hobnobbing with the rich and famous, who treated him like a Pekingese sitting on a needlepoint pillow for them to pet. An anonymous poem of the time went like this: *Truman Ca-pote...is not nearly as dotty... as some of the people...who went to his party.* The complete guest list, believe it or not, was published in *The New York Times.* A year later, the world was still abuzz about the ball(s) of Truman Capote. The Gods of Power (celebrity, cultural and political) spoke of it as Capote's greatest coup. Norman Mailer's deft backstab was, "To me, that party was greater than any of his books!" So I tried to put all the spin to rest with a final, sour-grapes Esquire cover depicting an eclectic and unmasked group sweetly sticking their uninvited tongues out at Capote. The only person with the hubris to ever outdo Truman Capote was the flamboyant Malcolm Forbes with his airlift shindig of 880 friends to Morocco in 1981 (see 110). Celebrities don't give parties like that anymore. Of course not. They're all dead.

THE PARTY POOPERS

BACK ROW:
NFL GREAT JIM BROWN
LEADING MAN TONY CURTIS
CALIFORNIA GOVERNOR "PAT" BROWN
BROADWAY REPORTER ED SULLIVAN

MIDDLE ROW:
SCREEN STAR KIM NOVAK
"GEORGY GIRL" LYNN REDGRAVE

FRONT ROW:
JFK PRESS SECRETARY PIERRE SALINGER
BASEBALL LEGEND CASEY STENGEL

69. THE ULTIMATE CELEBRITY CAMPAIGN. MUHAMMAD ALI LEADS THE FIGHT TO FREE RUBIN HURRICANE CARTER, AN INNOCENT BLACK MAN SENTENCED TO 300 YEARS IN JAIL FOR MURDERING THREE WHITES.

"March to prison with me Friday."

In the growing battle to free Hurricane Carter, Muhammad Ali will personally lead a People's March in Trenton, Friday, 9:30 AM!

In 1966 black middleweight boxer Rubin Hurricane Carter was arrested for the murder of three whites in a Patterson, New Jersey, bar. During a period of intense racial acrimony, Carter was convicted and sentenced to 300 years in jail. Eight years later two key prosecution witnesses recanted, while new lawyers unearthed the suppression of vital evidence that would certainly have helped exonerate Carter. I had read about the case like any fight fan and figured that the viciousness displayed in the ring by the shaven-headed, Fu Manchu-moustached Carter had somehow exploded into the streets. One day I received a call from a young fight fan who claimed Rubin Carter had been railroaded and begged me to read Carter's book, *The Sixteenth Round.* I read it, I talked to Carter's lawyers and I read and reread the trial transcript. Then I got back to the young white guy who had called me, Richard Solomon. "Let's get this guy out of jail," I told him. I designed a three-inch ad that ran on page two of *The New York Times* (see 37) that shook up the public because Rubin Carter, the vicious fighter they thought was a mad-dog killer, might actually be innocent! Through that one small ad we were able to organize a committee of distinguished citizens, white and black. That was no piece of cake. We had to convince businessmen, politicians, athletes, writers, entertainers (and their *very* apprehensive lawyers) of Carter's innocence. Fifty-four prominent citizens joined the celebrity-activist committee of The Hurricane Fund. Muhammad Ali became our chairman as soon as I convinced the heavyweight champ that Carter was framed. Ali spoke out at every occasion for a new trial, even dedicating his Las Vegas match with Ron Lyle to Carter, announced at a press conference with a shocking film I produced of Rubin, peering from behind bars in Trenton State Prison, making a militant, devastatingly emotional appeal to the hundreds of stunned reporters covering the fight. Each celeb wrote a letter to Governor Brendan Byrne pleading for a new trial, as we organized Hurricane benefits all over Manhattan. Howard Cosell stepped into a boxing ring we set up for one event as our MC to speak up for Rubin Carter. Committee members like Dyan Cannon and I appeared on TV talk shows, and the press ran hundreds of major stories, with dozens of TV news segments. We handed out thousands of leaflets. We staged a Christmas Eve vigil at the gates of the Governor's mansion. We ran radio spots (beautifully read by Earl Monroe of the Knicks). And Ali led a march of 10,000 past Trenton State Prison, where Rubin was incarcerated, all the way to the statehouse to meet with the New Jersey governor as press photographers clicked away. The Rubin Carter case had become famous. All this publicity inspired Bob Dylan to visit Carter in prison, learn his story and write *Hurricane*, an activism that Dylan had seemed to have all but abandoned. I convinced Dylan, who was on a tour with his Rolling Thunder troupe, to commit to a Night of the Hurricane concert in Madison Square Garden. He said he would do it only if it were a doubleheader: the Garden concert and a command performance in prison. The Garden concert on December 8, 1975, was the hottest ticket in town. The Hurricane cause was sweeping New Jersey. The demonstrations led by Ali had elevated the case to a cause celebre as Governor Byrne was overwhelmed with pressure demanding a new trial. Before long, Rubin's lawyers received overtures from the state for a pardon. But Carter insisted on being vindicated in a new trial! With mounting pressure, in March 1976 the New Jersey Supreme Court ruled unanimously in favor of a second trial. With a new judge, a new jury, and the distance of a decade since the first trial, there was reason to hope that Carter would finally be exonerated. Indeed, my mole at the statehouse indicated that the authorities wanted the whole case to go away and avoid the continuing publicity of a new trial. But suddenly, Carter, out on bail, was reported to have struck a Muslim woman (who was on our committee) and the powers that be decided he had stripped himself of "martyrdom." So a new trial proceeded, but with missing evidence, disappearing witnesses, and an obsession on the part of New Jersey prosecutors to nail this incorrigible black man, the verdict was the same. Rubin Carter was returned to prison, ending a nine-month interlude of freedom. But the case remained a thorn in the foot of justice, and in November 1985, citing "grave constitutional violations" by prosecutors, Judge Lee H. Sarokin of the Federal District Court in Newark threw out the second conviction. In 1988, the United States Supreme Court upheld Judge Sarokin's noble ruling that Carter had been unjustly convicted because the Passaic County prosecutor's office suppressed critical evidence. In 1990, all charges were dismissed. After 22 years, Rubin Hurricane Carter was freed. Ali! Ali! Ali!

P.S. In early 2002, I found myself seated next to ex-governor Brendan Byrne at a roast. "Governor," I said, "the last time I was in a room with you, Muhammad Ali, Joe Frazier, Ellen Burstyn, Jimmy Breslin and I were presenting a petition for a new trial for Rubin Carter signed by 10,000 people." A little shaken, he leaned over and in a raspy whisper said "that sonofabitch was guilty, y'know." Incredulous, I said "you gotta be kidding. You *can't* be serious." He was adamant. "I hired a detective–a *black* detective, mind you, and he reported to me that Carter was guilty!" "You're shittin' me," said I. "You *can't* believe that!" "Well," he insisted, "he may not have been the *shooter*, but he was *there*!" "Governor, you're telling me John Artis, a 19-year old college kid riding home in Carter's car to do his homework, stopped at a bar to kill 3 white people?!" "No, *he* didn't do it, but Carter was *there*!" "Huh?" I said.

70. WHERE HAVE YOU GONE, JOE DIMAGGIO?

The great Joltin' Joe DiMaggio, always a private person but always with
an eye for the ladies, came out of hiding when he surprised the world by marrying
the ultra-visible Marilyn Monroe, Hollywood's sex goddess. As a husband, he
modestly ducked behind her voluptuous curves and out of the limelight. Too proud,
classy and important to become Mr. Monroe, he and Marilyn split and
The Yankee Clipper was out of sight again. This July 1966 Esquire cover hauntingly
reflected on his absence (inspired by yet another classic Gay Talese profile).
Carl Fischer caught this dream-like apparition of Joe, in one of his tailored civilian suits,
frozen at the apex of the most classic swing in the history of the game,
hitting one into the empty stands at Yankee Stadium.
I almost asked No. 5 himself to pose, but even I don't have that kind of hubris.
So I cast dozens of lithe, athletic 52-year-old men, but finally chose
a 35-year-old who, as a kid, worshiped the ground Joe D walked on. Moi!
Two years later, Mrs. Robinson, from the hit movie *The Graduate*, sported a lyric
evoking all the nostalgia of the time: *Where have you gone, Joe DiMaggio?*

71. "BOB DYLAN, WHO HE?"

I was riding in a car with Muhammad Ali and a few others
who were trying – with political pressure, demonstrations and logic –
to get a new trial for the innocent Rubin Hurricane Carter,
convicted and sentenced to 300 years in jail for the murder
of three whites. I was telling the champ that we had taken Bob Dylan
to visit Carter at Trenton State Prison, and that Dylan was
so convinced of Rubin's innocence and so moved by his plight
that he was writing a song that would surely help
propagandize Carter's cause. We were certain Dylan would
record a masterpiece. Ali, whose favorite singer was
Elvis Presley, listened to my excitement and anticipation,
and finally leaned over to me from his front seat
and said, "Bob Dylan, who he?" Bob Dylan's explosive song,
Hurricane, added another emotional tool in the
fight that finally resulted in Rubin Carter's release from prison,
after 22 years of living hell.

72. BARBIE AS BETTIE, THE BLACK-BANGED QUEEN OF CURVES.

Barbie, the doll with curves, has become an icon of
American popular culture and a wildly popular toy, except
among feminists. (The National Organization for Women
objected that Barbie's figure "created unrealistic expectations for
young girls that could lead to low self-esteem.") In 1998,
the Barbie Doll people at Mattel asked me, along with dozens
of other graphic designers, to create a tribute to their
popular doll for a book celebrating the Barbie culture in America.
Since 1959, young girls have seen Barbie as the clotheshorse
they wanted to be. To totally infuriate the chicks at NOW,
I depicted Barbie the way we bad boys see her: a Bettie Page
of the early '50s with killer curves, black bangs, 6-inch
high heels and girl-next-door looks. Needless to say, the stiffs at
Mattel rejected my vision of their moneymaking doll,
but Soho's hot magazine *Paper* took it to their bosom.

73. THE NATIONAL ORGANIZATION FOR WOMEN VERSUS BROADWAY JOE NAMATH.

Among industrial design cognoscenti, Olivetti was synonymous with beauty,
but most people wouldn't recognize good design if they tripped over it.
To break through the IBM barrier, my *Olivetti Girl* TV and print campaign was directed
to America's secretaries, showing *Olivetti Girls* as the star performers in their office,
as the secretary who typed faster, neater, sharper, making her the girl in the
office most likely to succeed. Secretaries who wouldn't have been caught dead
without an IBM clamored for an Olivetti, and their sales in the U.S. doubled.
The campaign burst on the scene in 1972, just as the National Organization for Women
was flexing its muscles. NOW attacked the campaign for stereotyping
women as underlings (they were furious that only men were shown as bosses while
only women were shown as secretaries), and they called me a male chauvinist pig.
They picketed the Olivetti building on Park Avenue and sent hecklers up to my office
to un-n-n-nerve me. Something had to be done. Who can fight a woman's fury?
I capitulated. I would do an ad and a TV spot, with a woman executive giving orders
to a male secretary. I cast an actual woman exec (not an actress) as the boss.
I cast Jets great Joe Namath as the secretary (because he could type).
I invited the women of NOW to view the spot, but when they saw the boss ask her
secretary for a date at the conclusion of the spot, they were aghast.
(You do very good work, Joseph. By the way, what are you doing for dinner tonight?)
"It's an old story," I said. "The boss always tries to make the secretary." They cursed
me (I swear), walked out and never bothered this male chauvinist pig again.

74. SHOWING DOROTHY LAMOUR 30 YEARS LATER, FLYING ROYAL AIR MAROC TO MOROCCO, WAS A NO-BRAINER. (BUT SHE HAD LOST HER ONCE PETITE FIGURE.)

In the '40s, Bob Hope and Bing Crosby went off with Dorothy Lamour on the *Road to Morocco*. Thirty years later, still vividly remembered, the famous trio's female star shows up for a return flight, clad in her trademark sarong. This time her destination is not the sandy Hollywood movie lot, but the for-real exotic land of Morocco. When we shot Ms. Lamour, she was still a stunning beauty, but her legs had lost their curvaciousness. So I substituted the gams of a youthful gymnast, hoping that somehow she wouldn't be embarrassed by my somewhat arrogant substitution. When I showed this Hope and Crosby sex object her new, trimmed-down, juiced-up figure, she barked, "That's a lousy shot of my legs!"

Vanity, thy name is woman.

"I'm off on the road to Morocco ...again"

75. "WE BREATHLESSLY ANNOUNCE THAT THE TWO OF US HAVE TAKEN OVER THE FOUR SEASONS." (A WHITE ELEPHANT REGAINS ITS STATURE BY CREATING TWO SUPERSTAR OWNERS).

The '70s were shaping up as the disaster decade for New York's great restaurants. Landmarks like Pavilion and Chauveron went out of business. And by 1974, the 15-year-old Four Seasons restaurant, created by the legendary restauranteur Joe Baum, was losing money and sliding toward extinction. It had been part of a chain, Restaurant Associates, and was becoming a casualty of creeping neglect. It was perceived, increasingly, as a "tourist" restaurant, forsaking its power-base Manhattan clientele, and was regarded by the restaurant industry as a white elephant and, lamentably, a lost cause. With all these odds stacked against them, Tom Margittai and Paul Kovi bravely bought The Four Seasons and asked us to reposition the original appeal of breakthrough American cuisine. In the magnificent Philip Johnson-designed interior, set like a jewel on the first two floors of the greatest modern edifice in America (designed by the International Style master, Mies van der Rohe), the Seasons' pioneering reputation had once promised to change the face and ethos of fine dining in the U.S. So we boldly positioned the new owners as "The-two-of-us" shaking hands in front of their "store," and ran a full-page ad in *The New York Times*. The ad charmed New York food lovers who valued great food, service, ambiance and dedication to a work ethic as they flocked back. Overnight the hungry Hungarian expatriates became the hot restauranteur entrepreneurs in the Big Apple. Within weeks, we created the concept of the *Power Lunch*, which repositioned their neglected Grill Room as the most prestigious meeting place in town. Every piece of the printed material, all lovingly designed by my staff and I, was signed "From the-two-of-us," and each year-end we ran an "Annual Love Letter to New Yorkers" in *The Times* and *New York* magazine. We designed their classic recipe book, and originated and named their milestone *Spa Cuisine* concept, whose name and recipes attracted millions of devotees, and imitators, all over the world. Its landmark interior status (the only restaurant so designated in New York) attests to its classic aesthetic and spiritual splendor. The Four Seasons has prospered to this day.

TOM MARGITTAI

PAUL KOVI

76. THE TORCH IS PASSED.

A decade after defining Tom Margittai and Paul Kovi as the two superstar owners
of The Four Seasons, they groomed, drilled and encouraged two young,
ambitious restauranteurs as heir apparents. My new ads anointed them as
"The-*four*-of-us." Then the day came when we announced the retirement of
the dynamic duo of Tom and Paul with a clink of champagne glasses on
the grand steps at the foot of Picasso's welcoming ballet backdrop. In 1994, after
double-handedly bringing the Seasons way beyond even its former
eminence under the great Joe Baum, Tom and Paul passed the torch to their protégés
Alex von Bidder and Julian Niccolini (toasting farewell to their mentors)
and the occasion was memorialized in this full-page *Times* ad. It's a miracle that
The Four Seasons still flourishes in today's cost-driven world. When you
contemplate the high mortality rate of fine restaurants over the past decades,
The Four Seasons is the marketing miracle of the restaurant business.
The Four Seasons, forever!

ALEX VON BIDDER

JULIAN NICCOLINI

77. A NATION'S TEARS.

"Kennedy Without Tears" was an article by Tom Wicker that looked at JFK "objectively,"
seven months after the assassination. This Esquire cover defined an opposite symbolism—
of Kennedy himself, crying for his lost destiny. (Or are they, after all, the tears of the reader?)
For most Americans the murder of our president was an unrelieved trauma.
Nerves and emotions were apparently as raw in June as they had been in November.
Even though the issue was a big seller, prompting a big jump in circulation,
I caught hell for being "insensitive". But this image still brings a tear to my eyes.
The death of FDR, the saviour of our nation...the assassination of JFK, Dr. King, RFK...
the horrific 9/11 terrorist attack on my home town...bring tears to fortify the soul.

78. THE ANACIN ALL-TIME SUPERTEAM.
(GREATER THAN THE GREATEST OLYMPIC DREAM TEAM!)

When Hal Greer, the ex-Philadelphia '76er, became ill and was unable to provide for himself
and his family, a concerned group of retired NBA players decided that it was about time
they took care of their own. (Unlike Major League Baseball players, with a strong
pension plan for over 50 years, the once-struggling National Basketball Association
had neglected their retired players.) Dave DeBusschere, Oscar Robertson,
Dave Bing and Dave Cowens, among others, created the NBRPA (National Basketball
Retired Players Association). What a mouthful! So I convinced them to ditch that cacophony
of letters and be known by a familiar and memorable name: XNBA. To raise
funds, we organized an XNBA Sports Award Dinner, MC'ed by NBC anchor Tom Brokaw,
with a dais that included Muhammad Ali, Rev. Jesse Jackson, Senator Bill Bradley,
and Detroit mayor Dennis Archer, along with dozens of superstar athletes.
Then I enlisted 11 of the greatest men who ever played the game (and one legendary
coach) to be part of an Anacin Dream Team television spot. The group we formed
was truly mindboggling to any hoops fan. Each introduces himself in our Anacin TV spot:
Oscar Robertson! Bill Walton! Bill Russell! Rick Barry! Elgin Baylor! Bob Pettit!
Hondo Havlicek! Jerry West! Big George Mikan! Wilt Chamberlain!
The Couse!...and their coach, Red Auerbach! The great Celtics coach, as usual,
kept talking: *We share a love of basketball...* and in a group shot of the dynamic dozen,
they call out with perfect teamwork: *and Towering Headaches!*
A voiceover package shot proclaims, *The all-time superteam comes back to Anacin.*
Regular strength Bayer, Bufferin or even Tylenol can't get rid of Towering Headaches
like Anacin! Coach Auerbach brings the commercial to its climax with
Rediscover the power of Anacin!...and the greatest dream team to ever give
a testimonial to a product, bellows at the top of their lungs, *for Towering Headaches!*
Any production starring disciplined athletes is a piece of cake, and this shoot
was no exception, except GM Jerry West, under tremendous time pressure, was
frantically trying to convince Shaquille O'Neal, on the phone, to jump ship and
sign with his Los Angeles Lakers. When West rejoined the shoot for the umpteenth time,
armed with a winning grin, my dream team knew full well that
the victorious GM had snared O'Neal, ensuring years of championship teams.
Though a hated competitor to his Celtics, Red Auerbach called out,
"Discover the power of Shaquille O'Neal," followed by the whole gang screaming:
"for Towering Headaches!"

THE SEVEN YEAR ITCH
(7 HAPPY YEARS OF BLOOD SWEAT AND TEARS
BY LOIS HOLLAND CALLAWAY INC.)

79. MY SEVEN YEAR ITCH.

I left Papert, Koenig, Lois
(the first agency I started in 1960)
after 7 years, and this put-on of Marilyn Monroe's
now legendary scene in *The Seven Year Itch*
announced that I had spent another full 7 years
at my second agency, Lois Holland Callaway.
This composite of me on Marilyn was not loved by
everyone. "You're a board chairman,"
said my wife Rosie. "Why don't you grow up?"
"Is this your way of saying that you're not really a male
chauvinist?" asked my faithful secretary.
"Those aren't your legs," said my son Luke. And
my older boy Harry wanted the broad's phone number.
I was speechless. All I can tell you is that
thrill-seekers absolutely mobbed the TGI Gallery
in Manhattan to see an exhibition of 7 years of work at LHC.

80. WHOSE LEGS ARE THESE?

In the midst of my No nonsense American Woman campaign (see 36)
I conjured up a mystery celeb sweepstakes flashing the legs of six
stunning women and asked: Whose legs are these?
PR ace Roberta Greene rounded up Heather Whitestone,
Chris Evert, Susan Lucci, Kathy Mattea, Leeza Gibbons and
Rita Moreno (who each donated our
$25,000 fee to their favorite charity)
to show their gorgeous gams
in a four-page print spread of leg
art, with copy giving
clues as to their identity.

The promotion culminated
in a revealing press conference at The Four Seasons,
and a lucky lady from Omaha won the sweepstakes.
The spontaneous formation of a six-woman chorus line
of No nonsense American Women, high-stepping
Rockette-style for the TV cameras, wowed America that night
on national television. (The lady with the great set of wheels
shown on this page is none other than the then
65-year-old Rita Moreno, the flamboyant Latina actress,
winner of a Tony, a Grammy, an Oscar,
a Golden Globe, and two Emmys.)

81. FIND THE MISSING CELEBRITY IN THIS PICTURE.

In 1968, America once again anticipated a hot, troubled summer in that steamy time of racial conflict and "civil disorders." The "White-Devil" diatribe of Malcolm X and the fearsome threats of Huey Newton, Eldridge Cleaver, and their Black Panthers made clear to the white world that the black man, up to no good, had retribution in his heart. And it was abundantly clear to the black man that the racist society he grew up in would never blossom into Lyndon Johnson's proposed "Great Society." African-Americans in America had no future. So when the summer came, both jobless fathers and their neglected sons were in the streets, fuming, fussing and firing. Ralph Ellison had previously written of the "Invisible Man" of the '50s, but now that black man had become *too* visible, mugging in the alleys and rioting in the streets. James Baldwin published *The Fire Next Time,* foreseeing the rioting in the summer of 1964 in Watts, Newark, Detroit, Chicago, Washington, D.C., and other American cities. Esquire interviewed this powerful and prophetic spokesman of the "Negro" two days after the funeral of Dr. Martin Luther King, during a country-wide nightmare of riots and martial law. Baldwin's biting, embittered and fatalistic attack on the white establishment appalled many readers of Esquire. And this searing visual image of real-life, ass-kicking young black men, being urged to cool off in an actual Harlem ice house, added to the heat. It infuriated both black leaders and white neighborhoods that feared an all-out black revolution. It also scared the hell out of New York mayor John Lindsay, a no-show after he promised me he would pose in the shadows of the ice house along with his seven young constituents. Waiting in the eerie silence of the strangely beautiful ice-filled room, one of the brooding young men finally spit out: "You didn't really think that blond, blue-eyed motherfucker had the balls to show up in our 'hood, did you, Georgie-boy?"

82. IN 1967, BEFORE SHE WAS FAMOUS (AND BEFORE SHE WAS A MOTHER) A REDBOOK "YOUNG MAMA" SHOWCASES HER TALENT.

In the pre-career days of most young American women, Redbook magazine, traditionally, sought out the 21- to 35-year-old market of new mothers. We had to put a handle on this demographic to make Redbook's strategy seem like a fresh idea. So I labeled their readers *Young Mamas.* It marked the first time anybody spoke directly to the baby boomers, and we convinced Redbook to stick a tentative toe into the dreaded waters of their major competitors, television–unheard of for those times. I cast a striving actress who stepped up to the plate and delivered this soliloquy:

I remember one day I was at the supermarket, and Linda was only four years old. She pulled the bottom orange out of the display, and every last orange rolled all over the floor. I looked at the grocer and the grocer looked at me and I said, 'Well if it were my kid I'd kill her.' Then I ran around the corner, down the next aisle, called Linda, grabbed her and beat it out of that store. Never went back. (Then a voiceover: *The most interesting parents the world has ever known are Young Mamas. And Redbook is, frankly, written for Young Mamas.*)

Her first reading was stupendous, and the second was jaw-dropping. I grabbed her, hugged her, and she beat it out of that shoot. I never saw a better performance, her agent's phone rang off the hook, and she went on to become...Susan Sarandon. (Other talents I cast before they became stars were Peter Boyle, Ali MacGraw, Madeline Kahn, Sandy Duncan, Susan Blakely, Nancy Allen and Jason Alexander.)

83. STAR SEARCH ACCOMPLISHED: SANDY DUNCAN SINGS "I'M YOUR MOTHER." THE HOUSEWIVES' LAMENT ON KIDS AND CLEANING.

In 1965, I had been scouring the town for weeks trying to cast a pretty young mama
who could belt out a song, Ethel Merman style, for a Lestoil household-detergent TV campaign.
Time was running out. That weekend, my wife Rosie dragged me to a Broadway revival
of *The Music Man*. (As usual, I wanted to stay home to watch a Yankees game.)
"But George, honey," she purred, "maybe you'll find who you're looking for on stage tonight."
The overture played, the curtain went up–and there she was...a small,
peppy blonde with a big big voice. Her name was Sandy Duncan. A few days later she
pleadingly sang to "her kids," they sang back, and Lestoil cleaned up.
The unknown Duncan was followed by a black mother (and her kids) and an Asian mother
(and her kids). The singing campaign about mothers who toil to keep their homes
clean, but are largely unappreciated by their families, was startling advertising in the days
of grimy demo spots. It was a TV experience that only a mother could love.
I'm your Mother hit pay dirt as Lestoil sales climbed. And loving letters came flowing in from
thousands of appreciative moms. When I met Bill Pitts, the marketing consultant
for Lestoil, this Greek Orthodox kid gained a friend and "Rabbi" for over 25 years. In 1978,
I was thrilled to make him a partner in Lois Pitts Gershon, the third agency I launched.

SANDY DUNCAN SINGS:

I'm your Mother
Working morning, noon and night
Not complaining
But I work day and night
I keep this house clean
'Cause that's my job
So don't you track the dirt in
Debbie, Sue or Bob

DEBBIE, SUE & BOB SING:

She's our Mother
Wipe our feet at the door
Our Mother
Don't spill things on the floor
Tomorrow's Lestoil
She won't use the rest
Tomorrow's Lestoil
She says it's the best

SANDY DUNCAN SINGS:

But I'm your Mother
I can do it all with ease
Your Mother
I can do it in a breeze
I know a little secret
It's worth quite a lot
Tomorrow's Lestoil
Smartest friend a mother's got
I'm your Mother
Keep your mitts off the wall
Your Mother
Don't play ball in the hall
I'm your Mother
And with me you're number one
Tomorrow's Lestoil
It gets all my housework done
I'm your Mother
So don't scuff the floor...

84. AUNT JEMIMA WAS THE LEADING LADY OF PANCAKE MIXES. BUT QUAKER REFUSED TO MARKET A SYRUP. UNTIL OUR CUNNING RESEARCH "PROVED" PANCAKE EATERS LOVED NONEXISTENT AUNT JEMIMA SYRUP!

In the early '60s, while working on various Quaker brands, I didn't understand why the Chicago-based giant wouldn't market a syrup with Aunt Jemima's famous face on the bottle. They gave me several dopey "marketing reasons" why it was a bad idea. Huh? They had already sanitized the racial stereotype of a Dixie mammy wearing a telltale bandana, redrawing the overweight, broadly smiling Aunt Jemima to look like a black corporate lawyer. So I listed four popular brands at the end of a marketing "survey" of pancake-mix users and asked 100 consumers to check any brand they had bought that year. Eighty-eight out of 100 women *insisted* they were Aunt Jemima syrup users! We called Quaker and convinced a neophyte brand manager to set up a date to talk to Quaker's bigwigs. On the big day, the honchos were stunned because syrup was certainly not on the agenda. They were fuming when I stood up to make yet another plea for syrup. But when I proved that the women of America *already thought they had bought it*, they gave up and plunged into the syrup business. I poured it on with an ad campaign that asked: *Aunt Jemima, what took you so long?* Aunt Jemima became the No. 1 syrup within a year. A no-brainer if there ever was one. (With the instant success of the brand, my cohort in the adventure, their young brand manager Bill Smithburg, was labeled a boy genius. Some years later, propelled by his "brilliant marketing coup," he became the CEO and chairman of Quaker.)

85. RUTHLESS BOBBY THE CARPETBAGGER TAKES ON THE SILVER-HAIRED GRANDPA.

Less than two years after President John F. Kennedy
was assassinated, Robert, his "ruthless little brother," ran for
the Senate. Working with him he struck me as an honest,
principled leader who was desperately needed by New York,
even if RFK wasn't a New Yorker. We knew we had
to sweep the "carpetbagger" label, or his candidacy could
be stillborn. So months before any political advertising
blitz normally begins, we plastered New York State with this
straightforward message: *Let's put Robert Kennedy
to work for New York.* Our strategy paid off as the
"carpetbagger" handle evaporated. But as the campaign
entered its final week, I was shaky because I feared
Bobby might lose to incumbent senator Kenneth Keating
as a result of a large undecided bloc, including many
voters troubled still by the "ruthless" label. I begged Kennedy
and his campaign manager, brother-in-law Steve Smith,
to let me immediately produce and run a 20-second TV spot
that would cause voters to think hard as an ominous voice says:
When you're in the election booth, think about this...
followed by the words on the right, moving against a foreboding
black background. It was a powerful, unexpected way
to say that Robert Kennedy, warts and all, would make a truly
great senator, while Keating would go on being an
amiable hack. The large undecided bloc came to their senses
and made our assassinated president's brother their
senator from New York, with a plurality of 720,000 votes.
Some months later, when we were having lunch,
Steve Smith said to Bobby and me, "Maybe we would still
have won without that last-minute attack,
but that was the best political commercial I ever saw!"

Which of the
candidates for
the United States
Senate

has the better
chance of
becoming

a great
United States
Senator?

A *great*
United States
Senator.

86. WHAT KIND OF BABY WAS DR. SPOCK?

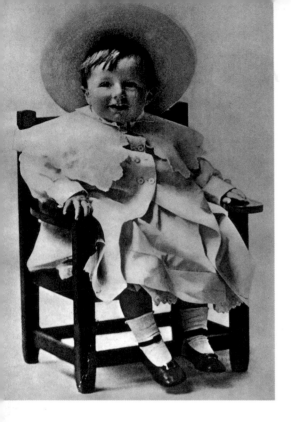

I owe a lot to Dr. Spock.
In 1960, when I started my first advertising agency,
Ladies' Home Journal asked us to come up
with a campaign to attract more readers, and they gave me
an advance copy of the upcoming issue.
I plucked out a story on the childhood of Dr. Benjamin Spock,
visited the good doctor, chose this sweet photo
from his family album, submitted an ad with the headline
What kind of baby was Dr. Spock? and got our
first client, paying the rent until we became the hottest ad agency
in the '60s. Although I'm not a Spock baby,
he was there when I needed him.

87. A KILLER CELEBRITY COVER.

In 1970, author John Sack and I conned the infamous Army lieutenant
William Calley to pose with Vietnamese kids. Calley was awaiting trial for his role
in the 1968 My Lai massacre, and Esquire scheduled an excerpt from
The Confessions of Lieutenant Calley, a book by John Sack. When the issue hit
the newsstands, the sight of Calley, posing with a wide, toothy smile, lovingly
surrounded by four Vietnamese children, chilled your bones. The image of this young
nobody who had suddenly caught the attention of the world, putting a magnifying glass
on the war, seemingly sitting among the very kids he killed, was totally devastating.
A brouhaha exploded all over America over what was described as another
outrageous "anti-war" Esquire cover. Editor Harold Hayes wrote "With the Calley cover,
Lois sought to make the point that Calley's assumed lack of guilt was a stupid innocence
shared by us all." To me the cover expressed—and decimates—Calley's view of
himself as a nice guy; he is oblivious to any connection between the kids he murdered
and the ones he posed with. Along with millions of anti-war protesters, graphic
statements on the covers of Esquire, a popular men's mass magazine (and of course,
the powerful articles they visually dramatized) helped wake up America, but not
until 58,000 Americans and 3,000,000 Vietnamese were killed. Correctly, our collective
national guilt continues because ultimately, our frightened, confused,
yet brave young men—even the notorious Lieutenant Calley—were fall guys,
scapegoats for an atrocious war.

88. CELEBRATING USA TODAY'S FIFTH ANNIVERSARY BY COUPLING IT WITH OTHER FAMOUS AMERICAN FIVE-YEAR-OLDS.

Preparing for USA Today's fifth birthday in 1987, marking a spectacular comeback from near extinction a few years earlier, even a great client like Al Neuharth expected an ad campaign of self-congratulatory puffery. The media pundits and advertising gurus of America had unanimously predicted that USA Today would be a stinker. I wanted to stick it to them with a joyous affirmation of the newspaper's vitality (and celebrate Al Neuharth's hubris in creating a national newspaper with a stunningly original style). My surprise solution was a series of sweet and engaging messages based on the theme, *Two of the most famous five-year-olds in history.*
The "other" five-year-olds were E.T., who came from outer space five years before and won the hearts of the entire U.S.A...the great Kelso, named Horse of the Year at age five–the greatest five-year-old who ever ran...Shirley Temple, the child film-star legend who made her debut at age five...Rin Tin Tin, the superhero dog who made his first film at age five...a pussycat from the five-year-old musical *Cats*...the most talented five-year-old who ever lived, Wolfgang Amadeus Mozart...and Michael Jackson, who became lead singer of the Jackson Five when he was five (to read my exchange with the weird one, see Obnoxious Celebs 2). The campaign, a gently humorous amplification of USA Today's brilliant five-year history, turned a traditional backslapping event into a memorable, witty campaign that said USA Today was not only a great success, but also had a lot of style.

WOLFGANG AMADEUS MOZART
AT THE AGE OF FIVE, MOZART WAS ALREADY COMPOSING SPIRITED MINUETS ON THE HARPSICHORD AND WAS ON HIS WAY TO BECOMING A VIRTUOSO VIOLINIST.

THE NATION'S NEWSPAPER
USA TODAY
NO.1 IN THE USA...5,541,000 READERS EVERY DAY ®

CATS!
THIS SMASH MUSICAL HAS BEEN PLAYING ON BROADWAY FOR FIVE YEARS AND HAS RECENTLY STAGED ITS 2,000TH PERFORMANCE.

E.T.
IT'S BEEN FIVE YEARS SINCE THE LITTLE VISITOR FROM OUTER SPACE LANDED ON EARTH, PHONED HOME AND TURNED ON THE HEARTS OF THE ENTIRE USA.

89. THE DUMMY ON LYNDON'S KNEE.

When Hubert Humphrey was shamefully defending LBJ's Vietnam war escalations, Esquire editor
Harold Hayes assigned a writer to do a major piece on the vice president. As the article was being written,
I designed this punishing image of HHH as LBJ's dummy. Lyndon Johnson was tied up at
the time picking out mud huts to bomb in Vietnam, so I never asked him to pose. The photograph
was shot in a studio using a model as large as LBJ. Then I decapitated the photo and
substituted the president's head (one of my pre-computer notorious transplants). When Hayes read
the article, he called me to kill my planned cover. The writer had done a *sympathetic,*
pro-Humphrey piece. But Harold thought the cover was too good to kill. So on the corner of the foldout
we said *But to be fair to the vice president, see page 76*, hoping we would do right by Hubert.
Two years later, when I was in the veep's office in Washington for a meeting on political advertising,
I was astonished to see the cover pinned to the wall of his anteroom. I gulped and
confessed to Humphrey that I was the creator of that
masterpiece. "You no-good sonofabitch," he told me straight out.
"Well then why do you allow it on your wall?"
I asked the vice president.
"Because," he said, "maybe it's right."

**"I have known
for 16 years
his courage,
his wisdom,
his tact,
his persuasion,
his judgement, and
his leadership."**

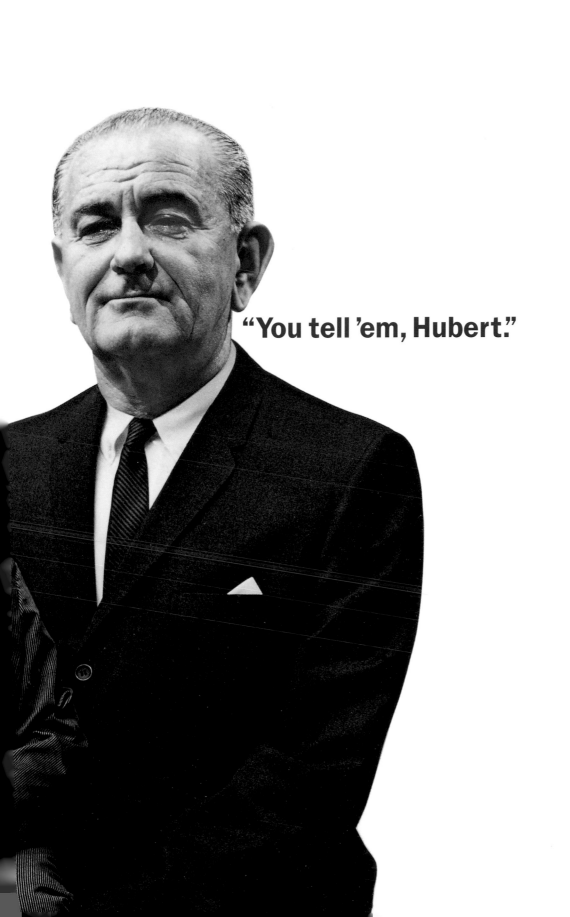

"You tell 'em, Hubert."

90. A COOL DUDE SUPERSTAR MODELING CLOTHES.

I had promised Esquire editor Harold Hayes I would do a men's fashion cover some day to satisfy the ad sales guys who sold to the fashion ad agencies. Walt "Clyde" Frazier of the Knicks, New York's man about town, was the world's coolest athlete (wide-brimmed hats earned him his nickname, Clyde, as in *Bonnie and Clyde*). The only question was how to show a dude jock so that he looked like a superstar rather than a superstiff, the way male models usually look. This way: Clyde, the quintessential smoothie, soaring over the court, ball in hand, being guarded by that hurly-burly Irishman, Kevin Loughery. Easier said than done. To heroically fly through the air without a rumple (in the prehistoric days before computers) required a harness and wires. Ordinarily not a big deal. However, a few hours after the shooting, Clyde would be on a plane with his teammates heading west to play the Los Angeles Lakers in the '72–'73 NBA finals. Without Frazier the Knicks' chances would nose-dive. If the harness slipped, or if a wire snapped and something happened to Clyde (a torn muscle, a stubbed toe, a bruised pinkie), Knick fans would never have understood that art comes before playoffs. I held my breath. We shot the best-dressed jock. We lowered him lovingly. Then I exhaled. (P.S. The Knicks beat the Lakers.)

Some of the best built men in America look terrible with their clothes on!

91. THE BODYBUILDER IS A TRAMP.

In 1989, Botany '500' was introducing Gladiator, a specialized line of tailored suits for men with overly athletic bodies (fuller shoulders, wider forearms and biceps, slimmer waist, fuller seat and thighs and an 8" drop from shoulder to waist). A guy built like Arnold Schwarzenegger had to have his wardrobe custom-made, or look like a mound of jelly in a tent-like fat man's suit. To visualize an image of their target audience in an ad to the trade announcing the new brand, you would think Arnold would come to mind, but the he-man symbol I chose was a silhouette of the skinny, mild-mannered "Little Tramp," Charlie Chaplin, the most famous celebrity in the world in his heyday. Readers got the joke, and the full-page ad in *Men's Wear Daily* drew the greatest response from retailers in the history of the shmatteh business.

92. THE FIRST-NAME FAME GAME

In the past, the most famous celebrities in America who were affectionately referred
to by their *first* names were presidents–Abe, Teddy and Ike; followed by jock culture heroes–
Babe, Dizzy and Yogi; followed by heartthrob crooners–Bing, Frank and Elvis.
Today, astoundingly, the three most famous first-name celebrities in the U.S. are all brand
name fashion designers–Calvin, Tommy and Ralph! This is my year 2003 approach
to adding the name of Rock 'n' Roll Hall of Fame guitarist Carlos (Santana),
to the exclusive *First-name* Hall of Fame, for his introduction of a new clothing line
for *young dudes with 'tude*. Only in America.

Calvin!
Tommy!
Ralph!
Who just joined the giants of first-name fame?

CARLOS!
BY CARLOS SANTANA™

*(He's dressing every young dude...
with 'tude!)*

93. "MY HUBBY ALAN KING MAY KNOW FUNNY, BUT I KNOW MONEY. HE MAKES IT, I INVEST IT." (IF YOU CAN'T AFFORD THE CELEBRITY, HIS MISSUS MAY EVEN BE BETTER.)

Two million people live on Long Island, but it's short on native-born celebs. Central Federal Savings, a bank on the island, needed identification as a distinctly and unmistakably Long Island bank– but its generic-sounding name was a source of confusion, while its identity as a Long Island enterprise was dim. So I created the theme: *Central Federal Savings–The Island Bank!* Perhaps the most famous Long Island celebrity was pop singer/writer Billy Joel, but his price was a million smackers. Fuhgedaboutit! I wanted comedian Alan King, but his tab was hefty, too. But (for bupkis) his wife leaped at the chance to deliver this stand-up pitch: *My hubby Alan King may know funny, but I know money...he makes it, I invest it...in fact, he's so big-hearted that if it weren't for me and Central Federal Savings, where would we be? Fuhgedaboutit!* Jeanette King became the ultimate spokesperson, the ultimate Long Island wife–smart, spunky, funny, tough, believable. And the price was right.
The campaign attracted immediate new business to Central Federal and made it an important, front-of-mind bank. Long Islanders (and the Long Island press) loved it.

94. I LOVE MY (CELEBRITY) MUG!

Pepsi suspected, after they bought a little-known root beer brand called Mug, that they had a real clinker. Beyond that fear, I had to change an old-fashioned, turn-of-the-nineteenth-century beverage into a modern, popular, mass-appeal drink. I told them: *I love my Mug!* The two memorable mugs I chose to belt out our self-effacing message were Richard "Jaws" Kiel, the shark-toothed villain of two popular James Bond 007 films, and the outrageous Phyllis Diller (whose mug changes every year). The double entendre of their delivery, raucously sung in a sunny, funny jingle, along with the enthusiastic acceptance of the campaign by Pepsi bottlers, made Mug the No.1 root beer in New York in a few short months.

95. THE SISTER POWER DREAM TEAM LOOKS UP AT THE GLASS CEILING!

In the '80s, Brit magazine queen Tina Brown landed in America, brilliantly resuscitated Condé Nast's ailing *Vanity Fair,* then pumped life into the old *New Yorker,* and in 1998 created *Talk* magazine for Harvey Weinstein, the Miramax movie mogul. When the clubby male bastion of the 107th Senate was invaded by a record total of 13 females (with the addition of 4 women in the recent national election in the year 2000) Tina Brown knew what a coup it would be for *Talk* to print an historic first photo of the 13 most powerful women in America. Photographer Jason Schmidt and I knew we'd only get a few minutes with the senators, who were rushing from press conference to press conference on the first day of their new term. I opted to shoot straight down at them,

in the Senate Appropriations Committee room, against a star-studded rug, with
Jason perched on a 20-foot ladder hanging over a precarious *Phantom of the Opera*
chandelier. After a quick preening, and swiftly composing them, we were set
to shoot when the dean of the girlfriends, Barbara Mikulsky, the Senate's 4-foot,11-inch
dynamo (nicknamed "The Mouth") blurted out: "My neck hurts. Posing like this
feels stupid. What are we supposed to be looking at? Get the damn camera down here
and shoot it straight!" I knew there would be a chorus of Sirens luring me to
mediocrity, echoing her demand for a stuffy, traditional pose, so, with no time to lose,
I yelled down,"Ladies, you're all looking up at the proverbial glass ceiling!"
They burst out laughing and each one nailed the camera with devastating charm.

96. WHOSE EAR IS THIS?

When I was a rookie art director at Doyle Dane Bernbach in 1958, my first assignment was to create a campaign for a new product, Kerid ear drops. Burrowing through Kerid's research I confirmed that most people cleaned their ears by poking around with pencils and bobby pins. I pushed that finding to its graphic brink by showing a colossal close-up of an ear, sprouting pencils and pins and assorted hardware. The ad screamed: Don't tinker with your ears, use Kerid ear drops. Outraged veteran creative people at DDB formed a posse and galloped up to Bill Bernbach's office to protest my "disgusting" campaign. Bernbach patted them on the head and herded them out the door. (In those days the buzzword was "tasteful." Taste, schmaste, my ear! There is imagery that shocks people for shock's sake–and imagery that can attract and hold attention because of a meaningful and memorable message!) My boss and I sold the campaign and Kerid sold a lot of ear drops, and a lot of people quit sticking bobby pins in the wrong place. The only *shameful* part of this story is the answer I gave when the client asked me who had posed for the shot. "An actor friend of mine," I answered, "but I had to promise not to reveal his identity." I had led them to believe the actor was well known, so the client's PR announcements spoke of their "Mystery Celeb." *Whose Ear is This?* became a headline in newspapers. The truth is the model was a pal of mine, John Cholakis, who *did* go to acting classes. A dozen years later, on the *Today* show, Gene Shalit, introducing me for an interview on my book *The Art of Advertising,* didn't know how close he came to nailing me. He intoned, "To read George Lois on advertising is to read Leonardo Da Vinci on art, Julius Caesar on warfare, Ted Williams on hitting...and Clifford Irving on fraud." Et tu, Brutus?

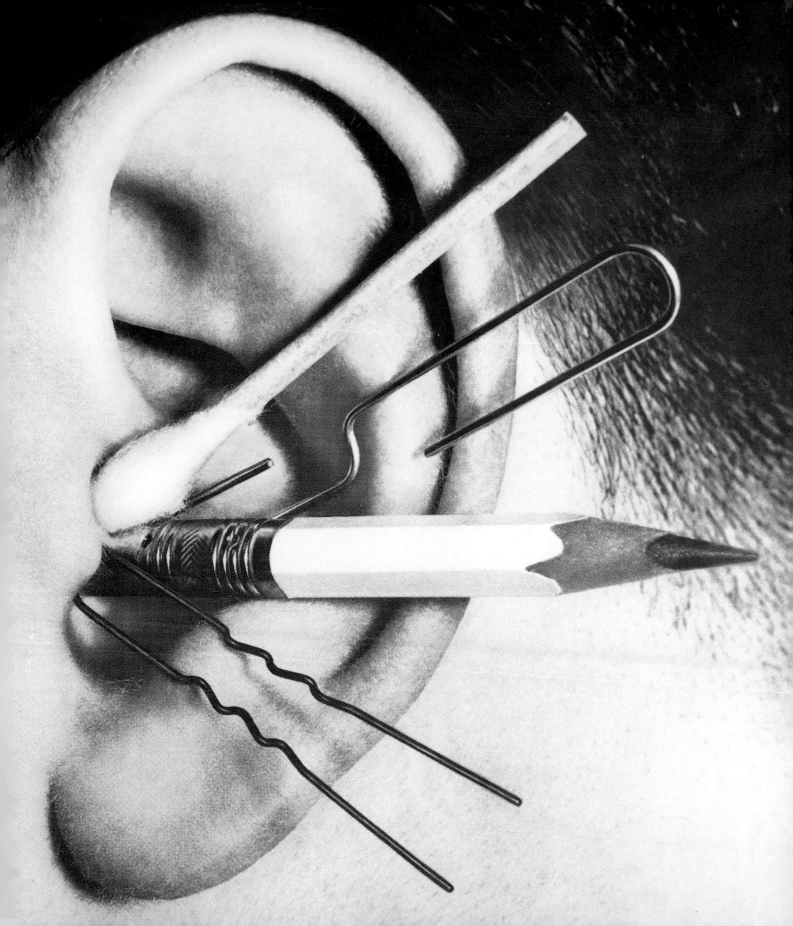

NEW YORK POST

SPORTS EXTRA

MONDAY, APRIL 10, 1989 / Partly sunny, 60s today; clear, 40s tonight / Details, Page 2

'35¢ in New York City **50¢** elsewhere

PHOENIX SIGNS EWING!

In a startling and sensational press conference, Patrick Ewing revealed that it was "'bye 'bye Adidas" and "hello Phoenix high performance basketball shoes!" The Knickerbocker superstar center said his reasons for switching are simple—"The Phoenix fit is phenomenal...and the Phoenix price is unbelievable. When my fans see me in Phoenix, they'll know I made the right move!"

"WHEN I GET INTO PHOENIX, I'LL FLY HIGHER THAN EVER!"

97. HOW TO ANNOUNCE A NEW CELEBRITY BRAND: SLAP IT ON THE FRONT PAGE!

When Patrick Ewing was at the top of his game, he rebelled against the Nikes and Reeboks of the world, and signed a shoe deal with a start-up company named Phoenix (that would sell at about half the price of the big brand names). So I rolled the presses and printed a blaring, phony front page of *The New York Post* (*Phoenix signs Ewing!*) and *The Daily News* (*Patrick jumps to Phoenix!*) and wrapped them around that day's actual newspaper, and had them waiting for dozens of sportswriters at a noon press conference in Manhattan. Ewing's defiant entrepreneurial venture got big press, including two New York TV stations who stopped *Knicks* fans in the streets, showed them the front pages that seemingly announced that Patrick had, unbelievably, been traded to the Phoenix Suns, and ran their shocked, expletive-filled reactions all over TV. The Phoenix brand was obviously not a serious threat to the giants of the industry, but the caper made them nervous enough to bury Phoenix by stealing Ewing with a lollapalooza contract the next season. Stop the presses!

98. LITTLE BIG MAN. A MEMORABLE COVER. (OR WAS IT?)

Doing covers for Esquire for a decade, I refused to produce a celebrity cover, as such. To this day, nine out of ten magazines choose (or vie for) celebrities for their covers, and nine out of ten do expected, uneventful covers. (Oh, I had my fun with famous people, but always with a purpose: Ed Sullivan in a Beatles wig, Warhol drowning in his own soup, Svetlana with her father's moustache, Ali agonizing as St. Sebastian.) Nevertheless, eight years into my Esquire covers, editor Hayes, after viewing a rough cut of Arthur Penn's *Little Big Man*, begged me to slap Dustin Hoffman's mush on the cover of the next issue. Hoffman, one of America's foremost actors, had a notorious rep with producers for refusing to promote his films. But Esquire covers were hot, so he agreed to pose. I showed the diminutive Hoffman, who had adopted New York as his home, standing tall, eyeball-to-eyeball with the Chrysler Building. Twenty years later, I found myself having breakfast with Hoffman and Steve Ross, the chairman of Time Warner, during a presentation to a packed auditorium of my ad campaign *Make time for Time*. Gobbling up my cereal (and feeling my oats) I proudly preened to Hoffman, "Remember me? I'm the guy who did that Esquire cover of you in 1970." Dusty replied: "Esquire cover? I was never on an Esquire cover!" Ouch.

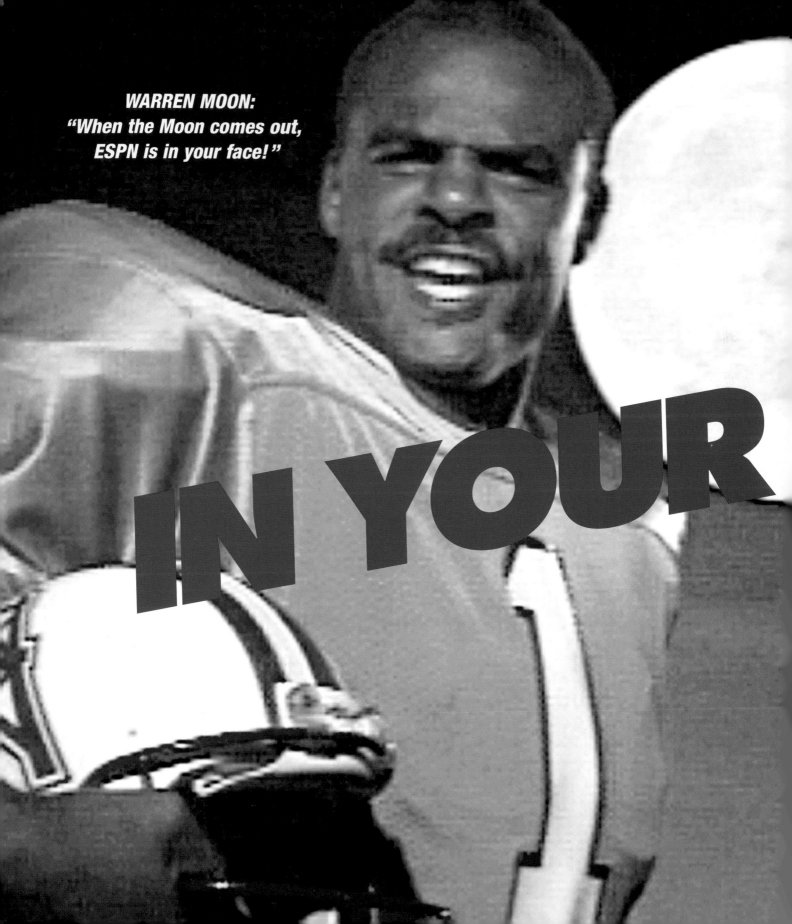

WARREN MOON:
"When the Moon comes out,
ESPN is in your face!"

IN YOUR

FACE!

**99. ESPN WAS PERCEIVED
AS A MICKEY-MOUSE SPORTS NETWORK...
UNTIL AMERICA'S GREATEST
ATHLETES SHOVED ESPN IN YOUR FACE!
(GRATIS!)**

Rodney Dangerfield's famous line, "I don't get any respect," had been precisely the insurmountable problem for ESPN, the 24-hour sports cable network. Even the announcement of my agency's appointment in *Adweek*, an advertising trade paper, took a below-the-belt shot at ESPN: "Lois will become familiar with aerobics and Demolition Derbies!" (A snide way to repeat the popular perception that ESPN was basically broadcasting junk sports.) To convince America that ESPN was indeed a dominant force in TV sports, I went nose to nose with their management to let me produce an in-your-face campaign. The ESPN honcho guffawed when I showed him a list of 15 of America's hottest sports personalities, insisting I could convince many to appear in the commercials...for zilch. "Lois, not one of them would cross the street for less than $50,000!" he barked. But I cajoled them all, and then some, including Roger Clemens, Thurman Thomas, Jim Kelly, Eric Davis, Boomer Esiason, Bobby Bonilla, Greg Norman, Gabriella Sabatini, Andre Reed, Darryl Strawberry, Dan Marino, John Elway, Bruce Smith, Richard Dent, Ronnie Lott, Howie Long, Marcus Allen, Warren Moon and coaches Mike Ditka, Joe Paterno and Rick Pitino. Because I knew two things they didn't know: ESPN had the possibility of becoming a giant and they hadn't scratched the surface...and an athlete is a sucker to appear in a TV spot if you can make them look like a million bucks! The results of the campaign were, in the words of an ESPN executive, a "Harvard Business School case study on how to turn around a company's image." ESPN sold out their Major League Baseball, NFL football and NCAA basketball (after a decade of cut-rate sales) and a few months after the campaign broke, a research tracking study showed ESPN suddenly going from worst to first, rating ahead of ABC, CBS and NBC, as having the best sports programming in America. They went on to implement a creative marketing plan that they thought was a pipe dream on my part. I recommended an ESPN 2. "You nuts, Lois? We don't have enough programming to fill ESPN!" I told them an ESPN magazine was a no-brainer. "Ridiculous, Lois. We're not journalists!" And among a host of licensing possibilities, I expounded about some kind of ESPN Sports Hotel and/or Sports Bar. With their newfound *In Your Face* imagery, they went on to do it all, and then some. The same way I used Rock stars to save MTV, *In Your Face* athletes transformed a mickey-mouse network into the Power Network of Sports!

"Fongool! I ordered *three* pizzas and *two* heroes!"

"No, this is not a gay bar!!!"

"Hello, is this the kindergarten teacher? Well, this is an obscene phone call: Ca-Ca. Stinky. Wee-Wee. Poo-Poo. Boom-Boom."

"Shit Sherm— there's no nickel in this coin return either."

100. MA BELL'S X-RATED CELEBRITY WALLS

In 1972 I made this proposal to Restaurant Associates: "Let's do a restaurant in Shubert Alley with a long, long bar opposite the theaters. We'll call the place Ma Bell's. Each table will have a 1930s telephone that works, phone calls on the house. Business people will be able to make calls during lunch, mothers can phone their sitters at night. The floor will be tiled, the furniture bentwood, the ceiling will have fans. We'll have a long-distance bar the length of Shubert Alley. Theatergoers will meet there before showtime, and anyone who needs a blast between acts will be able to run over for a quickie." Ma Bell's came into being with old-fashioned phones and its long-distance bar. Over the bar and all over the cavernous rooms I hung a gallery of dozens of gigantic photo blowups of celebrities on the phone making juicy remarks. Lots of out-of-towners blushed bright red when they read my in-your-face quotes, but preshow drinking and dining at Ma Bell's became part of the titillating Broadway experience, and the joint became a New York institution for over 20 years. (Damn those newfangled cell phones!)

101. GERMAINE GREER OGLES KING KONG MAILER.

The literary male-chauvinist monster goes ape for the female-liberationist doll. Germaine Greer looks ecstatic in the clutches of macho-Mailer. When Norman Mailer saw this 1971 Esquire cover he called editor Harold Hayes and challenged him to a fistfight. Hayes, an ex-Marine, chickened out and asked me to take him on. I refused. I told Mailer I wanted him to qualify first by taking on Germaine.

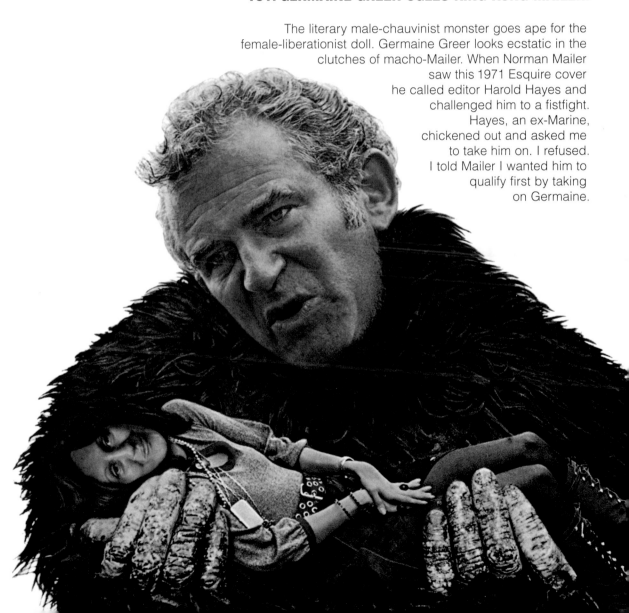

TIM ROBBINS CAME THROUGH A HURRICANE AND
DELIVERED HIS POWERFUL PLEA FOR BLOOD,
THEN GAVE HIS BLOOD...BUT HE DIDN'T WANT TO BE
SEEN IN A POSTER WITH THE DONALD.
(BUT THE 6'5" ACTOR WOULD HAVE FIT RIGHT IN,
STANDING TALL IN THE BACK ROW.)

102. THEY CAME THROUGH HURRICANE FLOYD TO GIVE THEIR TIME, THEIR TALENT, THEIR BLOOD.

There are eight million stories in The Naked City, and one million of them
have blood transfusions each year. Three out of four people in New York and
New Jersey are saved by a transfusion at some time in their lives.
Two hundred hospitals depend on the New York Blood Center and the
New York Blood Center depends on New Yorkers and Jerseyites
to give blood. To emotionalize the always acute shortage of blood, I enlisted
New York–area celebs to spread this compassionate message:
Give Blood. Save a neighbor. But things looked grim on the morning the poster
and TV ads were to be shot. On Sept. 16, 1999, as Hurricane Floyd
blew into town, these inspired, intrepid celebs weathered the storm to deliver
TV spots, pose for a poster, give blood, and save a neighbor.
Each actor expressed the need for blood from their own personal point of view.
Jason Williams of the New Jersey Nets shocked the studio with his
reading. (Jason's mother had once shot at his abusive father and chased him
through the 'hood with a butcher knife...and two sisters died of AIDS,
one after she was brutally raped and beaten with a hammer.) Jason said, almost
prophetically: *Sooner or later, tragedy strikes us all. And almost always,
blood transfusions are essential in saving the lives of the people we love.*
Tim Robbins (who insisted on writing his own heartfelt script):
What if you were rushed to an emergency room, needing blood? And there wasn't any?
Jimmy Breslin: *My beautiful daughter Rosemary is kept alive only because
of blood transfusions. Thanks, neighbor.*
Donald Trump: *Donating a pint of blood is better than giving someone a million bucks!*
Rebecca Lobo (the female basketball star whose mother survived cancer):
Girlfriend, why not celebrate your 17th birthday by saving a life!
Brian Dennehy (starring at the time on Broadway in *Death of a Salesman*): *Attention must be paid!*
Kim Raver (who played a paramedic on *Third Watch*):
This is no TV drama. This is a matter of life and death.
And former mayor Koch's punch line: *You can end this neverending problem
by clenching your fist and pumping out a pint for a pal.*
Give Blood. Save a neighbor." Adweek magazine commented, "It takes
a good cause–and an adman with clout–to convince celebrities
to brave a hurricane for a photo shoot." Maybe so, but these eight stalwart
New Yorkers surely performed above and beyond the call of duty.

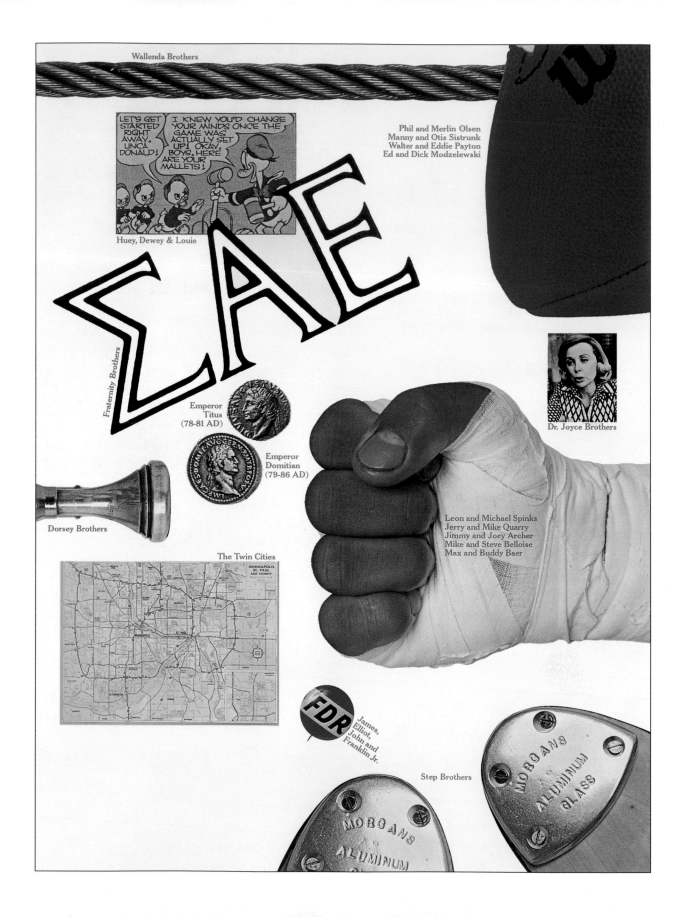

TOM & HANK AARON
DONNIE AND BOBBY ALLISON
THE ALLMAN BROTHERS
FELIPE, MATTY AND JESUS ALOU
JIMMY AND JOEY ARCHER
MAX AND BUDDY BAER
BEE GEES
BLUES BROTHERS
KEN AND GEORGE BRETT
CLETE AND KEN BOYER
DR. JOYCE BROTHERS
CAIN AND ABEL
HOSS AND LITTLE JOE CARTWRIGHT
BILLY AND JIMMY CARTER
RAOUL AND FIDEL CASTRO
MORT AND WALKER COOPER
DALTON BROTHERS
DIZZY AND DAFFY DEAN
JOE, DOM AND VINCE DIMAGGIO
JIMMY AND TOMMY DORSEY
DUCHAMP BROTHERS
HUEY, DEWEY & LOUIE
EARP BROTHERS
TONY AND PHIL ESPOSITO
EVERLY BROTHERS
FRATERNITY BROTHERS
FRANCISCAN BROTHERS
GEORGE AND IRA GERSHWIN
ALBERTO AND DIEGO GIACOMETTI
BROTHERS GRIMM
AMBROSIUS AND HANS HOLBEIN
MARK AND MARTY HOWE
JACKSON FIVE
FRANK AND JESSE JAMES
BERNARD AND MALVIN KALB
BROTHERS KARAMAZOV
LEHMAN BROTHERS
LEVER BROTHERS
BRET AND BART MAVERICK
DON AND DAVE MALONEY
MAYO BROTHERS
PHIL AND JOE NIEKRO
PHIL AND MERLIN OLSEN
OSMOND BROTHERS
LYNN AND MUZZ PATRICK
JIM AND GAYLORD PERRY
RICHARD AND MAURICE PETTY
DENNIS AND JEAN POTVIN
JERRY AND MIKE QUARRY
HENRI AND MAURICE RICHARD
RINGLING BROTHERS
RIGHTEOUS BROTHERS
RITZ BROTHERS
ROCKEFELLER BROTHERS
MANNY AND OTIS SISTRUNK
SMITH BROTHERS
SMOTHERS BROTHERS
SOLOMON BROTHERS
LEON AND MICHAEL SPINKS
STEP BROTHERS
SULLIVAN BROTHERS
EMPERORS TITUS AND DOMITIAN
FRANK AND JOE TORRE
THE TWIN CITIES
AL AND BOBBY UNSER
VAN ARSDALE TWINS
VANDERBILT BROTHERS
VAN EYCK BROTHERS
WALLENDA BROTHERS
LLOYD AND PAUL WANER
WARNER BROTHERS
ORVILLE AND WILBUR WRIGHT

103. THE CELEBRITY BROTHERS OF THE WORLD RECOMMEND THE BROTHERS DELI IN MINNEAPOLIS.

In 1980, one of the items on this menu read: "If you don't pick the $5.95 Rockefeller Brothers Prime Ribs Combination, it's your own vault!" Oh, Brothers! Groucho and Harpo impersonators slayed 'em on TV, and my brotherly menus (the back of the lunch menu shown at left) starring Huey, Dewey & Louie, the Dorsey Brothers, the Step Brothers, The Wallenda Brothers (even Joyce Brothers) were being ripped off by hundreds of drooling customers. The Brothers Deli became a hot spot in the Twin Cities and the talk of the Midwest. Brothers Len and Sam Rosen kept reprinting the menus as they happily dished out the best deli west of Broadway.

"You may hate this menu, but you'll love our food."

THE SIX BEST MAYORS IN AMERICA:

Alioto of San Francisco
who increases services but lowers taxes.

Massell of Atlanta
_the fastest-growing city
in the South._

Landrieu of New Orleans
_who preserved
the splendid French Quarter._

White of Boston
_who brought city government
back to his people._

Maier of Milwaukee
_whose sensible curfew defused
a riot situation._

And our own Lee Alexander
_for making Syracuse New York's only
major city that isn't broke. We consider him
one of the six best mayors in America.
Let's make him our mayor again._

104. LEE ALEXANDER OF SYRACUSE:
ONE OF THE SIX BEST MAYORS IN AMERICA.
(MY OUTRAGEOUS POLITICAL CLAIM
BECOMES A SELF-FULFILLING PROPHECY.)

In 1973, Lee Alexander, a handsome Greek (that's redundant), was running
for a second term as mayor of Syracuse. He had virtually stolen the first election
from a slumbering Republican machine; this time around the power brokers
of upstate New York were gunning for him. And the working-class people of Syracuse,
a bastion of tough, blue-collar, conservative Poles and Italians, weren't too happy
about Alexander's programs for the poor and the elderly. He was an activist liberal in
a decidedly conservative town and the polls showed he was going to get
clobbered. We knew that what was needed was a campaign that would popularize
the Democratic mayor's innovative programs, reinforce their validity, and turn
the perception of him upside down. So I did a campaign that ordained Joseph Alioto
of San Francisco, Sam Massell of Atlanta, Moon Landrieu of New Orleans,
Kevin White of Boston, Henry Maier of Milwaukee, and, of course...
Lee Alexander of Syracuse as *The Six Best Mayors in America!* Whether or not
he was or *wasn't* one of the six best mayors in America became the issue
of the campaign, and his confused, blindsided opponent spent most of his time
tripping over himself, arguing that Alexander *wasn't*. In no time, his campaign
to insist that Syracuse wasn't one of the six best-governed cities in America became
an affront to civic pride! Finally the Republicans simply threw in the towel when
the leading Republican newspapers in Syracuse both admitted editorially that
perhaps Syracuse's own Lee Alexander *was* one of the six best mayors in America!
In a conservative Republican town, Alexander was re-elected by a whopping
68% of Syracuse voters. Lee Alexander went on to become the head
of the National Conference of Democratic Mayors, president of the United States
Conference of Mayors, and kept Syracuse in the black while serving four terms.
The New York Times called Lee Alexander a "wizard," and Syracuse became
the envy of urban America at a time when cities in America were in the dumps.

talk

THE
PRODUCERS
FLAUNT IT,
BABY!

105. HOW A STINKER BECOMES A WINNER...

Editor Tina Brown was a first-nighter at Mel Brooks' big, cocky musical production about show biz.
The next day she svengalied the producers of *The Producers* into an exclusive cover
shoot of their newly anointed kings of Broadway. Early the next morning, before a 2:00 pm matinee, a
bleary-eyed Nathan Lane and a yawning Matthew Broderick stumbled into photographer
Albert Watson's studio, and came to life as they portrayed the maniac producer

...BECOMES A LOSER (AND ENDS UP THE BIGGEST WINNER ON BROADWAY!).

Max Bialystock and the quiet-riot accountant Leo Bloom. Soon thereafter Talk hit the newsstands and scooped every magazine in America. When Talk went silent in January of 2002, *The New York Times* sneered that Tina Brown's "black-and-white" *Producers* cover was an example of her many "last-minute switches." Certainly *this* "last-minute switch" was a Tina Triumph. P.S. Study the cover again. Black-and-white?!

106. THE UNKNOCKABLES.
IN A DOG-EAT-DOG WORLD, I CHOSE EIGHT FAMOUS PEOPLE BEYOND REPROACH.

The '60s were a time when Americans were becoming suspicious of celebrities, politicians, even their sports heroes. From a balcony above these "Unknockables," Carl Fischer and I asked them to look up at his camera for an Esquire cover. Norman Thomas was suffering from a painful spinal paralysis and couldn't move his neck. I was getting ready to lower the camera angle when Joe Louis leaned over and said gently to the old socialist, "Oh, Mr. Thomas, you never had trouble sticking your neck out before."

107. DICK SCHAAP, THE NEW YORK TIMES AND ME.

Thursday, July 2, 1994, I got a call at 8:00 am from the legendary, ubiquitous, people-collecting sports journalist, Dick Schaap. The silver-haired writer was a gleeful, unrepentant celebrity-hound who actually met and became close pals with most of the names he dropped. "Lois," he rasped, "I've been a newspaper editor, a magazine editor, I've written dozens of best-sellers, I've reported on sports for NBC, ABC and ESPN for over 40 years, I won three Emmys, but I *never, ever* had my name in a *New York Times* crossword puzzle. Fuck you!" and hung up.
I grabbed my unopened *Times* and there it was, 56 Down: Ad exec George_____.
My buddy Dick died tragically December 22, 2001, and he got a mournful but glorious half-page obit in the very same *New York Times*.

BACK ROW:
EDDIE BRACKEN
KATE SMITH
JOHN CAMERON SWAYZE

MIDDLE ROW:
JIMMY DURANTE
JOE LOUIS
HELEN HAYES

FRONT ROW:
MARIANNE MOORE
NORMAN THOMAS

Crossword | The New York Times   THURSDAY, JULY 7, 1994

ACROSS
1 Gutter site
5 Insomnia cause?
9 Marmon ―― (first auto to win the Indy 500)
13 Sick as ――
14 Onetime Aegean land
16 Actress Chase
17 Start of a quotation by 9 Down
20 Neighbor of Braz.
21 Popular machine
22 Detroit products
23 Kind of code
25 25, e.g.
28 Runway
30 ――-daisy
31 Signal since 1912
34 Indulgent
35 Sister of Selene
36 Straddling
37 Middle of quote
41 All ―― (attentive)
42 Zinger
43 Acht, ――, zehn
44 1994 U.S. Open golf champion
45 Star of "Mon Oncle"
46 Tidy up
48 Poznan's location
50 Seats, slangily
52 Peacock "eyes"
55 Addition
57 Suffix with insist
58 End of quote
62 "―― boy!"
63 Ruth's mother-in-law
64 Western star Richard
65 Admit, with "up"
66 Girlie show props
67 Certain investor's agreement, for short

DOWN
1 Gobble
2 More than appreciates
3 1985 Tom Hanks comedy
4 Kind of maniac
5 Losing proposition
6 Offerings of 7-Down
7 Rest stop
8 Noisy bird
9 See 17-Across
10 ―― Romeo
11 Potato part
12 Mountain route
15 1991 Sondheim show
18 Bag
19 Like a haunted house
24 Hamas adherents
26 San ――
27 Savvy about
29 Galatea's sculptor, in myth
31 Salisbury Plain attraction
32 Comic strip reaction
33 Aix-les-Bains, e.g.
36 Chills
37 One of 18
38 Movie computer
39 Bit
40 ――, Minn. (1862 Sioux uprising site)
45 Highway robbery?
47 Ballpoint part
48 Guilty and others
49 Stuffed deli delicacy
51 Dictator's aide
52 One of five Norse kings
53 Île de la ――
54 Salamanders
56 Ad exec George
59 Capture
60 Gunk
61 ―― Lingus

Puzzle by Edward Early   7/7/94 (No. 0707)

Answers to any three clues in this puzzle are available by touch-tone phone: 1-900-884-CLUE (75¢ first minute, 50¢ each extra minute).

ANSWER TO PREVIOUS PUZZLE

A	S	O	F		S	W	E	E	P		S	A	D	R
F	A	I	R		P	E	S	T	O		O	N	E	A
E	R	L	E		E	A	T	A	T		N	D	A	K
W	I	S	E	A	C	R	E		B	O	D	I	N	E
			T	R	I	S		D	E	A	R			
M	A	R	I	N	E		S	U	L	T	A	N	A	
I	C	A	M	E		H	E	E	L	S		E	R	R
E	T	T	E		B	E	T	T	Y		G	R	O	H
S	U	E		C	O	A	T	S		T	O	T	S	Y
	P	R	I	O	R	T	O		B	I	A	S	E	S
			M	O	D	S		D	E	L	T			
S	T	A	P	L	E		B	I	A	T	H	L	O	N
Y	O	R	E		R	E	A	C	T		E	A	S	Y
N	O	O	N		O	N	S	E	T		R	I	S	E
C	L	O	D		N	E	E	D	Y		D	R	A	T

108. TAMEST EVENT ON KIDS TV THAT DAY: RUBY KILLS OSWALD.

November 24, 1963, was a definitive TV moment,
as Jack Ruby shot Lee Harvey Oswald dead, live,
in front of millions, old and young.
On an Esquire cover, I show the moment when
an all-American kid started to grow up with
real violence in his carpeted den, complete with
an all-American hamburger and Coke.
Oswald killed our president and our dreams
for building a better America,
and Ruby killed our chance to make any
sense of what went down.
May the two most infamous men in
American history burn in hell.

*"Awwk!
I want my MTV!"*

109. CASTRO AND HIS REVOLTING PARROT.

After a year of unprecedented publicity and success,
MTV head Bob Pittman asked me, begged me, *ordered* me–
to omit my slogan *I want my MTV* in future MTV advertising
(see 6). "But, Bob, it's incredibly famous. It saved your
ass. Why kill it?!" "Because," he pleaded, "I hear it a thousand
times each day and I can't take it anymore. It's *everywhere*!"
So I *very* reluctantly shot three new spots, ending the campaign
that made MTV a cultural phenomenon. A bellowing,
born again Christian berated MTV's sordid influence on the
youth of America, a Communist commissar went red in the face,
and a Fidel Castro look-alike, smoking a big, fat Havana
in the Cuban jungle, spitted out his disdain for MTV as a degrading
product of capitalist imperialism. His punch line: "It's garbaaage!"
I showed the finished spots to Bob Pittman and his
wunderkind gang, saving Castro for last. They guffawed at the
politically incorrect parody of the apoplexed preacher
and booed the Russian. Then, as Fidel's diatribe against MTV
came to a close, with the spot fading to black, a parrot
perched behind Castro squawked, *I want my MTV!*
When the whiz kids got off the floor, honcho Bob Pittman,
gasping for breath, said, "Touché!"

Neil Cole was a ballsy advertiser who had made a name for his No Excuses Jeans with bad-girl spokespeople like Donna Rice (who sank Senator Gary Hart's quest for the presidency in 1988 when a photographer caught them monkeying around on a boat named *Monkey Business* off Bimini). There were no more bimbos in sight, so he asked me to make waves by creating a campaign that was wired into the pop/gossip culture. A man after my own heart. I conjured up the No Excuses Award of the Month that would be "given" to a public personality right out of the day's headlines who "made us remember that to err is human, but to take the heat and make no excuses for it, is divine." Admittedly, it moved into that gray area where "invasion of privacy" could rear its ugly head. But what the hell. The campaign started with a time bomb, with a timely tribute to our lamebrain VP-elect J. Danforth Quayle (*Eager for his place in history, he is industriously doing his homework, crossing his i's, dotting his t's, getting ready to lead*). After weathering a storm of publicity (which was the name of the game) I followed with one newsmaker after another: LaToya Jackson, fresh off a *Playboy* spread (*For showing that any resemblance to her famous brother is from the neck up*)...Exxon for its Alaska oil spill (*For moving the Black Sea to the Alaska coastline*)...Actor Rob Lowe for his porno videotape caper (*How Lowe can you go?*). A mea culpa from convicted tax evader Leona Helmsley (for using corporate monies to renovate her opulent apartment): (*Hey...since when is it a crime to redecorate?*) My No Excuses ad brought down the house. Finally, I selected Malcolm Forbes at the crest of his notorious publicity for that singular 70th birthday party in Morocco, an internationally publicized bacchanal that outdid anything the world had seen since Nero and Caligula. Under his photo I ran the caption: *To Malcolm Forbes: For feeding 880 hungry people in Africa!* I must admit I was concerned about possibly sacrificing my friendship with Malcolm Forbes, but I would rather *lose* a friend and run a good ad than *keep* a friend and lose a great ad. The morning our ad ran, my pluperfect assistant, Emily Paxinos, fearfully told me Malcolm Forbes was demanding to speak to me on the phone. Cowering, I said "H-h-hello, Malcolm?" The great champion of capitalism bellowed: "George, I *love* that ad! Can you get me 880 reprints?!"

no excuses

AUGUST 1989

AWARD OF THE MONTH:

Dedicated to the principle
that to err is human,
but to take the heat and
make no excuses for it,
is divine!

To Malcolm Forbes

For feeding 880 hungry people in Africa!

A Dear John letter to John Fairchild from Pauline Trigère...

PAULINE TRIGÈRE

Dear John,
after all these years
and so many terrific
collections—is it really
over between us?
You don't call.
You don't write.
I still love you.
Pauline

111. THE LEGENDARY COUTURIERE PAULINE TRIGÈRE DEFINED HER MARKETING PROBLEM IN ONE SENTENCE: "GEORGES, PEOPLE THEENK I AM DEAD!"

The inimitable Pauline Trigère, a forthright, unpretentious, aristocratic lady, with her strong face and impervious Gallic accent, was dead right–and to define her predicament so candidly was a revealing clue to her honesty and courage. During the '50s and '60s, Trigère was properly regarded as a great talent, one of the first of the fashionistas. By 1988, the elegant lady was of a certain age, and her longevity problem was compounded by an intramural industry vendetta: The most influential trade paper in the fashion world is *Women's Wear Daily*, headed by the dynast John Fairchild, who had been known to banish any mention in *WWD* of anyone who had offended or slighted the Fairchild power. According to Pauline, Fairchild's displeasure concerned her son criticizing the banishment of Geoffrey Beene. At one time or another, Fairchild had also blacklisted Hubert de Givenchy, Giorgio Armani and Bill Blass. They all kept their mouths shut and took it on the chin. John Fairchild, the self-styled dictator of the fashion world, had set me up to make Pauline Trigère the Joan of Arc of Seventh Avenue! To deal with the Fairchild banishment head-on, I showed Madame Trigère *A Dear John letter to John Fairchild from Pauline Trigère* in her signature red-ink handwriting, surrounded by her tortoiseshell shades, her fountain pen and her well-known turtle jewelry. After being warned by Geoffrey Beene and all her pals in the business that my ad would be her ruination, she said "Screw it, Georges, run it!" A few days before the ad ran in *Fashions of the Times* (a *New York Times* magazine section), the *Times*' alert marketing columnist spotted the ad in a preview copy, and blew the lid off our counterattack with the lead piece on the front page of the *Times* business section, and zee shit hit zee fan! Pauline Trigère instantly became the heroine of the fashion world as congratulatory letters and phone calls were received from around the world with ongoing stories on TV, newspapers and full-scale magazine pieces for over a year. The great lady batted her Gallic eyelashes while disarming the Establishment, her customers flocked back to her, and today she is more revered than ever for shaming the arrogant bullyboy of the fashion world.

112. ANN-MARGRET TAKES ON WOODY ALLEN.

In a photo session for a 1965 Esquire cover on Sex in Hollywood, I showed a young Woody Allen laying face-to-face, smack-dab on an adoring Ann-Margret, both seemingly nude but with a bath towel tied around the vivacious redheaded actress' chest. But we couldn't quite get a clean shot because the towel kept peeking out. Finally, in feigned exasperation, she said, "Woody, get the hell off me!," peeled away her towel, and we continued the shoot with Woody laying on two exposed, bodacious breasts. (Woody did everything he could to prolong the shoot.)

**113. DURING A POWER LUNCH
WITH EX-KNICK DAVE DEBUSSCHERE,
A FIRE BROKE OUT IN THE KITCHEN.
READ ALL ABOUT IT:**

The New York Times

THURSDAY, MARCH 16, 1995

Fire at the Four Seasons: Everyone Who's In Is Out

By LAWRENCE VAN GELDER

For the movers and shakers who arrived to have lunch as usual yesterday at the elegant Four Seasons, yesterday was decidedly unusual.

Former Secretary of State Henry A. Kissinger never got in at all.

"There's no sense having a power lunch if you're not seen by the powers," he lamented. He ate, instead, at La Grenouille.

Alberto Vitale, the chairman of Random House, got in but soon left. He lunched at the Nippon Restaurant.

Ron Perelman, the chairman of Revlon, started at the Four Seasons but finished at San Pietro. And George Lois, the advertising mogul who was planning on having veal, had to settle for smoked salmon.

The salmon wasn't the only thing that was smoked yesterday at the landmark restaurant in the landmark Seagram Building at 375 Park Avenue between 52d and 53d Streets.

At midday, a two-alarm fire in a kitchen duct in the building's other restaurant, the Brasserie, sent smoke curling through the 38-story structure and forced the evacuation of nine floors and the two restaurants.

The situation was brought under control at 1:30 P.M., but not before one firefighter was treated for minor burns and another for a possible fractured wrist. Three other people, including two firefighters, were treated at the scene for smoke inhalation.

David Kratz, a spokesman for Restaurant Associates, which owns and operates the 215-seat Brasserie, said, "We expect to be reopened in four to five days, as soon as the duct system is examined and repaired." The Four Seasons was closed last night but planned to reopen today.

In the restaurant, whose entrance is dominated by Picasso's backdrop for the 1919 ballet, "The Three Cornered-Hat," and whose dining areas surround a square pool, the luncheon crowd was gathering when it became clear that something was wrong.

Alex von Bidder, the general manager and a partner, said the Four Seasons was three-quarters full, with some 150 people. "By about 12:40, there was too much smoke in our kitchen," he said. "We couldn't function any more. It didn't endanger any patrons. It didn't endanger any employees, but we decided it was smarter to go out in the street."

Mr. Lois, the chairman and chief executive officer of Lois/USA, said the ice skating star Katarina Witt had just walked in. "My eyes were not on the smoke," he admitted. "Then we realized the streets were full of fire engines.

"The captains came by and said, 'Oh, my God, the kitchen's full of smoke. The cooks can't work.' People began to get up."

Mr. Lois said, "Listen, in honor of the occasion, let's have smoked salmon. Run it out here, slice it fast and we'll eat it."

And he added: "I hate to be picky. Is there any way you can get us egg yolk, onion and capers? The captain said, 'Mr. Lois, what about a lemon?' I said, 'Why not?'"

An island of culinary calm in the midst of the storm, Mr. Lois had an emergency plan.

"I said, 'Listen, if it's a real fire, I'll dive into the pool.'"

114. THE FACE OF A HERO.

For an Esquire College Issue in 1965,
in a time when we still embraced heroes,
I created this composite of the men
I chose as the leading heroes of American youth.
Bob Dylan, Malcolm X, Fidel Castro
and John Kennedy are divided (and joined)
by the crossbars of a rifle sight.
Kennedy and Malcolm had been murdered,
and Castro (we now know) escaped
assassination attempts, and is still regarded
by many as a romantic revolutionary.
The poet Dylan remained to compose and sing
of that violent, revolting age.
(Today, alas, without heroes, we must do
with celebrities.)

CLIFF ROBERTSON *My ancestor, Lt. John Robertson, was decorated by General Washington. Now this revolutionary Scot is going home...to Greece.*

SALLY STRUTHERS *My grandparents came to America from a little fishing village in Norway. And now I'm going home...to Greece.*

HARRY MORGAN *My father came from Norway and my mother from Sweden. Now this Scandinavian is going home...to Greece.*

JOE NAMATH *My folks came to this country from their farm in Hungary. And now I'm going home...to Greece.*

SHECKY GREENE *My mother vas coming from Russia to this vunderful America. Now I'm going home...to Greece.*

EVA MARIE SAINT *My grandmother came to America from London in the late 1800s. And now I'm going home...to Greece.*

BRENDA VACCARO *My father Mario came from Sicily in 1905. And now I'm finally going home...to Greece.*

RODDY McDOWELL *I was born in London and came to America when I was 12 years old. Now, at last, I'm going home...to Greece.*

LLOYD BRIDGES *Mama used to tell me that my ancestors from the British Isles came over on the Mayflower. Now I'm going home...to Greece.*

E.G. MARSHALL *My great grandfather came to this country from Oslo, Norway, in 1850, and now I'm going home...to Greece*

ZSA ZSA GABOR *I was born in Hungary. Now, darling, I'm finally going home...to Greece.*

JOHNNY UNITAS *My people came from Lithuania at the turn of the century. Finally, I'm going home...to Greece.*

AUDREY LANDERS *My grandmamá came to America from Marseille. Now this mademoiselle is going home...to Greece.*

RALPH BELLAMY *My ancestors came from England, Ireland, France, Spain and Italy. Finally, I'm going home...to Greece.*

NEIL SEDAKA *My grandparents left Poland and Russia and came to Brooklyn. Now, at last, I'm going home...to Greece.*

115. IN 1985, PRESIDENT REAGAN WARNED AMERICANS NOT TO TRAVEL TO GREECE. PLANES CARRYING TOURISTS STOPPED MID-AIR! SO WE RECRUITED 39 CELEBS (OF NON-GREEK LINEAGE) TO TELL AMERICA THAT THEY WERE "GOING HOME...TO GREECE!"

This was mission impossible. We were up against international terrorism *and* the White House. That summer, skyjacking and hostage-taking in the Middle East had become rampant, and President Reagan put the last nail in the coffin when he warned Americans in a news conference to stay clear of the Athens airport. The tourism that Greece relied on vanished. Hotels were empty, cruise ships were being beached, and nobody was dancing in the aisles of Olympic Airways, TWA or the isles of the Aegean. A miracle was needed– a miracle that *can* happen, through the power of The Big Idea. As a proud Greek American, Zeus struck me with his lightning bolt when the Greek National Tourist Organization begged me to somehow contain this terminal damage to tourism to their homeland. The Big Idea: *I'm going home...to Greece!* But instead of recruiting famous Hellenic-American celebs such as Telly Savalas, Jimmy the Greek or Olympia Dukakis, I made a 180° turn from the obvious, and went after Americans of *non*-Greek ancestry, who were "going home to Greece," the birthplace of democracy, "where it all began." We offered free flights to a celebrity and his family (on empty planes), free hotel stays (in empty hotels), free passage through the Greek isles (on empty ships). Celebrities lined up in droves. Their obvious delight in their surprising destination was a sublime assurance of a safe trip. Our commercials were picked up by the networks and ran gratis as newsbreaks, demonstrating how Greece was fighting terrorism by dramatizing how famous Americans would not kowtow to the terrorists! Olympic and TWA flights filled to capacity. The Greek economy enjoyed a landslide tourist season, their most glorious ever. (Creativity can solve any problem. The creative act, the defeat of habit by originality, overcomes everything. I believe that.)

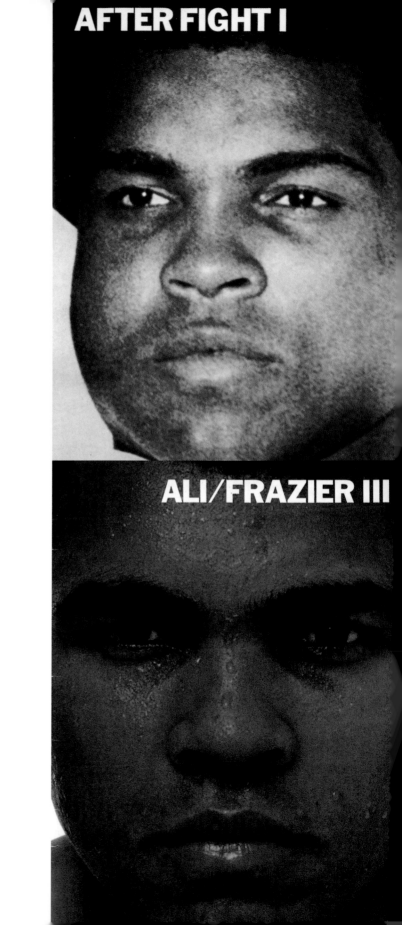

AFTER FIGHT I

ALI/FRAZIER III

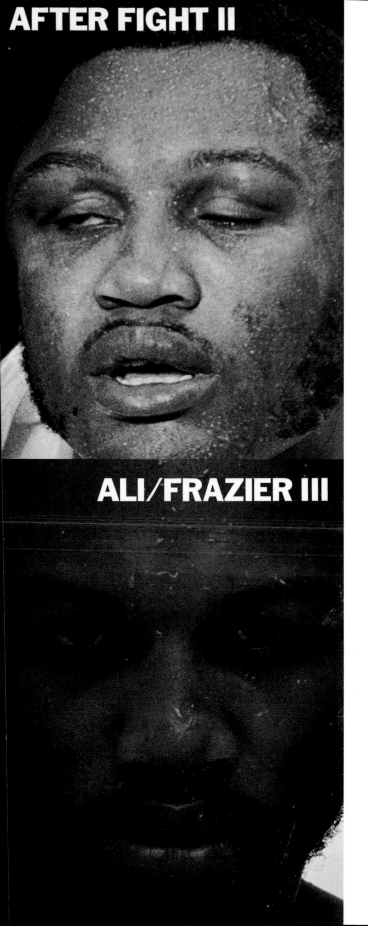

AFTER FIGHT II

ALI/FRAZIER III

116. "WOULDN'T IT BE GREAT TO DO THE ULTIMATE FIGHT PROGRAM (FOR THE ULTIMATE FIGHT) AND GIVE IT AWAY FOR NOTHING!"

Don King (the Mike Todd and P.T. Barnum of the fight game) was promoting the fight of the century, the grudge rubber match between Muhammad Ali and Smokin' Joe Frazier. I told King that I had convinced one of my advertising clients, Cutty Sark, a Waspy kind of scotch trying to earn its way into the lucrative Black market, to let me produce a free fight program to give to the hundreds of thousands of people in America who would attend closed-circuit locations, instead of the traditional media choice of running a couple of ads in *Ebony* magazine. The concept would expand the Cutty market, it would be a prestigious achievement for Don King, the most talented megalomaniac who ever lived, and I could even get a plug in the program for Rubin Hurricane Carter, who I was trying to spring from the slammer, by having Ali and Frazier handwrite their support (see Favorite Celebs 1). My old Esquire chum Harold Hayes and I had hilarious "interviews" with Muhammad and Joe, dissin' each other in our fight program that became an instant collector's item. A few weeks after the now legendary "Thrilla in Manila" (Sept. 30, 1975) I was gabbing with a veteran cab driver about the stupendous brawl that went a thrilling 14 rounds, a fight that solidified Ali as the iconic sports figure of our time. "It was the greatest heavyweight fight I ever saw in my whole life," he said, "almost as good as that ape-shit fight program those beautiful girls in Cutty Sark T-shirts handed out."

117. PAYING HOMAGE TO THE GREAT FLORENCE KNOLL.

In the early 1960s my agency, Papert, Koenig, Lois, was contacted by a banker in Florida.
His name was Henry Hood Bassett, and without a lot of fanfare he gave my agency
his advertising account–on one condition: all the work had to be approved
by his wife. At the time I didn't realize who his wife was, so I said, "Well, I've had a lot
of kibitzing wives kill my work." He then sheepishly mentioned his wife was *the*
Florence Knoll, and I believe my exact words were "Holy shit!" He asked me,
"Does that scare you?" I said, "Hell no, it's thrilling. I'd much rather have her as a client
than you." And a truly great client Florence Knoll and her husband became as they
approved and approved logos and ad campaigns for his group of avant-garde banks.
Forty years later, *Metropolis*, the superb architecture, culture and design
magazine, honored me by asking me to create a cover to celebrate the first interview she
had granted in decades. And the legendary interior-space planner and designer
who had an iconoclastic influence on modern design as the driving force of Knoll Designs
in the '40s, '50s and beyond, had plenty to say to today's designers.
When the great lady received the first issue of the July 2001 *Metropolis*, hot off
the presses, she called me from her home in Florida and once again,
appreciatively, approved my work.

118. THE VERY FIRST HOWARD HUGHES HOAX.

This issue sold like hotcakes because at long last the
"invisible" Howard Hughes was finally "discovered."
Which proves once more that you can fool all of the people
all of the time. I was simply trying to spoof the idiotic
interest in America's best-known, least-seen mystery man.
The guy in the white bathrobe is an actor playing
Howard Hughes. The woman in the bathing suit is an
actress who looked like Hughes' wife, Jean Peters.
And the lug playing a bodyguard came from central casting,
all staged at a pool in Miami and photographed to look
like the Hughes entourage had spotted us as we clicked away.
(Photographer Tasso Vendikos played the paparazzo
so well he was detained by the Miami cops.) Everyone thought
the sighting was the real thing when this issue came out,
but the big thinkers at *Time* magazine figured out that it was
a hoax. The press pounced on editor Harold Hayes
for an explanation, and he summed up the silly hoo-ha over
the mystery celebrity: "What we're doing is an attempt
to satirize the whole obsession with the idea that the world
is constantly pursuing Howard Hughes." I wonder
if Clifford Irving saw this cover in 1969, three years before
he wrote his bogus "authorized" Hughes biography—
an incredible caper that landed him in the cooler.

METROPOLIS

The Soul of Knoll

Florence Knoll Bassett

Eero Saarinen
Gae Aulenti
Isamu Noguchi
Marcel Breuer
Don Petitt
Charles & Ray Eames
Walter Gropius
Hans Knoll
Herbert Matter
Mies van der Rohe
Anni Albers
George Nakashima
Hans Wegner
Harry Bertoia
Warren Platner
Jens Risom
Richard Sapper
Yrjö Kukkapuro

"Evander,
do the Bart-man
on the old geezer!"

119. THE BATTLE OF THE AGES:
A YOUNG EVANDER HOLYFIELD VS. OLD MAN GEORGE FOREMAN,
KID-STAR BART SIMPSON VS. 50-YEAR-OLD BUGS BUNNY.

Men are from Mars (they love the masculine combat of boxing).
Women are from Venus (they *abhor* the brutality of boxing).
Can a direct-response TV campaign prompting immediate phone response for
a world championship heavyweight fight, bring them together?
Read on. In 1991, the controversial merging of two communications giants,
Time and Warner, seemed to promise an extraordinary synergy. But it wasn't happening.
My ad agency, Lois/USA, worked with the young Seth Abraham, the dynamic HBO sports head,
to create an ambitious plan to catapult Time Warner onto center stage in the sports marketing
and programming arena. I created the name TVKO, and Abraham signed the first event,
the Holyfield-Foreman championship bout, positioning it as the Battle of the Ages to attract far more
than the devoted fan, and break the mold of "sweaty boxer" formula advertising.
We began our TV campaign with the 42-year-old Foreman sitting in a rocking chair in the corner
of a ring, saying: *Some folks think I'm too old to be fighting for the heavyweight title again.*
I'm just a big old baby boomer–and I'm going to lower the boom on that baby, Evander Holyfield.
Holyfield counterpunches by saying: *My mama taught me to always respect my elders.*
But Mr. Foreman, if you think you're going to beat me, you're off your rocker! In Holyfield's corner,
the young Knicks center Patrick Ewing says to George: *Evander's gonna stuff you, old man!*
Billy Crystal, rooting for Foreman, fires back: *Patrick, you made a mistake. You should never say*
stuffed to George–because George translates that to stuffing, which means he's gonna
eat this kid! Finally, Bart Simpson tells his man Evander to *Do the Bart-man on the old geezer!*
And Bugs Bunny, celebrating his 50th birthday, gets
into the act for his aging hero George Foreman,
by declaring: *Oh, brudder...George'll pulverize the kid!*
Our TV campaign charmed America's boxing fans
(including wives who normally object to their working-
class husbands blowing 40 smackers on a fight).
The event was seen by the largest Pay-Per-View
audience ever, 1.4 million homes plunking down 40
bucks each, for a record-breaking gate of $60 million.
P.S. After a two-week ad campaign, everybody
in America, young and old, was rooting for George.
The old guy fought valiantly, but in a helluva
battle, lost on points.

"Oh, brudder...
George'll pulverize
the kid!"

120. "SVENSON, HANG OVER THIS CLIFF OR I'LL THROW YOU OFF IT!"

In 1964, Puss 'n Boots was ready to introduce what they called "a revolutionary semi-moist cat food," packaged so it remained fresh in individual cups that contained one serving, 12 in a pack. I created two spots: My pal Dick Lynch starred as a helicopter pilot flying over a tiny Caribbean island, making an emergency landing after spotting a distress signal on the beach. He runs up to a vigorous-looking cat marooned on the island who was miraculously surviving because of his cache of Puss 'n Boots Semi-Moist. Lynch and the pussycat discuss the benefits and great taste of the new product. The handsome, athletic and charismatic ex-Giants star was perfect casting.

For the second spot we searched high and low for a Nordic type with an accent, who had experience as a mountain climber. We found a young, manly actor named Bo Svenson. I was ecstatic as he described his climbing feats in an understandable Swedish accent. But at the shoot on a Colorado mountaintop, as we positioned Svenson to be photographed, seemingly climbing the mountainside to rescue a stranded tiger cat– he coiled back in fear. He had never mountain-climbed in his life! He was too frightened to approach within six feet of the edge of a thousand-foot cliff. But the show must go on. I pleaded, then screamed, then warned him, then *pushed* the six-foot-five, safety-belted Svenson over the edge. Our cat trainer positioned the cool cat, and we filmed a hilarious commercial, as a dangling Svenson wet his pants. Hollywood directors saw the commercial on the air and Bo Svenson went on to have an up-and-down career in Hollywood starring in he-man action movies (*Walking Tall Part 2*), transforming his yumping-yimminy Swedish accent into a dang-good, shit-kicking American twang. Cat owners lapped up the spots and Puss 'n Boots Semi-Moist leaped off the shelves. With the most successful month in Puss 'n Boots history, parent company Quaker planned to build a new factory to keep up with the demand. But a month later, sales went south. Felines all over America raised their noses to it, and no cat owner ever bought it a second time. (As it turned out, the answer to our slogan *Who knows more about cats than Puss 'n Boots?* was...everybody!)

121. I NEEDED AN EMOTIONAL KIRK DOUGLAS–TYPE VOICEOVER FOR A TVKO SPOT TOUTING AN EVANDER HOLYFIELD VS. MIKE TYSON CHAMPIONSHIP BRAWL. I GOT IT! HOW ABOUT KIRK DOUGLAS?

The great megastar who powerfully depicted a corrupted pugilist in
Mark Robson's film *Champion* seemed to enjoy the witty conceit of
lending his voice as spokesman for the upcoming war in Las Vegas
between two superb heavyweights at their prime.
He read these words over memorable, historic footage:
Where were you that incredible day
*   man stepped on the moon?*
Where were you when Bobby Thompson
*   hit the shot heard 'round the world?*
Where were you when LBJ startled the nation
*   with his decision not to seek re-election?*
Where were you when the Beatles
*   premiercd on TV?*
Where were you that Sunday Broadway Joe
*   pulled off that super upset?*
Where were you when our boys covered
*   themselves in glory by*
*   beating the Russian hockey team?*
And where will you be the night Tyson fights Holyfield
*   for the Heavyweight Championship?*
But somehow, his read didn't have enough oomph.
So I stammered, "Mr. Douglas, great, but, er...
could you give me a reading where you impersonate
Kirk Douglas in the movie *Champion*?"
He knew exactly what I meant, gritted his teeth,
and belted out a classic.

122. 12 ANGRY MEN AND A NO-SHOW.

In November 1969 I did my third Ali cover for Esquire (see 16 and 58).
At the time, Muhammad remained stripped of his title for refusing military service.
Harold Hayes and I enlisted 12 good souls to climb into the boxing ring
and publicly support Ali's right to resume his illustrious career. One giant who had
agreed to join my cover protest was his fellow Muslim, Kareem Abdul-Jabbar
of the L.A. Lakers. I envisioned the seven-footer standing tall in the midst of the literary
great Truman Capote, Pop artist Roy Lichtenstein, sports announcer Howard Cosell,
director Sydney Lumet, actor James Earl Jones, and anti–Vietnam War senator
Ernest Gruening (I tried to enlist a female celeb, but no dice). Photographer Ira Mazer
had a full-size ring constructed in his studio for the shoot. As they patiently
waited for Kareem to show up, one side of the ring broke down and my dozen heroic
combatants started to topple like bowling pins. Mortified, I rushed to their help.
Graciously, the octogenarian senator Gruening said to me, "Don't concern yourself,
young man. If we all *have* to go down to speak up for Muhammad Ali, so be it."
Kareem Abdul-Jabbar, alas, was a no-show. His explanation to me for his embarrassing
absence was that he feared "retaliation," not by the white establishment, but by
competing factions in the Muslim world. Finally, in 1970, the Supreme Court stood
in Ali's corner and Muhammad went back to work.

123. IN AN ERA OF DISPOSABLE CELEBRITIES, ELVIS LIVES!

1988 was the 75th anniversary of the American Cancer Society. Over the years,
media traditionally but grudgingly ran their "public service" TV spots, usually
ostracizing them to Siberia in the wee hours of the morning when the world was asleep.
We needed a campaign that excited TV stations to give us prime-time coverage,
gladly and willingly. So we convinced the Elvis Presley estate to allow us to use Elvis'
anthem-like *If I Could Dream* with lyrics we wrote that appealed to the emotions
of the good and generous people of America. Leslie Uggams of *Hit Parade* fame
leaped at the chance to deliver our message, knocking America out with her stirring
tribute to the inspiring work of the American Cancer Society, along with our call
to action for the future, as Cliff Robertson said: *There are three million Americans
alive today who have cancer. And now, one out of two cancer patients gets well.
This year the American Cancer Society commemorates 75 years...of life!*
Thanks to Graceland, and the grace of Leslie Uggams, our startling, hopeful and
inspiring campaign was run gratis five times more that year than any other previous
American Cancer Society ad campaign, raising more than twice the monies of
any other year. (In today's world of celebrity licensing, Elvis remains the top-earning
dead celebrity in history. Long live the King.)

We believe this:
Muhammad Ali deserves the right to defend his title.

1 Richard Benjamin
2 Theodore Bikel
3 Truman Capote
4 Howard Cosell
5 Ernest Gruening
6 Michael Harrington
7 James Earl Jones
8 Roy Lichtenstein
9 Sidney Lumet
10 George Plimpton
11 Budd Schulberg
12 José Torres
And inside,
90 others.

124. TWO MACHO MEN (AND TWO HOLLYWOOD SEX SYMBOLS) WHO LOVE PUSSYCATS.

Cat lovers *love* their cats (nobody loves living with a pussycat more than me). To break the myth that a real man only goes for dogs, I chose two mythic macho men, the legendary Manassa Mauler, Jack Dempsey, and the irrepressible Casey Stengel. In a studio crawling with cats, Big Jack said, "I like cats better than dogs, take it or leave it," ending up with "I hope my boxer doesn't hear this commercial!" In Casey Stengel's TV lecture for Tabby cat food, the Ol' Perfesser, nose to nose with a tabby cat, delivered his lines in machine-gun Stengelese, proving that all cat owners ain't sweet old ladies with scratches on their wrists. (And I swear the cat understood every word Casey said.) To round out our cat food campaign, our client Lorillard asked us to produce a couple of spots using females, and we wowed them with glamourpuss WWII G.I. pinup Betty Grable and the va-va-voom Jane Russell. Russell sexily stroked a purring male cat and said, *He eats Tabby day and night.* Then she looked into his eyes and asked suspiciously, *By the way, where were you last night?* (a line *she* wrote that was edgier than ours, a remarkable feat). Copywriter Ron Holland was working in front of the camera with Betty Grable when he got a phone call from a friend who directed Broadway plays and regarded ad men as sell-out stiffs. "Can't talk to you now," said Holland. "I'm right in the middle of directing Betty Grable." Ron's friend said, "Oh" and hung up.

125. THE CLAIRVOYANT MAYOR OF NEW YORK IN 1924 PROUDLY ANNOUNCES THE BIRTH OF LITTLE EDDIE KOCH.

On Mayor Ed Koch's 60th birthday (December 12, 1984)
the Democrats in town threw him a fund-raising dinner dance to celebrate.
For a theme, I researched who the mayor of New York City was, way
back when Edward was born. I swiped a baby photo from the Koch family album
and my retoucher sat little Eddie's Jewish tush on Mayor John F. Hylan's
Irish knee, as the Teddy Roosevelt look-alike proudly announced the birth of the
precocious baby that would follow in his footsteps over a half century later.
I was told baby Ed's first words were "How'm I doing, Mr. Mayor?!"

PETER VECSEY

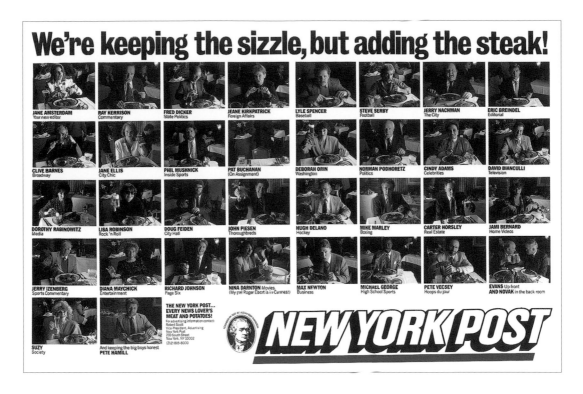

126. MAKING THE NEW YORK POST THE PRIME TABLOID IN TOWN.

Don't worry, Mr. Hamilton, your newspaper is in good hands.
This reference to founder Alexander Hamilton (see 11) captured the New York Post's
irrepressible gall, and we then underlined it with our coup de grace slogan:
We're keeping the sizzle, but adding the steak. The "steak" was new columnists, new
features, new reporters, and a new editor. The "sizzle" was the tabloid style
that had made the Post distinctive (and infamous) over the years. In 1988, new owner
Peter Kalikow brought in the liberal columnist Pete Hamill to add some balance to
the Post's conservative bent, and he hired Jane Amsterdam to be the only woman editor
of any newspaper in the tri-state area. So I shot two 60-second spots starring
no less than 34 (34!) Post reporters eating steak at a famous Manhattan steak joint.
Each of the 34 well-known Post stars interrupts their eating by informing us of their duties:
Jerry Nachman–*The City!* Clive Barnes–*Broadway!* Pat Buchanan–*Washington!*
Jeane Kirkpatrick–*Foreign Affairs!* Richard Johnson–*Page 6!* Suzy–*Society!*
Peter Vecsey–*Hoop du jour!* Pete Hamill–*Keeping the big boys honest!*
And Cindy Adams (as she stabs her steak with a vicious knife thrust)–*Celebrities!*
The rallying cry in the corridors of 210 South Street became "More steak! More steak!"
One frantic day at the Post I heard Kalikow, after receiving the previous day's issue
on his yacht in the waters off the Bahamas, bark on his ship-to-shore phone,
"There's not enough steak in this [bleep] issue to pour ketchup on. I paid for a 3-lb.
porterhouse and you clowns give me a [bleep] hamburger!"
I believe great advertising should reach slightly ahead of the product. (Gertrude Stein
said to Picasso: "I don't look like that!" Picasso replied, "You will!") And the
Post kept serving steak until New Yorkers bit. Circulation went from 460,000 to over
600,000, while the crass image of the Murdoch years (phony Wingo-hyped
circulation, lurid headlines, typified by the classic "Headless Man in Topless Bar")
had been upgraded, making the New York Post the prime tabloid in town.

"Is this any way to run an airline? You bet it is!"

127. A STAR IS SCORNED.

In 1962, 36-year-old former jet pilot Lewis (Bud) Maytag's young, troubled
National Airlines needed a campaign to tell travelers that he was running his airline
in a lively way–like dressing their stewardesses in outfits by Oleg Cassini,
coming out first with fan-jets and introducing special meals on certain flights. I believed
a theme was needed to actually *force* National into continuing exciting innovations.
I wanted an ad campaign where the product had to work overtime and keep up with their
imagery. Rather than messages that focused on flight schedules, we convinced
National to be the first airline ever to run *image* advertising on television. Our edgy theme:
Is this any way to run an airline? You bet it is! I wanted a down-home Doris Day beauty
to be National's TV stewardess. I spotted Andrea Dromm, a young print model,
on a Manhattan street. She was no drama whiz, but she looked perfect. Within a week
of TV advertising our slogan became famous, and the New York-to-Miami market
filled the planes. A year later I was having lunch at The Four Seasons, when a man
in a safari jacket stuck his nose in my face and asked, "Are you George Lois...
from Papert, Koenig, *Lois?*" "Uh huh," I said suavely. (I recognized him as Norman Jewison–
wow, my name had spread to *Hollywood!*) "So *you're* the schmuck," he barked.
"So you're the genius who discovered Andrea Dromm! I was going crazy looking for
a fresh face for an important part in my *The Russians are Coming, The Russians are Coming,*
and one night–there she *was*, doing a National Airlines spot on TV. I was behind
schedule so I gave her the part without an audition, and she damn near destroyed my
movie. Then I realized about the only thing she said in your commercials was
'Is this any *fucking* way to run an airline?!'" I added, "You bet it is!"

128. THE RINGING CRY OF 12 MILLION WORKING PEOPLE IN AMERICA: "UNION, YES!"

In 1989, the AFL-CIO asked me to address their one thousand
rough-and-tough kick-ass delegates in a smoke-filled convention hall, and
convince them to ask their rank and file,12,000,000 men and
women strong, to kick in one buck each, each year, to run a fighting
TV ad campaign to educate the younger segment of our nation
about the necessity for a strong labor movement in America. Labor was
in trouble with Nixon, Ford, Reagan and Bush in the White House,
and the AFL-CIO needed a catchy, populist concept to halt their decreasing
power of influence in fighting for the respect and dignity of America's
labor unions. Did I have trouble coming up with a punchy concept? Hell, No!
I created the ringing cry *Union, Yes!* When I belted out the line, and read
spots that would star Edward James Olmos, Tyne Daly and
Jack Lemmon expounding the virtues of trade unionism, the delegates
sprang to their feet, chanting *Union, Yes! Union, Yes! Union, Yes!*
When the commercials were shot, the power of the message delivered
by Olmos, Daly and Lemmon was gripping. The campaign ran for five years,
and *Union, Yes!* continues to be used for organizing, on picket lines,
on T-shirts, and is still chanted by the working men and women of America.
Was the labor movement worth fighting for? 12,000,000 working people
say, *Union, Yes!* Am I proud of helping the labor movement in America?
Hell, Yes!

UNION YES ✓

JACK LEMMON:

*Today's union movement is
all about giving people a
voice in what goes on at work...
and in supporting one
another. I believe
in that! I say...Union, Yes!
(Chorus Sings:)
America works best
when we say, Union, Yes!*

129. THE PHANTOM OF THE OPERA, AZANIA OF THE JUNGLE AND ROBIN HOOD WANT THEIR LIFESTYLES CONDOMS!

As AIDS became rampant in America, the condom industry expected sales to explode. By 1988, sales had risen, but decidedly short of the industry's expectations. Something had to be done. Any advertising of condoms on television had previously sent a grim message: *Condoms or Die!* (To get clearance to run *any* commercial, a condom spot had to be developed as an anti-AIDS message, with a public service flavor, with minimal emphasis on the condom brand paying for it.) Marketing condoms was also beset by a social bugaboo that made it almost impossible for many people who wanted condoms to use that taboo word with store clerks. (It's tough to ask a clerk for condoms if you can't say what you want–sign language is worse!) I told John Silverman, the head man at LifeStyles, that to break down social fears against buying condoms, *humor* was a must. Copywriter Elaine Kremnitz and I wanted to have fun with the subject with an audacious attitude. Our theme: *It's a matter of condom sense!* We created three 15-second TV spots that cast famous personalities from the theater and the movies as users of LifeStyles condoms. Our first condom consumer was The Phantom of the Opera, who surreptitiously tells a clerk: *I could use some LifeStyles.* The dizzy blonde store clerk tells him with a straight face: *Oh...but you don't have to wear a mask to ask for them!* In a second spot, the voiceover introduces us to a primal sexy creature, Azania, who he announces as *The Queen of the Jungle, shopping for LifeStyles condoms!* Azania reels off her shopping list to the store clerk: *I need sunscreen, hair mousse and a year's supply of LifeStyles.* Unfazed, the male clerk congratulates his customer: *Good thinking, Azania–'cause it's a jungle out there!* And in our third spot, the customer is Robin Hood. In a cunning allusion to our venerable gay brothers, he tells the clerk: *Shampoo for the fair Marion, and LifeStyles for all my merry men!* (The gay community loved it.) All three vignettes come to a climax with the announcer popping our slogan: *LifeStyles. It's a matter of condom sense!* Not surprisingly, the networks said no, no, no. But finally, six cable networks agreed to take the spots. An historic breakthrough! It was a milestone that changed the fear of dying to the love of living, helping make "safe sex" not just essential but pleasurable–while significantly pumping sales and market share of the LifeStyles brand. *Adweek* columnist Barbara Lippert made this incisive observation: "These commercials take a taboo subject and make terrible, hokey jokes, to our great relief. Unafraid, unashamed, they allow everybody access to the message. In that, they're so dumb, they're smart. Nah, they're so unabashedly idiotic– they're brilliant."

**ROBIN HOOD
(TO STORE CLERK):**

*"Shampoo for the fair Marion,
and LifeStyles
for all my merry men!"*

"More than 20,000 flashbulbs
go off in the stands...
but (sob) not one of those fans
is taking a picture of yours truly."

"I'll take your picture, Bill.
Say Cheese...with Ritz!"

130. FOR RITZ CAMERA, BILL WENNINGTON (NOT FAMOUS) SUBSTITUTES FOR MICHAEL JORDAN (VERY FAMOUS).

Ritz Camera Centers sounded snobby and expensive.
But not after America heard: *"Say Cheese...with Ritz!"* Our picture-perfect slogan
developed 500 Ritz Centers into 900 and growing. A lineup of *affordable*
celebrities brought style and showmanship to a basically nuts-and-bolts operation.
Faith Prince of Broadway fame brought the house down, jockey Julie Krone
rode home a winner and Darryl Strawberry lied through his teeth (see 35).
Who could possibly afford Michael Jordan? So I looked at the very end of the
champion Chicago Bulls bench, spotted reserve center Bill Wennington and put him
into the game. Looking perplexed and unappreciated, the 7-foot Wennington
blubbered, *I play on the winningest basketball team ever. Every game more than
20,000 flashbulbs go off in the stands...but (sob) not one of those fans
is taking a picture of yours truly.* A 14-year-old kid butts in and, spotting a tear
in the big fella's eye, says, *I'll take your picture, Bill.* The Bulls benchrider
looks at our camera and triumphantly comments, *Now that's a real fan!* The youngster
looks at us and says, *As they say at Ritz Camera, 'say Cheese...with Ritz!'*
The totally delighted Wennington triumphantly exclaims, *Say Cheese...with Ritz!*
Which proves, if you can't afford star power, come up with the power of a Big Idea!

131. THE ONLY BEARDED ANCHORMAN IN AMERICA RETURNS TO HIS NEW YORK ROOTS.

To welcome the bearded, well-respected anchor Dave Marash back to the Channel 2 Newsbreakers in 1981, I enlisted goalie Billy Smith along with five fellow National Hockey League champion New York Islanders, sportswriter Peter Vecsey, Knicks guard Earl Monroe, middleweight champ Vito Antuofermo, and other illustrious types like gory writer Edward Gorey, folk singer Pete Seeger, ballet master Robert Joffrey, jazz critic Nat Hentoff and art guru Henry Geldzahler to appear in a multi-celeb TV spot. Conductor Mitch Miller ended the spot by schmoozing: *Welcome back to New York, Dave–you're one of us!* Nothing special, except when the spot faded to black, a million viewers realized that, besides being New Yorkers, all 15 celebrities all had one other thing in common. They all had beards.

132. WHO *WAS* THAT HANDSOME MASKED MAN? 15 MASKED CELEBS MAKE RIO THE BIG WINNER IN VEGAS.

The demanding Zagat Survey rated the off-strip and unknown Rio All-Suite Casino Resort as the best hotel in Vegas. Rio management took a perverse pride in calling themselves the "best-kept secret in town!" But a huge problem loomed. In 1997, their new president, Dave Hanlon, found that repeat customers and slowly spreading word of mouth created enough business for its 1500 suites, but it would never suffice for Rio's $220 million expansion to 2500 suites, plus Masquerade Village, a complex of gaming, retailing and entertainment. A month before opening day, Hanlon was shocked that Rio had no advertising or PR planned. He threw the dice and gave us the job of making Rio famous, fast. We took the gamble out of Rio's enormous 1997 launch. First, Ron Holland and I punched up the logo to *Rio...Vegas style!* Then we added a compelling identity with the symbolism of a mask, echoing the masquerade theme with the slogan *Where the Hidden You comes out to play!* The playful graphic image of a mask is at once powerfully visual (especially on famous celebs), mysterious, sexy and more than a little naughty. Our TV and print campaign starred masked celebrities who dramatized each of Rio's attractions. Over a driving big band delivering our *Rio...Vegas style!* showbiz tune, a masked seven-foot Wilt Chamberlain exclaims, *Everybody gets a suite big enough for the Big Dipper.* Nancy Sinatra, with shoes made for walking, adds, *How suite it is!* Carol Channing, with "Hello, Dolly" pizzazz, flashes a *He-llo, Rio!* The brilliant dancer Donald O'Connor sells their nightclub with *Put on your dancing shoes and meet me at Club Rio!* Baseball Hall of Famer Reggie Jackson chips in with *At Rio I'm still an MVP... a Masquerade Village Person!* And a provocatively masked Downtown Julie Brown reacts with *Who was that handsome masked man?* In response to NBC's Gene Shalit belting out *I hear everybody gets a suite, but who can sleep with that Mardi Gras going on?!*, a beguilingly masked Leslie Ann Warren pantingly whispers *Who was that moustached masked man?!* The parade of stars continues with Rita Moreno, Adam West (TV's Batman), Hector "Macho" Camacho, the Pointer Sisters and a purring Eartha Kitt, who steals the show with *her* inimitable rendition of *Who was that masked man? Me-yeoww.* Overnight (literally) the campaign catapulted Rio into the front rank of Vegas' hottest casinos. The 2500 suites were grabbed up, gaming take soared, and Masquerade Village is now on every visitor's "must see" agenda, guaranteeing a near-captive clientele for their 22 retail shops and 14 restaurants. My coup de grace was a tough sell because of its overt sexiness, but every guest, whether sleeping with a roommate or alone, finds two masks lying on the bed pillows when they enter their spacious suites. When worn in the casino, Rio security doesn't know if they're planning to gamble, or hold up the joint!

133. MY DREAM DAY WITH ERNIE KOVACS TURNS INTO A NIGHTMARE.

In the early '50s, Ernie Kovacs became one of TV's greatest innovators, a brilliant combination of offbeat humor with pioneering special effects. His slick black hair, his omnipresent cigar dangling from his mouth, his moustache bristling with every expressive twitch of his Hungarian puss, looked square into the television camera and dared you not to laugh. (His loving wife Edie Adams said he looked like a B-movie villain.) Kovacs played with TV technology and used the camera as a comic tool, turning fades, wipes and split screens into visual puns. A pair of shapely high-heeled legs might strut onto the stage, sans a torso. Or a hole might appear in a cast member's head, with Ernie intently staring through it. He once sat on a tree limb, casually sawing away at it...the *tree* toppled, with Ernie sitting on the branch, remaining suspended in mid-air. His surreal characters were a howl: El Stupido, Matzoh Hepplewhite the Magician, Rod Lovely, Superclod, Percy Dovetonsils the Poet. In the era of live television, Ernie Kovacs was the mad genius of the TV tube. In 1961, Papert, Koenig, Lois got the Dutch Masters account from the Consolidated Cigar Co., who had been sponsoring Ernie's TV shows. I wanted a shot at convincing Kovacs to incorporate some of his most memorable schtick into Dutch Masters TV spots, so I was dispatched to L.A. to try to talk him into it. I was greeted by the beautiful actress/singer Edie Adams at his house on a steep Beverly Hills hillside, done up in an outlandish free-spending Kovacs way (featuring a driveway that was a giant turntable so you didn't have to turn your car yourself. The wine celler lacked the proper aged look, so Kovacs sprayed it with fake cobwebs). We sat by the swimming pool as an elegant lunch was served, and I detailed how a dozen of his blackout gags could be flipped, without compromising the integrity of his humor. (One was Ernie performing his famous Nairobi Trio: Three men in gorilla suits, one tinkling on a piano, another banging bongos, and Ernie on xylophone, casually rapping a fellow gorilla on his noggin every 10 seconds or so, to the syncopation of the staccato song. All I wanted was the three gorillas to have lit Dutch Masters dangling from their mouths!) We hit it off, and Kovacs enthusiastically agreed to shoot a dozen spots. I had to hustle to be in New York the next morning, so Ernie insisted on driving me in his Corvair station wagon to LAX airport to catch the red-eye home. We hugged as we said our good-byes, and off he went to a party at Milton Berle's home. I was ecstatic as I landed at 6:00 am at Kennedy, eager to regale the troops at my agency with the story of my successful day with the ingratiating Kovacs. I strutted with my carry-on to get a taxi to go straight to my office. But laying at the door of a still closed newsstand was a stack of morning New York newspapers, still bound, with the blaring headline: *Ernie Kovacs Dies in Car Crash.* How in the world, I thought to myself, could that madman, known for his practical jokes on friends, have arranged for this gag headline

to have greeted me at the airport?! But, of course, it was, unbelievably, true. He had been drinking and as he was speeding home down a rain-slicked highway, spun off and wrapped his Corvair around a telephone pole. On January 13, 1962, Ernie Kovacs died, not yet 43, at the height of his career. The coroners who arrived at the scene found a cigar near his left hand. It was suspected that his death was caused by losing control of the steering wheel as he was trying to light his goddamn cigar.

134. THE LAST OF THE MARX BROTHERS LEAVES US LAUGHING.

In 1972, on the occasion of Groucho Marx's 81st birthday, Harold Hayes and I, both Groucho-lovers, craved gracing the cover of Esquire with his memorable countenance. I wanted a simple shot of him with his birthday cake ablaze. But the last remaining Marx Brother insisted on sharing the cover with his female companion. ("Do not go gently into that good night...Rage, rage, against the dying of the light.") When I thanked him for coming, he told me he was an avid Esquire reader and said he loved the cover where I drew Stalin's mustache on Svetlana's pious puss, tweaking his mustache as he said it. I had been warned that at age 81 and in failing health, Groucho was animal crackers. But when I addressed him as "your Excellency," he instantly repeated his exchange with Margaret Dumont in *Duck Soup* (1933): "You're not so bad yourself." When photographer Carl Fischer asked him to sign his standard photo release, he mulled it over, so I told America's greatest wit to read the "sanity clause." Groucho fired back with Chico's wisecrack from *A Night at the Opera*: "You can't fool me. There ain't no Sanity Claus." After a repartee-filled photo session, Groucho meticulously washed his hands in his dressing room. His parting words were: "I'm going. And I'll never darken your towels again." *Some* ga-ga!

135. MY CAT ROUSSEAU FOLLOWS IN THE FOOTSTEPS OF PUSS 'N BOOTS, THE MOST FAMOUS CAT EVER.

I've got nothing against those charming drawings in children's books, but what could be more exciting than a real live pussycat stepping into his boots, throwing his knapsack over his shoulder, and stepping out for a stroll! The Puss 'n Boots people at Quaker thought so, too. To my great dismay, my cat Rousseau took his acting gig on the road and fled our Fire Island summer vacation home soon thereafter. Alas, after a sad summer of searching, the Lois family hasn't seen hide nor hair of him since.

136. MISSING BOY.

When I was growing up in the Bronx in the '30s, my Papa, an amateur wrestler, took me to each Tarzan movie, the only movies we attended together, in an unstudied act of father and son bonding. Superman, Batman and Captain Marvel were okay, but Tarzan was good, brave, fearless, athletic and, alone among superstars, a *family* man. So in a 1970 issue of Esquire that featured a nostalgic look back at the movie heros of the '30s and '40s, I leapt at the chance to lionize an aging, fully clothed Tarzan and Jane, the legendary lovers of the silver screen. Tarzan, the swinging Lord of the Apes, and Jane, the sophisticated Englishwoman, proved that social barriers disappeared when hearts beat like native drums. Still ruggedly handsome, the great Olympic swimming champion Johnny Weissmuller, and his mate, the elegant, high-toned Maureen O'Sullivan (the mother of Mia Farrow), got a big kick out of posing for an Esquire cover, along with Cheetah, their faithful madcap companion. But looking back at this warm reunion always saddens me, because there's a missing person...Boy. The only issue of their jungle love match, Boy, played by young John Sheffield, was the loyal, loving son all we kids in the Bronx were trying to be. When John Sheffield expressed reluctance to complete my family portrait, I had Tarzan call. John finally agreed to fly to New York for the family reunion. But he never got off the plane. He was embarrassed to be seen by Tarzan, Jane, Cheetah and our prying camera. Boy had ballooned to over 370 pounds.

137. SINGING CELEBRITIES (WITH VARYING DEGREES OF TALENT) CROONED "I READ IT EVERY DAY FOR NEWS AROUND THE USA TODAY!"

Gannett media mogul Al Neuharth credits four full-page ads that ran the same day on the back page of the four sections of *The New York Times* with saving the first mass newspaper in the USA (see Heroes 8). The quartet of ads won over a previously derisive Madison Avenue after a full year of their ignoring an obviously big marketing idea. But what truly clarified the advertising power of Neuharth's brainchild were the following two celebrity TV spots. To fix clearly in people's minds the various sections of USA Today, we lined up Senate Majority Leader Howard Baker (an incredible coup) to talk about the News section, Joe and Deborah Namath to talk about the Sports section, hotel honcho Bill Marriott Jr. to talk about Business, British sexpot Joan Collins for Entertainment and the basketball giant Wilt Chamberlain for Weather (*Everybody asks me, 'How's the weather up there?'*). Because that commercial rescued USA Today from extinction, Gannett CEO Neuharth fired his direct-response agency and gave us the account. Research showed that over a million people bought USA Today only once or twice a week, so I came up with the slogan *I read it every day for news around the USA Today!*, starring a broad spectrum of tone-deaf celebs who, believe it or not, *sang* their praises of USA Today: Chicago mayor Jane Byrne (News), discount broker Charles Schwab (Business), a duet of Willie Mays and Mickey Mantle (Sports), Diahann Carroll (Entertainment) and Willard Scott (Weather) sang out at the top of their lungs, *I read it every day...* The direct response was, according to the usually ball-busting Neuharth, "Ten times more successful than our previous TV spot in promoting daily readership," and goosed the paper's sales to make it the biggest selling newspaper in the USA, and moved them, hot off the presses, into the black, big-time.

"I read it every day for news around the USA Today!"

CHICAGO MAYOR JANE BYRNE:

I read it every day,
for news around the USA!

CHARLES SCHWAB:

I read it every day,
for mergers on the way!

DIAHANN CARROLL:

Every day,
for movies, books and plays!

WILLARD SCOTT:

I read it every day,
for weather on the way!

MICKEY MANTLE
WITH WILLIE MAYS:

I read it every day,
just like my pal, Say Hey!

138. FOUR CUTTING-EDGE WRITERS OF THEIR TIME GO TO CHICAGO, BUTCHER OF THE WORLD.

Only Esquire editor Harold Hayes had the guts and the nuts to assemble this stunning team of underground intellectual mavericks to go to the fateful Democratic Convention in Chicago in 1968 and report, *their* way, to the nation. A debilitated LBJ had shocked the nation by bailing out, lobbing his Vietnam hot potato to a succeeding president. The television coverage of bitter wrangling in the arena, intercut with Chicago cops splitting open young demonstrators' heads as they chanted "the whole world is watching," laced together by film footage of GIs in mortal combat in Vietnam, traumatized the nation. Originally, Carl Fischer had been sent to Chicago to shoot a portrait shot of the unholy quartet at the convention. But watching the carnage on TV, I envisioned a cover idea of a Christ-like image of a jeans-clad student, lying in a bloody gutter at the feet of the wildest literary men of the time: Jean Genet (the French high priest of decadence), William Burroughs (the Beat Generation expatriate spokesman), Terry Southern (the irreverent, bad boy *Candy* man) and John Sack (the anti-war war correspondent). I called Carl and described the shot. When he tried to stage it in the streets of Chicago, he damn near got himself and the fearsome foursome reporting team beat up and arrested. So I told them to hot-jet it back to New York and we grabbed this dramatic image in the safe streets of Harlem. (The convention went on to nominate the shell of Hubert Humphrey, who had shrunk to being a yes-man to his president. HHH fell victim to the bitterness of the fray, ran an inept campaign and got beat by Tricky Dick's "secret plan" that promised to bring our boys home by Christmas. 27,000 dead GIs later, home they came.)

139. AN APOTHEOSIS OF OUR ASSASSINATED LEADERS, THE THREE MOST MOURNED AMERICANS SINCE FDR.

I plead guilty to shockingly irreverent concepts for many of the Esquire covers I created. But the '60s, at times, pleaded for equally shocking reverence. Three martyred American leaders hauntingly watch over the sacred ground of Arlington National Cemetery. For Esquire's definitive 35th anniversary issue, in a hagiographic fantasy, we pay homage to an idealized, saint-like John F. Kennedy, Robert F. Kennedy and Dr. Martin Luther King in this dreamlike epitaph on the murder of American goodness.

OBNOXIOUS CELEBS (MY DIRTY DOZEN)
"YOU GO URUGUAY AND I'LL GO MINE."
GROUCHO MARX

OBNOXIOUS CELEBS
1. LAUREN BACALL
CELEBRITY FROM HELL.

With Bacall's clean-cut, yet magnetically sultry come-hither look, Bogie and all the world fell for her, and she went on to become an American icon. We negotiated for the great lady to do a gig as a masked celeb at the grand opening of Rio's Masquerade Village, a cavernous new gambling casino in Las Vegas with 2,500 new rooms and a vast complex of stores, restaurants and Vegas showbiz entertainment. The classy Lauren Bacall had to be a thrill to work with! And a New York gal to boot! Fuhgedaboutit! I take pride in being a gentleman with the ladies, but this dame was the celebrity from hell– and I'll leave it at that. This is one guy who would never put my lips together...and whistle!

RON HOLLAND AND I SUGGESTED TO MS. BACALL THAT SHE WEAR THIS BLUE FEATHERED MASK (KIND OF A NO-BRAINER AT A MASKED BALL) AND SEDUCTIVELY REMOVE IT WHEN INTRODUCED ONSTAGE. SHE LOOKED DOWN HER NOSE AT IT (AS WELL AS AT ME). BUT IT WAS AN EYEPOPPER ON THIS RIO BEAUTY.

OBNOXIOUS CELEBS
2. MICHAEL JACKSON
"MAKE MY NOSE THINNER, SLIM DOWN MY NOSTRILS, AND LIGHTEN MY SKIN."

The first time I dealt with the world's most famous moonwalker, he threw me for a loop. In rounding up *Fabulous five-year-olds* for USA Today's 5th anniversary print campaign (see 88), I equated a five-year-old Michael Jackson with the wunderkind Wolfgang Amadeus Mozart, the magnificent thoroughbred Kelso, and the out-of-this-world five-year-old E.T. This was before Jackson's surgical transformations, when there seemed to be no clue to his strange perception of his appearance. But he laid a clue on me when he sent this sweet photo, and insisted I retouch his five-year-old face. "Make my nose thinner, slim down my nostrils, and lighten my skin," asked the surreal one. Huh?! I ran the photo unretouched (although my advertising lawyer warned me to heed his demand) and Michael's picture survived the surgical knife. Soon thereafter, I was asked to brand a planned campaign for his Heal the World philanthropies to benefit children, pro bono. I created a charming logo of a Band-Aid slapped on a kid's drawing of the earth, along with a proposal that Johnson & Johnson market a dozen Band-Aid designs I created with a Heal the World message–proceeds going to Michael Jackson's foundation. But Jackson gave my Band-Aid concept a thumbs-down, with barely a thank you.

To illustrate a self-serving piece by attorney Roy Cohn in which he rationalized his skullduggery as the demagogue senator Joe McCarthy's favorite gofer, I asked him to pose as the angel he thought he was. I made no bones about the photo: he was to be shown wearing a halo that was visibly attached, a self-applied halo. He somberly posed for the shot and said as he was leaving Carl Fischer's studio: "I suppose you left-wing crackpots are going to pick the ugliest one." "You bet," I said. "I hate your guts." For once in his life, the mouthpiece of McCarthyism was speechless.

OBNOXIOUS CELEBS
4. ROBIN GIVENS
EXTRA! EXTRA! EX SLUGS IT OUT WITH ADMAN!

On the morning of January 13, 1990, leafing through the *New York Post,* I was punched in the face when I spied Page 6 (a daily gossip page) with the headline *Ex Slugs It Out with Adman.* The Ex was Robin Givens, and the adman was *moi*! The first sentence read: "Robin Givens–who went the distance with Mike Tyson in their matrimonial battle–is now going 12 rounds with Madison Avenue heavyweight George Lois." The piece, initiated by Givens' press agent, concerned a meeting with Neil Cole, the president of No Excuses jeans, Robin Givens and me, where Cole and I were offering 200,000 smackers to the ex-Mrs. Tyson to follow such luminaries as Donna Rice, Joan Rivers and Marla Maples as a TV spokesperson for No Excuses. In the Page 6 article, Givens more than implied that I was a racist by saying I was "condescending like a white man trying to sound black so a black girl could relate." Huh? She went on with the blatant lie that "every other word out of Lois' mouth was mother[bleep]." Now, I admit I sound like a mug from the streets of the Bronx, but I take pride in being a gentleman and would never, ever, use the word mother[bleep] in the company of a lady. Her final shot at me was that I was trying to "exploit her reputation in connection with Tyson." The world would never have heard of Robin Givens if she hadn't married and divorced the embattled champ, but it was she who, astoundingly, kept insisting that she could get Mike Tyson to appear in a spot with her, because she said, "I can get him to do anything I want," going into excruciating detail about how she could whip him into an encore of her notorious Barbara Walters interview, where she embarrassed Tyson in front of the world. After fielding dozens of calls from friends that day, my wife Rosie and I were awakened at 1:00 in the morning by Don King and Mike Tyson calling from the champ's training camp in Vancouver. "George Lois, you are the greatest friend the black man has in America!," bellowed the outrageous fight promoter, and Mike Tyson sweetly pointed out that Robin Givens was a...oops, let me remain a gentleman. In the next morning's *Post,* yet another missive, but this time it was Don King and Mike Tyson, in print, coming to my defense: "For anyone as self-serving, vindictive and vicious as Robin to say that George Lois, of all people, is a racist, well, we can't let good people be besmirched." Thanks, Don. I really appreciate it, Mike. And Robin, you're a mother[bleep]!

OBNOXIOUS CELEBS
5. RUBIN HURRICANE CARTER
NO GOOD DEED GOES UNPUNISHED.

After the New Jersey prosecutors were embarrassed into dismissing all the charges against the innocent Rubin Hurricane Carter in 1988, Myron Beldock, one of Carter's inexhaustible lawyers, said, "The real story is that good triumphs over evil, and how hard it is to get there." The publication of the incarcerated fighter's book *The Sixteenth Round* (The Viking Press, 1974) inspired *New York Times* reporter Selwyn Raab who inspired Richard Solomon who inspired me who inspired Don King who inspired Muhammad Ali who inspired Howard Cosell who inspired Jimmy Breslin who inspired Ed Koch who inspired Bob Dylan... and the beat went on (see 69). Each and every celebrity who spoke up for Rubin Carter took a heroically unpopular stand. A free man today, Rubin Carter maligns that help, claiming one and all were motivated to gain attention for themselves, or to reap profits. "I'm not grateful enough to anybody to give myself to them," he angrily states. Mark Twain once said, "It is a worthy thing to fight for one's freedom; it is another sight finer to fight for another man's." I still believe that.

A FOLLOW-UP AD (SEE 37)
THAT RAN THE FIRST WEEK
OF ENLISTING CELEBRITY SUPPORT.
(THE FIRST TIME ADVERTISING
WAS USED TO FREE A MAN FROM PRISON.)

OBNOXIOUS CELEBS
6. CALVIN KLEIN
DEFINITELY NOT A GOOD SPORT.

A $200,000 ad campaign made the totally unknown Tommy Hilfiger famous and successful within a few days, triggered by an outrageous poster plastered on telephone kiosks on the sidewalks of New York (see 33). In *Newsweek* and *People*, Calvin Klein, a threatened competitor, insisted we had spent $20,000,000, three zeros too many. (I've always said a great advertising campaign can make a million-dollar budget look like 10 million, but I never said it could make it look like 20 million!) A few months after the T _ _ _ H _ _ _ _ _ _ _ ad appeared, Mr. Klein, obviously livid as he watched Tommy's growing fame, saw me having dinner with my wife and friends one night at Mr. Chow's, strode over, stuck his finger in my face and blurted out: "Do you know it took me 20 years to get where Hilfiger is today!" I politely grabbed his finger, bent it, and answered: "Schmuck! Why take 20 years when you can do it in 20 days?!"

OBNOXIOUS CELEBS
7. WILLIE MAYS
"WILLIE DON'T CRY."

Being a sports pervert, nothing was more thrilling to me than creating advertising with the great sports figures of our time, including Broadway Joe, The Big O, The Manassa Mauler, The Brown Bomber and The Big Dipper, and every single one was a sweetheart to work with. (Nasty Nastase was one of the sweetest.) The only athlete I ever found overbearing, pompous and uncooperative was Willie Mays. Robertson, Mantle, Chamberlain, Unitas, et al., all got into the swing of my *I want my Maypo* shoot, crying so hard they were laughing. Then it was Mays' turn. The Say Hey Kid looked dully into the camera and kept saying, I swear, "Willie don't cry, Willie don't cry." He kept that up for a full half hour. Finally, I got a half effort, and he lost a fan. A few months later, I caught an interview with his great manager, Leo Durocher. The Lip described the terrible first days of Willie Mays' rookie season with the New York Giants when he went 0 for 27. Leo said, "After another oh-fer game, I went into our locker and found Willie sitting next to his locker, bawling away, tears streaming down his face. Willie cried a lot."

OBNOXIOUS CELEBS
8. LISA LING
80% OF LIFE IS SHOWING UP.

Talk show personality Lisa Ling had agreed to deliver an emotional appeal in a TV spot for the New York Blood Center (*Give Blood. Save a neighbor.*) on the crucial shortage of blood in the metropolitan area, as well as appear in a group photo shot for a jumbo bus-stop poster (see 102). The morning of the shoot, Hurricane Floyd hit New York, making travel in the city extremely hazardous, with torrential flooding on approaching highways and in the streets of Manhattan. Bravely, our drenched ex-mayor Koch, Donald Trump, Brian Dennehy, Tim Robbins, Rebecca Lobo, Jimmy Breslin, Kim Raver and Jason Williams of the New Jersey Nets (who had undergone a career-ending operation on a broken leg the previous day!) sloshed their way to a studio in the lower Village. But Lisa Ling was missing. I needed a representative Asian American to complete my melting-pot New York montage, and our wet gang of intrepid New Yorkers was waiting for her. When we reached Ms. Ling at ABC Television, where she was part of *The View* (a gabby daytime TV show, along with Barbara Walters, Meredith Veira, Joy Behar and Star Jones), rather than sweet-talking her way out of her commitment, she told us to "fuck off," and slammed down the phone.

OBNOXIOUS CELEBS
9. ROSEANNE BARR
WE'RE TALKIN' SERIOUS OBNOXIOUS HERE!

In 1990, HBO didn't get enough recognition in the press for their brilliant
Original Comedy productions, and needed a campaign to bring their comedy shows
front-of-mind to attract more cable viewers. I conceived the slogan
We're talkin' serious comedy here! (an oxymoron if ever there was one) with the idea
of getting the gang of comedians that performed gratis on "HBO Comic Relief"
to react to my slogan, on camera. With a film crew in La-La land I approached Billy Crystal,
Robin Williams, Dennis Miller, Whoopi Goldberg, Steven Wright, Louie Anderson,
Elaine Boozler, Robert Klein, Paul Rodriguez, Bob Goldthwait, Gilbert Gottfried, Jon Lovitz,
Judy Tenuta, Carol Leifer, Jim Morris and Roseanne Barr. Each and every one
performed an impromptu standup routine, twisting and turning the slogan into sidesplitting
double entendres...until I got to Roseanne Barr. Huhboy! She lambasted me for not
having a prepared script, on teleprompter yet, ready for her to read. When I played back
a hilarious Billy Crystal monologue delivered off the cuff, she did everything
short of grabbing her crotch, *Star Spangled Banner*-style, and barreled away, cursing
like a longshoreman. (Someone once said, life is a tragedy to those who feel,
a comedy for those who think. Personally, I think life is serious comedy.)

OBNOXIOUS CELEBS
10. JACKIE ROBINSON
THIS ONE HURTS!

This one hurts. I had been a homegrown fan of the Bronx Bombers.
King Kong Keller, Tommy Henrich and Joe D were my gods,
but when the Dodgers brought Jackie Robinson to Brooklyn I fell in love
with Dem Bums for their decency–while I worked up a hatred
for the Yankee brass, who refused to field a black player. The year Jackie
retired, Tom Hawkes, the president of Piel's Beer, and I arranged
a lunch with the indomitable legend, to offer him an executive position to be
in the front office for the Brooklyn-based beer. I had approached a
representative of Robinson's to test the waters, to be sure he had no moral
objection to having a stake in the beer business. Hawkes and I
were led to understand that he was, indeed, interested, and that he "loved beer
with a good steak." The compensation was more than he had ever
made as an athlete, and we were excited that we could offer the pioneering
Jackie Robinson a substantial living now that he had lost his baseball
income (as well as knowing it could be a dramatic public relations
coup for the beer from Brooklyn). The second we met we knew we were
in trouble. It was a humiliating experience for all of us because
Robinson, eyes hardened, looked right through us, and berated us throughout
the lunch (with us refusing to return fire). Halfway through a plate of
clams I strongly suggested we end the Piel's discussion, talk baseball or
politics, or discuss the weather–but he slowly ate a full-course lunch
and chewed our ass. (Cheez–I had given up Mantle and Maris
and Berra and Ford to root for Robinson!)

OBNOXIOUS CELEBS
11. RUDOLF NUREYEV
WHO SAYS A GENIUS CAN'T BE A JERK?

In 1978, after a prolonged strike at the New York Post, an impending
settlement caused Rupert Murdoch to ask me to produce a TV campaign
to promote its return. So I enlisted celebs to welcome the popular
tabloid back. Calvin Klein, Mets manager Joe Torre, Mayor John Lindsay,
Henry Fonda, Peter Gallagher from the Broadway play *Grease*, and
the coup de grace; Rudolf Nureyev (the greatest dancer of all time, who leaped
like a stag, pirouetted like a faun, and defied gravity to become birdlike).
I prepared sharp scripts for each, and as always, the celebrities did exactly what
I asked of them, nailing the camera with their eyes and engagingly reading
a script. I agreed to film in Rudy's apartment, and when our crew arrived,
I attempted to show him my script, but Nureyev had other ideas, and he waved me off.
An entourage of his boys preened and prepped him, and Rudy, wearing
a sweeping mink coat, prattled on, ludicrously overacting whatever it was he had in mind.
When I tried to gain control of my shoot, the raving Russian went rabid.
I didn't know how to say "fuck you" to him in Russian, so I said it to him in English,
fled his apartment, *en pointe*, and danced to a stage where Henry Fonda
elegantly obliged me by proclaiming, *I'm Fonda the Post*.
Welcome back, New York Post, welcome back.

OBNOXIOUS CELEBS
12. IVANA TRUMP
ALL THAT GLITTERS IS NOT GOLD.

In the days when Ivana was still on the Trump team, the Donald anointed her
as head honcho of Trump Castle in Atlantic City, and gave me the
advertising account. A few weeks after his plump-lipped, smooth-faced Czech-mate
took command, I had to endure hearing her berate a pretty young secretary
because she thought her attire "vas awful" (and actually sent her home
to change her dress!). After only a few weeks in command, her marketing group
was in total confusion, and her purchasing people were bitching about
hundreds of brass cigarette urns she ordered that cost $5,000 apiece.
I presented a hot ad campaign, *Live the Trump Life!*, but she insisted on making
what I considered shlocky changes. As much as I respected Donald Trump,
I had to resign the account, but not without a parting shot.
My last words were "Donald, everything Ivana touches turns to brass."
He guffawed.

OBNOXIOUS BONUS LIST

JACK NICHOLSON *Esquire*
To dramatize a story on the high jinks of Hollywood stars,
Jacko enthusiastically posed for an Esquire cover,
sitting bare-ass on the edge of his pool. He loved the shot.
But a month later when we were on press, he suddenly
objected, Esquire management chickened out (even though
he signed a release) and they stopped the presses.
Shortly thereafter, editor Harold Hayes and I kissed off Esquire,
and the magazine of the '60s took a dive.

ROGER CLEMENS *ESPN*
Roger the Rocket kibitzed in the outfield at a spring training workout
in Florida, keeping my film crew waiting for two hours.

LESLIE ANN WARREN *Rio Casino & Hotel*
She breezed through a dozen knockout gowns, but none
to her liking, as dance partner Tommy Tune cooled his heels.
(But she was a knockout when the camera rolled.)

PETER GRAVES *Greek National Tourist Organization*
He was so upset when I gave him a quick reading
(for time, as well as performance) that he chewed me out.
When I told him to leave my set, he sheepishly stayed.

PAT RILEY *Data General*
Coach Riley said yes, then no, then maybe, then yes, then no
to filming a television campaign. So I got fired.
(When I asked their CEO to reconsider his decision, he said no.)

ERICA JONG *Olivetti*
A meeting with the author of *Fear of Flying*
left me with a fear of reading.

RAQUEL WELCH *Wolfschmidt Vodka*
A lunch with the attractive Raquel Welch drove me to drink.
(There is nothing more *unattractive* than the behavior
of star-driven hubris.)

MY ALL-TIME FAVORITE CELEBS
"HOW DO I LOVE THEE?
LET ME COUNT THE WAYS."
ELIZABETH BARRETT BROWNING

Many people are calling this fight between me and Joe Frazier a grudge fight. It's not that, We just don't get along. But we do agree to one thing, and that is We dedicate ourselves to doing all we can in helping free Rubin Hurricane Carter, a Great Man Who Was unjustly imprisoned,

Muhammad Ali.

MY ALL-TIME FAVORITE CELEBS
1. JOE FRAZIER
THE "GORILLA" SHOWS HIS CLASS.

In designing the Ali/Frazier III fight program (see 5 and 116) I didn't dare schedule the two champions for a photo shoot at the same time. (I was afraid for photographer Carl Fischer's equipment.) Ali's characterizing Joe Frazier as the "Gorilla" he would tangle with in the Thrilla-of-a-Chilla in Manila was great theater and helped make the fight the most talked-about bout in boxing history. But Joe was deeply insulted, deeply maligned, deeply hurt. When I orchestrated a full-page written statement by Ali for the fight program in support of Rubin Hurricane Carter, nobody in the Ali camp thought Frazier would touch it with a 10-foot pole. Anything Ali was part of, the wounded Frazier would surely reject. But I approached Joe, with trepidation. Frazier gulped, thought about it and said, "Gimme a pen," and signed it with great care. When I thanked him profusely, Smokin' Joe mumbled, with resignation, "Ali is doing a good thing." Joe Frazier was a class act. Alas, Muhammad kept up his pre-fight abuse. (In Harold Hayes' interview for the program, he quoted Ali as telling him, "I called Frazier ignorant...I only have use for him to make a living. After that he can go on back to his diamond rings and his Cadillacs.") Twenty-five years later, the pain and resentment that tortured the still smokin' Joe Frazier was finally put to rest when an ill, chastened Ali publicly apologized to his old foe.

MY ALL-TIME FAVORITE CELEBS
2. JAMES BEARD
THE MONUMENTAL DEAN OF AMERICAN CUISINE (COMING AND GOING).

Jim was a pal from my 35 years
of designing and advertising for
The Four Seasons restaurant, where his
talents and influence flourished.
James Beard declined to give his
endorsement or do TV spots
for hundreds of products, but in 1967,
the most honest food authority in
the U.S. of A. hypnotically, almost angrily,
scolded American housewives into
using "only" Hecker's Unbleached
flour (since 1927, my mama had written
"Only Hecker's," in Greek, on all her
recipes). A few years later, I convinced
big Jim to introduce Mouton Cadet,
an affordable Philippe de Rothschild wine.
Then in 1983, I knew the greatest
coup for any food magazine would be a
"testimonial" from the most important
name in the history of American cuisine.
With monumental good humor,
wolfing down chicken legs, the
legendary 6'5" food giant posed for a
foldout cover, displaying the
back and front of his imperial, bald head.

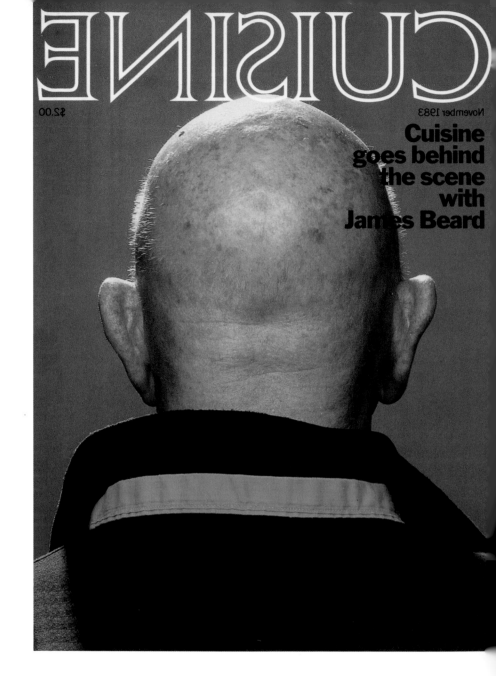

CUISINE

November 1983 $2.00

**Cuisine
goes behind
the scene
with
James Beard**

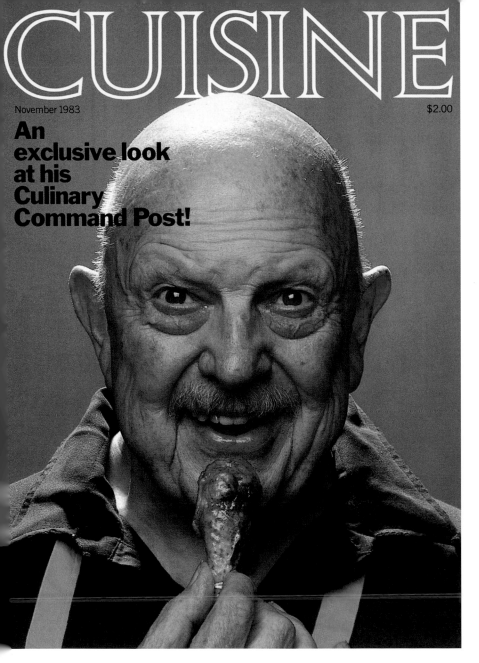

CUISINE

November 1983

$2.00

An exclusive look at his Culinary Command Post!

MY ALL-TIME FAVORITE CELEBS
3. ANDY WARHOL
THE INAUDIBLE VOICE OF THE AVANT-GARDE.

A few years after drowning him in a can of Campbell's soup (see 4) I asked Pop-art guru Andy Warhol to meet heavyweight champ Sonny Liston on a Braniff Airways plane (see 50). Big ugly bear meets short bewigged painter. Silent spade meets honkie bullshitter. Meanest man alive meets weirdest artist ever. Andy, in his quiet monotone, says to a sullen, disbelieving Sonny Liston: *Of course, remember there is an inherent beauty in soup cans that Michelangelo could not have imagined existed.* When Andy got to our punchline, *When you got it–flaunt it,* his whisper was inaudible, and I gave up after badgering him for a bunch of retakes. So on the Q.T., I dubbed in a fey impersonator in the final production, hoping Warhol wouldn't spot it. I sent the whole "odd couple" campaign to Andy's Factory, and he immediately called me and said: "I lo-o-ove the commercials. I love Dali and I love Ethel Merman and I love Marianne Moore and I love George Raft and I love Satchel Paige... but everybody here insists I said *When you got it–flaunt it* the best!"

MY ALL-TIME FAVORITE CELEBS
4. JOE NAMATH
THE BABE RUTH OF HIS TIME.

Broadway Joe guaranteed victory for the underdog New York Jets in the '69 Super Bowl, echoing the gold standard of cockiness when the Babe pointed to the stands and hit a clutch home run during the '32 World Series. Namath was bold, charismatic, and *delivered*. Men rooted for him, kids wanted to be him, women fell in love. I first met Joe Willie Namath, the superstar of them all, later that year, after a shouting match with his aggressive redheaded Bronx Irish lawyer, Jimmy Walsh. I had made a deal with Walsh for Namath to be a focal point for my *When you got it–flaunt it* TV campaign for Braniff, and he was hustling me for more money the very morning of the shoot! But an hour after our screaming match on the phone, Walsh arrived with his Pennsylvanian-Hungarian client. Sugar Ray Robinson was there, also Miss Universe, Tab Hunter, Leonard Lyons, Mickey Rooney, Emilio Pucci (who designed his signature-style dresses for Braniff stewardesses), Gina Lollobrigida, Paul Ford and the whole "odd couple" gang (see 50). At most shoots, the ho-hum film crews look at celebrities like any stiffs in the street. But the grips and gaffers, out of control, swarmed over Broadway Joe, begging for his autograph. "For my kid," they all said. He signed them all (he always does). I've worked with super-celebrities as electrifying as Bobby Kennedy and Muhammad Ali, and in those times he was in their class. "Joe Namath, Joe *Namath*," cooed Lollobrigida, "oooh, he's so hondsummm." Joe was always his own man. He let his hair grow long and infuriated the front-office wheels of pro football with his bad-boy antics. He wore white shoes on the field and grew a Fu Manchu moustache. He was cocky because he knew he had it and he wasn't afraid to flaunt it, but Joe Willie was never a put-down artist or a trash-talker. He was always a gentleman, unbelievably warm toward his fans and caring with youngsters, knowing full well they thought of him as their hero, and indeed, he *was* the Babe Ruth of his time.

MY ALL-TIME FAVORITE CELEBS
5. SALLY RAND
FAN-TASTIC STRIPPER.

When I talk about using celebrity for the shock of their seeming irrelevance to a product, a real knockout was a testimonial for a Wall Street brokerage firm from a burlesque queen. I coveted Sally Rand as the performer because her signature act involved her waving two gigantic feathered fans, shifting adroitly to give her audience a fluttering peek at her monumental nude body. Sally, the best-built grandma ever, stood center stage at the shoot, selling her heart out, as the crew and I stared in worshipful admiration. At the end of the spot, when Sally's fans come to rest, a voiceover delivers the punch line: *Edwards & Hanly, fan-tastic brokers!* In 1967, ultra-traditional Wall Street, that straight-arrow, starched-collar, scaredy-cat business, was shocked out of its communications coma when the great Sally Rand, fans and all, was seen on television, delivering a testimonial to the rhythm of shifting feathers.

1965 was pre-Friedan, pre-Steinem, pre-Abzug.
Before the hoopla about the women's movement had caught
the public's eye, I wanted to do a spoof of a movie star
caught in a manly act. The budding movement wanted liberation from
women's traditional roles. Like any Greek male, I wondered
where it would take us. The best way to draw attention to a trend on the
horizon in the '60s was with a cheeky Esquire cover. But I got
turned down by every uptight American beauty queen in Hollywood,
including Kim Novak, Marilyn Monroe and Jayne Mansfield.
Then the molta bellissima star of *How to Murder Your Wife*, Virna Lisi,
visited New York for a movie preview, and I hoped there was a
chance an Italian actress had the macho to pose for it. I contacted her,
and explained what I wanted. She laughed with gusto, slapped on
some shaving cream, and took it off on the front cover of
America's leading men's magazine.

MY ALL-TIME FAVORITE CELEBS
7. YOGI BERRA
90% OF SHOOTING A COMMERCIAL WITH YOGI
WAS HALF MENTAL.

In 1961, my very first celebrity TV spot starred the great Yankee Hall of Fame catcher,
part-time right fielder and full-time malapropist, Lawrence Peter Yogi Berra (see 3).
It's still one of my pet commercials, in no small part due to Yogi's attentive, delightful demeanor
gabbing nose to nose with an athletic cat. A decade later I took advantage of the
warmth and fame of Yogi's malapropisms, now a catchy part of American colloquial language:
for a Subaru spot welcoming a Japanese baseball star to America (see 54)
and for Jiffy Lube, co-starring with his be-yoo-tiful wife Carmen, depicting an all-American
couple in need of an oil change. His Yogi-isms ("I didn't say half the things I said"),
all emitting from his guileless puss and fireplug body, have made Yogi Berra one of the most
beloved cartoon characters in American popular culture: more cuddly than
Smokey the Bear, funnier than Fred Flintstone, more handsome than Shrek, more heroic than
Buzz Lightyear, and a *much* better hitter than Popeye.
P.S. Behind schedule at the Puss 'n Boots cat food shoot in 1961, I asked
Yogi what time it was. He answered, "You mean *now?*"

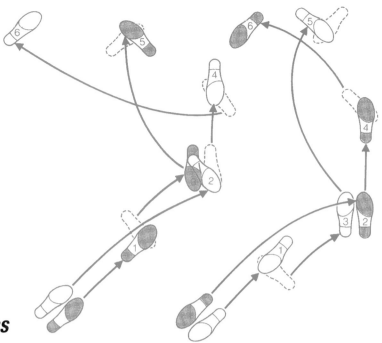

MY ALL-TIME FAVORITE CELEBS
8. JACQUELINE KENNEDY
"GEORGE, MAY I HAVE THE PLEASURE OF THIS DANCE?"

The great photographer Irving Penn told me this story.
In 1958, on assignment by *Vogue* to photograph Democratic minority leader
Lyndon Johnson, he reported promptly with his assistants for the scheduled shoot.
When Johnson's secretary entered his room to tell him of Penn's arrival,
a violent diatribe against New York, fashion magazines, and Penn's relationship with
his mother was heard by one and all in the Senate building. A shocked Irving Penn
fled LBJ's office, but on the way out spied the office of the young freshman senator
John F. Kennedy. Not wanting to return to New York empty-handed, he meekly
asked Kennedy's secretary if *he* might pose for his camera. Young Jack didn't have a clue
who Penn was, and called his wife Jacqueline at their Georgetown residence for advice.
His fashion-conscious wife yelped, ordered him to accept the offer, and showed up
15 minutes later with his best suit and supervised a Penn shooting. A month later her
ambitious young husband graced the chic, influential pages of *Vogue*. Jackie, an
amateur photographer, fashion plate and professional status-seeker, knew her stuff.
In 1964, a year after America's loss of the inspirational young president,
Jacqueline and the whole dang Kennedy clan were invited by Jack's baby brother
Robert to view (and OK) a TV campaign designed to make New Yorkers
elect him their senator. The campaign was conceived to destroy the "ruthless" tag that
the Republican incumbent Kenneth Keating was sure to exploit (see 85).
I presented the spots to Robert's mother, wife, kids, sisters, in-laws, nephews, nieces,
as well as his brother's widow. The "documentary" black-and-white spots starred
Robert F. Kennedy handling tough questions and making good sense with realistic,
easygoing, unrehearsed charm and power. Bobby, shocked by the in-your-face
imagery of the finished spots, wanted, *needed*, his family's approval.
After viewing the 24 commercials, there was a stunned silence in the darkened screening
room, finally interrupted by Jacqueline proclaiming,*"Wow!!!!"* The family broke out
in applause as Bobby proudly gave me a thumbs-up sign from across the room.
We had arranged a brunch accompanied by Ella Fitzgerald recordings, and without
missing a beat, Jackie strode up to me and asked me to dance.
Spontaneously, the viewing session turned into a celebration dance.

MY ALL-TIME FAVORITE CELEBS
9. FRANCO COLUMBU
THE SARDINIAN SUPERMAN.

After the surreal Surrealist Salvador Dali, the most *memorable*
celebrity I've worked with was the world-famous bodybuilder Franco Columbu,
a training mentor to Arnold Schwarzenegger, a two-time Mr. Olympia,
best-selling author of bodybuilding books, movie producer, actor,
and doctor of chiropractic to the rich and famous. At the height of the
body-building *Pumping Iron* craze in the '80s, I had "Muscle-lini"
Franco Columbu pump up in a TV and print campaign for Vitalis hair spray
(*The Pump! The Pump! And see how it built my biceps!*) Columbu's
Mediterranean charm and unchanging molto-Sardinian accent emits from an
astounding body, a man of Herculean strength, with a wit to match.
His retort to an admiring TV host asking how long he would have to train to have
a body like his: "Three generations!" Another TV interviewer supplied
an iron bar, defying Franco to bend it,
thinking it would be impossible to
bend. Columbu deftly twisted the
prodigious hunk of metal like a pretzel
around the wiseacre's neck, and
walked out of the studio. Not finding
a parking space on Rodeo Drive,
he bodily lifted a full-size
vehicle out of its space, and calmly
parked his Aston Martin. At a freezing
Thanksgiving Day parade in New York,
the muscleman walked backwards,
pulling the gigantic lead float...
with his *teeth*. Dining with Columbu
created havoc at restaurants; he
would take a fork off the table, move
it out of sight, and bring it back in
10 seconds flat, tied in a perfect knot
(all done using only one hand!).
Besides an enduring friendship with
Dr. Columbu, his talent for body
manipulation has kept me playing
basketball at the 23rd St. YMCA, long
after a sane man hangs up his jock.

The Businessman's Minutes-a-Day Guide to Shaping Up

Dr. Franco Columbu

John F. Kennedy Jr. was a product of a band of brothers, who each sought power, and then fought to defend the powerless. "John-John" knew privilege and fame, but he also knew suffering. After the shocking series of tragedies in the Kennedy family, the outpouring of emotion when young John Kennedy's plane crashed echoed America's pain at the death of his father and his Uncle Robert. When he worked for the New York D.A., many guessed he would run for office. But he left the law to found *George*, hoping to create a popular political magazine. I told John that, from the get-go, his covers should proclaim that *George* would be an irreverent read with uncensored, politically incorrect commentaries on serious issues. In a world of sycophantic magazines, *George* covers should knock your eyes out, should outrage the mighty, anger some advertisers, and infuriate more than a few readers. He asked me to take a crack at a hypothetical article on the sicko-fan relationship between Hollywood stars and the new president, Bill Clinton (he for them and them for him). I showed him an in-your-face image of an adoring Barbra Streisand...with a brown spot on the tip of her prominent nose! His backers were shocked at its outrageous audacity. But John loved it. Finally, however, he took the advice of his "publishing experts" and ran reciprocal brownnosing celebrity covers (you kiss mine and I'll kiss yours). Two years later, with his magazine failing, he was forced to reconsider his *George* covers, and called to set up a meeting. A few days before our scheduled powwow, he plunged into the sea, his promising future and his magazine succumbing with him.

Cady Huffman, the 6-foot blonde bombshell who plays the Swedish sexpot
Ulla Inga Hansen Benson Yonsen Tallen-Hallen Svaden-Svanson, newly basking in the glow of the limelight
thanks to her high-profile, high-stepping, Tony Award–winning role in *The Producers* (see 105), was the least affected
new star I've ever worked with. (Many of the new Brit Rock stars I shot for MTV were a pain in my arse.) I love
working with ladies with megawatt smiles and flashbulb eyes, troopers who work in front of the camera and seemingly
enjoy every exhausting second of it. Of the many hundreds, almost all have been professional and performed
up to, or beyond, my expectations. But there are those who, with their enthusiasm for nailing a photo or a performance
on camera, receive my admiration and special thanks: Ethel Merman, Hermione Gingold, Governor Ann Richards,
Betty Grable, Madeline Kahn, Jane Russell, Claudia Cardinale, Rita Moreno, Kim Novak, Julie Newmar, Tina Louise,
Pam Huntington, Downtown Julie Brown, Lauren Hutton, Leeza Gibbons, Rebecca Lobo and Ellen Burstyn–
all warm and wonderful women who flashed their pearly whites and went to work, relishing what I was trying to
accomplish, sometimes under trying circumstances. When flustered Ellen Burstyn was marching hand in hand with
Muhammad Ali in the midst of a protest march for Rubin Carter (see 69) she whispered to me, "I love marching
with Ali, but he keeps grabbing my ass." "Ellen," I said, loud enough for Muhammad to hear me above the din of the
10,000 chanting marchers, "either let him...or throw a punch at him." (She never told me her decision.)

MY ALL-TIME FAVORITE CELEBS
12. MELBA MOORE
MELBA MOORE GOES TO PRISON.

Developing a publicity campaign to force a retrial for Rubin Hurricane Carter, I met with the incarcerated boxer once a week for a period of 16 months. I was subjected to body searches by scowling guards, then escorted through the seething corridors of Trenton State Prison, an American Bastille, past the prison's population, as a surly guard rattled his billy club against the iron bars to announce my unpopular arrival to his fellow security officers. Among the dozens of courageous women celebrities helping our cause (Dyan Cannon, Ellen Burstyn, Lola Falana, Joan Baez, Joni Mitchell, Candice Bergen, Gladys Knight, Congresswoman Millicent Fenwick), the talented Melba Moore told us she very much wanted to meet Carter. I was unable to escort her to the prison that day, so I asked my wife Rosie to accompany her, knowing full well it could be a scary and maybe humiliating experience. They entered Trenton State, gulped hard, endured a body search, and walked the long walk. The maximum-security prison, with its predominantly black population, was buzzing with the news that the popular Melba Moore was visiting that day, and all eyes were on the beautiful black singer/actress and my leggy, blonde wife. As the two brave ladies were leaving after the embattled Carter received them, they reached the last steel door, gasping in that oppressive atmosphere, when a burly prisoner leaped out of nowhere, suddenly between them and the door! For a brief second, they feared the worst. But the convict, eyes downcast, sheepishly handed Melba Moore a *present*. It was a portrait he had painted from a fashion photograph of her in *Vogue* magazine! In the car taking them back to the city, Melba Moore wept.

HEROES

"NOT ALL OF US CAN BE HEROES,
 BECAUSE SOME OF US HAVE TO SIT ON THE CURB AND CLAP."
RALPH WALDO EMERSON

HEROES
1. MUHAMMAD ALI
HE WAS A SELF-FULFILLING PROPHECY.
HE *WAS* THE GREATEST!

Muhammad Ali was an illiterate, narcissistic self-promoter who eventually became a man of principle
through a journey of tests. I did three Esquire covers of Muhammad Ali during the Vietnam War
(see 16, 58, 122), all protesting his being punished for refusing to fight in an unjust war. That terrible wrong
was righted in 1971 when the Supreme Court threw out his conviction as a draft dodger. In 1975,
an essential part of my master plan to get Rubin Hurricane Carter out of the slammer was to convince this active
symbol of peace and reconciliation to publicly lead a propaganda war against the legal authorities
in New Jersey. The boxer who had stunned the world with his dazzling fists and dancing footwork, audacious
rhymes and his passion for life, had by now become popular among whites, and a god-like figure
to blacks. Ali helped change the despair of a bad, bad time in America.
It didn't take much for me to convince Ali that the Hurricane was innocent. I've always suspected, because
of my support of him on the covers of a mass magazine (political heresy at that time), that initially he worked for
Carter more for my sake than for the incarcerated fighter. But Ali, with all his magnetism and gift of gab,
was tireless in speaking out for Rubin Carter, becoming the catalyst in bringing the injustice to the attention of the
entire world. Years later, in 1997, he graciously attended a star-studded XNBA (retired NBA players) awards
dinner I organized. Muhammad, by now a mythical symbol of faith, defiance, athletic courage and racial pride,
arrived an hour early, escorted by his wife and entourage, and was sitting alone at a table in an empty
ballroom. I approached him gingerly, afraid that in his obviously ill condition, he would not recognize or remember
me. Ali, suffering with Parkinson's disease, was seemingly asleep, his head down, his chin resting on
the bow tie of his tuxedo, and I was reluctant to bother him. But his constant companion, photographer
Howard Bingham, urged me on. I sat down next to Muhammad, waiting for him to open his eyes.
Finally one eye opened, then two. He glared at me and instantly poked his index finger into his chest and
leg once, twice, three, then four times, mimicking arrows piercing his martyred body (see 58),
and said, "Hi, George, how's Rubin?"

HEROES
2. MICKEY MANTLE
AMERICA'S HEEERO!

I'm in awe of any man who can keep producing under the eyes of the world year
after year. When he becomes a legend, like Mickey Mantle, there's a truth to the legend
and usually a decency in the man. The Mick was no braggart. He once told me,
"George, when I was 16 I was the best ballplayer who ever lived, and it scared me."
Then he stopped for a moment and drawled softly, "But you take a guy like Hank Aaron–
he's twice as good as I *ever* was." He understood the pressures that went with the
role of America's hero. One early evening I got a frantic call from his teammate Billy Martin,
begging me to collect Mickey at the bar at the nearby Pierre Hotel and "get his ass
to JFK" where his concerned wife had booked a flight to Dallas so her philandering husband
could be home for the holidays. I ran over to the Pierre, and sure enough, there was
the great Yankee legend, surrounded by adoring fans, charmingly unloading his repertoire
of baseball stories–getting loaded. I pulled the tipsy Mickey off his stool and guided
him to the checkroom to retrieve his suitcase. He peeled off a $100 bill to tip an attractive
hatcheck lady. But she gave him back the hundred and handed him a blank sheet of paper
and a pen. "Please, Mr. Mantle," she said, "I don't want the money, but if I could have
your autograph for my eight-year-old son that would be wonderful. His name is *Mickey*,
and he idolizes you!" Mantle would much sooner part with a hundred than sign an autograph,
and he reached out...and fondled her! I reprimanded him, he wrote a lovely note
to her son, and the bewildered young mom gave America's superstar a kiss on the cheek.
I was really pissed at his behavior as I grabbed his suitcase and pushed him into the
revolving door. I shoved it hard, following with his baggage. When I got outside he was gone.
I looked around to see if he was spun back into the bar. But he was nowhere.
Then I saw him. He was lying in the Fifth Avenue gutter, his cheek on the edge of the
sidewalk by the curb, with slush from a recent snowstorm on his face. I had
pushed the revolving door too hard–he tripped on the way out and went into a dive, landing
on his handsome puss. "Holy shit, Mickey," I said leaning over him, "are you hurt?"
He sheepishly looked up at me and sweetly said, "Fi-i-ine place to be for America's *heeero*."
Mickey made it home safely, a Band-Aid on his cheek.

HEROES
3. SENATOR HUGH SCOTT
"THE ONLY THING THAT SEPARATED RICHARD NIXON FROM FASCISM... WAS HUGH SCOTT."

In 1970, after having done Senate campaigns for Democrats Robert Kennedy and Warren Magnuson and growing up as an FDR liberal, I was asked to work for the opposition, Senate Minority Leader Hugh Scott of Pennsylvania, not only a Republican, but his party's top man in the Senate. After coolly turning his people down, I got conned into a supper with him. After two hours of conversation about art, the moment of truth approached. "Senator Scott," I said, "you are the most intelligent politician I've ever met. On top of that you're a formidable art scholar, and I adore the book you wrote on Chinese art. You also happen to have a fatherly warmth that reminds me of Gene Hersholt. I know you're no great favorite of the White House, having organized the vote against Nixon's absurd Haynsworth Supreme Court nomination. But I've been a Democrat all my life. How can I *possibly* explain to my (as yet unborn) grandchildren that during the Nixon Administration I helped to re-elect the top *Republican* to the Senate! Give me one reason a guy like me should work for you!" Scott put his pipe in his mouth, chugged on it, looked at me square in the eye, and said: "Tell them this. The only thing that separated Richard Nixon from Fascism... was Hugh Scott." I went to work for the Senate's top Republican with relish. Scott's campaign occurred in the middle of the Vietnam War, which was going badly. I put a young boy at his side in all our advertising, with the senator saying obliquely that we were going to get through this nasty war, that a new generation of young people faced a fine future, which Scott would help bring into being. I filmed them fishing together, in a Bethlehem steel plant and in his Senate office, where he had a marvelous grouping of photos with each of the six presidents he had worked with. He spoke of his experience with them and ended with the line, *C'mon Billy, I'll buy you a Coke.* We called him *Scott of Pennsylvania,* a heroic image in the genre of Lincoln of Illinois and Charles de Gaulle (Charles of France). And we described him as *The most powerful Senator Pennsylvania ever had.* This line was the Big Idea and everything in our advertising led to it. We were telling the voters of Pennsylvania *don't lose this guy.* He needed a decisive vote by at least 100,000 to remain Senate Minority Leader, because Nixon was gunning for him. He won by 220,000 votes (while the popular gubernatorial candidate, Democrat Milton Shaap, won by 900,000 votes – a turnaround of more than a million votes). P.S. The senator then went on to help torpedo Nixon.

The most powerful Senator Pennsylvania ever had

HEROES
4. BOB DYLAN
THE COMPOSER OF "HURRICANE" VISITS RUBIN CARTER, BEHIND BARS. (BEHIND BARS?)

In 1975, after years as a recluse, Bob Dylan went back to his roots, hitting the road with his Rolling Thunder Revue. In the midst of his whirlwind tour, our Rubin Carter defense committee was raising hell publicizing the story of how the outspoken fighter had been framed (see 69). Dylan had read Carter's searing account of his conviction and maximum-security prison life, and was totally convinced of his innocence. I delicately goaded the passionate poet, songwriter and performer that the time had come for him to pull the trigger by writing a song and "maybe even, er, well, maybe even a concert, Bob?" He composed the song protesting Carter's conviction, performing it to tremendous emotional response from his young audiences, and planned two special concerts, the first one held where Rubin was incarcerated. To pump up publicity about the concerts and their cause, I enlisted the help of Ken Regan, one of the greatest photojournalists ever, and he pre-sold a photo to *People* magazine that he would take on the night of the December 7, 1975 prison concert. The previous week, Carter had been inexplicably transferred to a minimum-security women's prison! With Carter in hand, I started scouting around for bars to separate Dylan and Carter for a dramatic prison shot.

In Larry "Ratso" Sloman's epic book *On the Road with Bob Dylan*, he writes, "Lois is looking around the building. 'I didn't know it was this open. I can't find any fucking bars! Where are the bars, Rubin?' 'There ain't none,' Carter shrugs. 'What a fucking image,' the adman shakes his head, 'This joint looks like a country club. You spent ten years in hell, and they want to make it look like you were at a girls camp!' They start to stroll down a hallway when Lois suddenly stopped short. 'What's that?' He points to a grill built into the ceiling. 'It's a gate, sir,' one of the unctuous guards smiles. 'What does it look like when it's down? Does it look like bars in a goddamn prison?' 'I suppose,' the guard agrees. 'Pull it down, pull it down,' Lois is screaming and the guard complies. It's a steel grill gate, running horizontally, that looks fairly ominous. 'We got our bars,' Lois shouts. 'Hey Ratso, go get Dylan, fast. Tell him Rubin has to talk to him, now!' I go get Dylan. Dylan pokes his fingers through the bars to meet the boxers. 'Hey Rube, how you doin' man?' Lois whispers something to Ken Regan, armed with his ever present Nikon and Regan fires away, capturing the hatted, multiscarfed Dylan on one side of the bars and the boxer on the other. I laugh to myself as Regan shoots away and a few feet out of frame Lois just smiles like a Cheshire cat."

HEROES
5. ROBERT REDFORD
MY HERO (AND NO.1 FAN).

As a dedicated actor, director, mentor, political activist and fighter against the Hollywood Establishment, Robert Redford has been a heroic practitioner of intelligent, deeply felt humanity in American film. His Sundance Institute and Film Festival has given filmmakers with more talent than money a way to launch commercially successful careers, changing the look and feel of "independent" film, transforming it into a creative and profitable art form. The word Sundance has come to signify a sphere of movie creativity more vibrant than Hollywood itself. Robert Redford studied at Pratt Institute (my alma mater) to be a designer before he achieved film stardom, and before he had visions of Sundance in his head. In the early '60s (dare I say it) I was such a design hotshot that he became a fan of *mine*. In 1968 he came through for me and the American Museum of Natural History, driving every dog within earshot nuts with our "wolf calls" record (see 46). In 1981, a few months before his *Ordinary People* opened, Paramount thought they had a real dog on their hands. The first-time director was desperately trying to prevent the movie moguls from chopping up his film to make it "less boring." Redford called from L.A. and asked me to rush to a private screening room in New York to view his finished edit. Barry Diller, the boss of Paramount, wanted to slice up the film with a hit list of over 40 edits, and although Redford was a supremely confident artist, he needed a fresh opinion. I sat all alone in Paramount's private viewing room in the Gulf+Western building staring at his film about the death of a young man and the consequences on his family. It was a searing experience (it was only a few years after the tragic death of my 20-year-old son, Harry). When I got home, Redford was frantically calling to get my opinion. I told Bob not to touch one frame of his film. Buoyed by my analysis of why every scene and every nuance counted, he manned the barricades and stood his ground. That year, *Ordinary People* won the Oscar for Best Film and Robert Redford won the Oscar for Best Director. He sent me a case of Dom Perignon the morning after.

A MAGAZINE AD I CREATED
FOR THE PARAMOUNT PICTURES RELEASE
OF ORDINARY PEOPLE.

HEROES
6. JOE LOUIS
THE ICON IN MY SON'S BEDROOM.

Joe Louis' return-bout KO of Adolf Hitler's hero, Max Schmeling,
was a seminal event in the beginning of America's fight against Fascism.
This beautiful portrait of Joe Louis posing with my son, Harry Joe,
hangs in a lonesome bedroom in my home. The iconic Brown Bomber
posed with Harry in 1967 when my boy was eight, after going
through six or seven wonderful takes for the first stockbroker commercial
ever to appear on television (see 48). Joe looked into the camera,
and in his warm and mumbly way, with that sad twinkle in his eye, said,
Edwards & Hanly–where were you when I needed you?!
Then he gently grabbed my son and sat him on his knee.
I look at the picture now that hung an inch from Harry's breath
where he slept for his short life of 20 years, and grieve
for greatness unfulfilled.

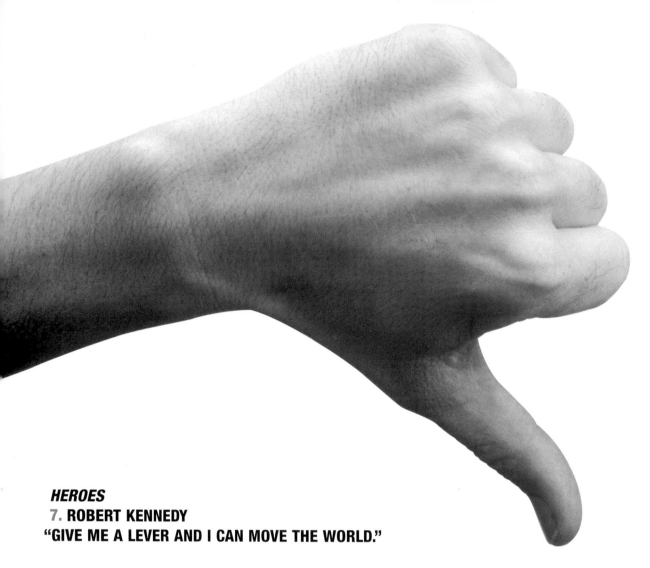

HEROES
7. ROBERT KENNEDY
"GIVE ME A LEVER AND I CAN MOVE THE WORLD."

Robert Kennedy was fearless and decisive when I showed him ads and brochures and TV spots
I wanted to produce for him for his successful run for the Senate in 1964, and we (usually) enjoyed
dueling with each other. One day, however, I was in a limo with Bobby, headed for a rally
in the mean streets of Brooklyn's Bedford-Stuyvesant, known in those days as a black "ghetto."
His give-and-take conviction in the streets was turning New York on. He loved to quote Aeschylus and
he was no slouch on Archimedes. "One thing I learned when working with President Kennedy,"
he would say, "is that one man can make a difference. As Archimedes once said,
'Give me a lever and I can move the world.'" As he bit off the line, he would thrust a thumbs-up
fist at the audience. In the limo filled with his top aides, going over the Brooklyn Bridge,
I told Bobby, "I like the Archimedes line, especially since a Greek wrote it. But you're not going to use
it on the corner of Bedford and Nostrand, are you?" Bobby jumped all over me, implying–
hell, *accusing* me of being a racist. Instead of arguing over the use of intellectually elitist allusions,
I became enraged and blurted out something like "Your old man was a *Nazi* and you worked
for that fascist Joe McCarthy and you're busting *my* balls?!" We didn't say another word all the way to
Bed-Stuy. Bobby was in rare form that day, and the enormous crowd was spellbound.
Suddenly, he leaned forward and built up to "as Archimedes once said, 'give me a lever and
I can move the world'" with his shirtsleeved arm thrust out with his thumb up.
He drew a complete blank. Bobby paused, searched the all-black crowd and spotted
my lone white face, stared into my eyes at least a hundred feet away,
and turned his thumb straight down.

8. AL NEUHARTH
"GODDAMMIT, LOIS...THERE IS NO AMERICA!"

One of the most important innovations in modern journalism was the creation in 1982 of the first national newspaper, USA Today. It was the brainchild of Gannett's gutsy chairman, Al Neuharth, and readers took to it immediately, but advertisers stayed away in droves. In his biography, *Confessions of an S.O.B.*, Neuharth wrote: "Lois told us 'Your product is better than the competitors, but you're not communicating that to the advertiser. The truth is your advertising sucks.' Lois came into a room of poker-faced Gannett execs--many of them skeptical journalists--to hype his ideas. One proposed ad Lois prepared tackled the question of USA Today's identity head-on. Was it a newspaper or a news magazine? The ad showed a drawing of a creature that had a body of a rooster but the tail of a fish. *A lot of media people are saying USA Today is neither fish nor fowl*, his copy said. *They're right. The truth is...we don't care what you call us, just as long as you call us.* I liked Lois' bright new approach. but it left us with a dilemma-- it wasn't easy for a new product to ditch the country's largest ad agency (Y&R). And they ran a lot of ads in our other Gannett newspapers. So I asked Lois what people would say if we switched agencies. 'They'd probably say you're finally getting your head screwed on straight,' Lois replied. 'You're doing pussy advertising now. You ought to be doing triumphant fucking advertising.' The man spoke my language...I gave Lois the advertising. It worked." My most unforgettable lesson from this Dakota country boy who became one of the world's mightiest media S.O.B.'s involved pride and brand integrity. He was obsessed with preserving the purity of the USA Today brand. A few years after the paper became a winner, at a meeting with Neuharth and Cathie Black (his USA Today honcho) I presented an ad that blared, *USA Today is now the No. 1 newspaper in America!* Neuharth exploded. "Goddammit, Lois," he said in deadly earnest, "when are you going to learn that *there is no America*!" The great man had banished "America" from the language as long as there was a USA Today!

HEROES
9. PAUL ROBESON
OUR MOST BELOVED, PERSECUTED HERO.

Legendary heroes who perform superhuman deeds are at a minimum in our time. (Ours has been an age of the anti-hero.) The gods have been supplanted by the likes of Godot. A hero of my youth was a giant among men, Paul Robeson, the son of a 16-year-old escaped slave who fought for his freedom in the Union Army. Robeson's greatness began with his talent, but his courage against the evil forces of racism and fascism in America during the terrible days of McCarthyism makes him, to me, the greatest man I ever met. Abuse was heaped upon him, but he never faltered. "Courage" is one of the smaller words in judging Paul Robeson. No "professional" in the business world would touch him, for fear of political recrimination. He was even deprived of making a living overseas when the government stripped him of his passport. So both my wife Rosie and I, barely out of our teens, designed record album covers for him in 1951. Today, his good name is legendary. And the black community, which had regarded him as a pariah in those dark days in America, now reveres him as one of their most beloved, persecuted heroes.

HEROES
10. DR. SPOCK
THE GOOD DOCTOR SAVES THE WORLD!

Dr. Benjamin Spock was impressed with my Ladies' Home Journal ad starring him as a baby (see 86) and asked me to do a New York subway poster that I've always been proud of. Before the Atomic Test Ban Treaty in 1963, nuclear testing in the atmosphere by the U.S. and Russia was threatening the continuation of life on our planet. Dr. Spock, one of the brave leaders of The Committee for Sane Nuclear Testing (SANE), was instrumental in alerting the public with factual warnings by Nobel scientists (true *super* celebs!) that the fallout of radioactive materials would result in a growing number of birth defects, and asked me to create a subway poster. I showed the image of a saintly silhouette of a conspicuously pregnant woman– (my secretary at that time) with this absolutely factual headline: *1 1/4 Million unborn children will be born dead or have some gross defect because of Nuclear Bomb testing.* Spock and the Nobel scientists were rewarded for their warning about the perils to unborn children by being called Communist sympathizers. The Cold War was getting hotter and the country's mood was poisoned by hateful political passions. McCarthyism had left a legacy of paranoia and fear, and protest against nuclear testing was tarred as "peace propaganda." Speaking out for SANE was like waving a red flag, with the press (especially the Madison Avenue trade press) attacking me as a pinko. Today, almost four decades after the Test Ban Treaty of 1963, it seems incomprehensible that protests against SANE (and a poster that told the truth about the real and malignant peril of nuclear fallout) could ever have caused such extreme reaction. But Dr. Spock and the Nobel laureates who manned the barricades in those scary days were a band of heroes who truly saved the world.

HEROES
11. MICK JAGGER
THE PATRON SAINT OF MTV.
(HE TOOK MTV FROM ZERO TO HERO)

MTV, the 24-hour rock 'n' roll video channel, now regarded
as a "sure thing from the start" and "an idea whose time had come"–
was an absolute failure after a full year of operation (see 6).
When I got Rock fans to call and yell *I want my MTV,* cable companies
called WarnerAmex and begged them to stop running the spot.
They didn't have an army of telephone operators to answer the calls.
So the cable companies surrendered and put MTV on the air.
But it couldn't have happened, no way, if the climactic moment of my
commercial wasn't delivered by a legitimate Rock star. Of the
dozens we approached, the only one with the foresight, the moxie,
the hubris, was Mick Jagger, who first brayed the
industry-transforming words, *I want my MTV,*
to the rock fans of the world. Twenty years before the
bad boy of Rock became a Knight of the Realm,
Sir Mick had already been anointed...
the Patron Saint of MTV.

HEROES
**12. GARRY KASPAROV
THE KING AND EYE.**

I can't think of a single celebrity I've ever worked with in my life who caused me to remotely characterize myself as "starstruck." (Although I've been struck dumb at the sight of Kim Novak, Jane Russell and Claudia Cardinale.) But working for Garry Kasparov, the reigning world champion of chess, gave me goose bumps. And when his creative brain and eagle eye immediately grasped the visual trick on my poster announcing his 1990 World Championship war with Anatoly Karpov (see 17), I was his subject forever. In over 40 years of selling with celebrities I made it a point to never ask for an autograph. But I made my move and shoved my well-worn chessboard in Kasparov's hands, nervously asking my hero to autograph the back of it. My only autograph!

MY MOST MEMORABLE CLIENTS

THERE ARE THREE KINDS OF CLIENTS:
1. ANALYSIS PARALYSIS
2. THE ABOMINABLE NO-MAN
3. "YOU'RE A GENIUS, LOIS—RUN IT!"

La Fonda del Sol doesn't give you this Gaucho knife to cut your tacos, Hombre.

This Gaucho steak knife is used at LaCabaña in Buenos Aires, the best steak house in South America. It is also used at the best steak house in North America. La Fonda del Sol. *La Fonda del Sol?* La Fonda del Sol. 123 West 50 St. PLaza 7-8800

MY MOST MEMORABLE CLIENTS
1. JOE BAUM
"RUN THE SHIT."

Restaurant Associates was a network of classy restaurants, including The Four Seasons, The Brasserie, Tower Suite, La Fonda del Sol, and other stylish eateries. Their big enchilada, Joseph H. Baum, was leading a personal, pioneering crusade to convert eating in America into a theatrical and aesthetic experience. Joe Baum, the man I called Little Caesar, was the most cultured tyrant I've ever known. (He later created all the dining facilities at the ill-fated World Trade Center, including the marvelous tourist attraction Windows on the World. He then went on to breathe exciting new life into The Rainbow Room atop Rockefeller Plaza.) The word *perfection* is almost inadequate in describing this demanding entrepreneur. Nothing was ever exactly right for Baum and he hated to praise anything because praise might imply that perfection had been attained. In 1960, the first time copywriter Ron Holland and I asked him to react to a proposed campaign for The Four Seasons Restaurant, we knew we were ahead of the game when Joe barked, "Run the shit!" Besides the aforementioned restaurants, we helped the great man create the Bavarian snack bar Zum Zum, Spats, Paul Revere's Tavern, Trattoria, Charley O's, Charlie Brown's Ale & Chop House and many others, each one a memorable gem. The late Joe Baum, a legendary figure to the food entrepreneurs and chefs of the world today, enjoyed my shenanigans because he was witnessing a fellow pain-in-the-ass madman in pursuit of perfection, and he welcomed the comradeship of this crazy Greek.
I was also his perfect audience. One evening at the bar of his spectacular Forum of the Twelve Caesars, Baum checked to see if I was watching his every move as he ordered a Bloody Mary. Before sipping his drink, he asked the bartender, "Is this the *best* Bloody Mary you can make?"
"Yes, Mr. Baum," the bartender answered with assurance.
"Taste it," Baum ordered. The bartender sipped and reflected.
"It's good," he decided. "Can you make a better one?" asked Baum. The bartender mixed a new Bloody Mary.
"Now taste this one and tell me what you think," said Baum. His lips had not yet touched either drink. The bartender took a sip. "This is *very* good, Mr. Baum. It's perfect."
The magic word was finally dropped. "Then why the *fuck* didn't you make it that way in the first place!" asked Baum.

I don't care how talented you are. If you're the kind of creative person who gets your best work *produced,* here's how you *must* spend your time: *1% Inspiration, 9% Perspiration, 90% Justification.* Selling and protecting your work (to those around you, to lawyers, to TV copy clearance, and ultimately to your client) is what separates the sometimes good creative person from the consistently great one. Charles Revson was one tough cookie, but when he was sold, he was sold (see 12). I admit that I sometimes go on and on in a kind of rapture about my campaigns, and Charles nailed me once with, "Lois, don't knock on an empty door." (Al Neuharth's zinger was "Lois, you can't take yes for an answer.") Like many of the benevolent tyrants of American business, Charles Revson had a keen understanding of power. He also understood mass preferences. Back in the '60s he sponsored the TV quiz show *$64,000 Question* and made Revlon a household name. One afternoon, in the last year of his imperial life, Revson summoned a marathon meeting with his four advertising agencies–on Christmas *Eve,* for chrissakes!
He herded all of us into his private office, where we sat and fumed while he made long-distance calls to his top men at home as they were trimming their trees, wishing them interminable greetings of the season. The last of the calls dragged on with the most syrupy praise I've ever heard royalty pour on a subject. Then, after gushing compliments for a great year's effort, Charles paused, looked coldly into his gold phone (*gold*–I kid you not) and said without a trace of humor, "But fuck up *once* next year, and *out* you go!," and slammed down the phone.

3. SAM BRONFMAN
MASSA SAM AND HIS PIG-FUCKING AGENCY.

There is nothing quite as thrilling as earning the respect of genuinely tough clients. The power elite of my own ad agency life began with Samuel Bronfman, the former Canadian bootlegger and fabled boss of Joseph E. Seagram & Sons, Inc. They called him "Mister Sam." I called him "*Massa* Sam." When Bronfman was in his majestic prime, he sat dumbstruck as he watched me create an outrageous Wolfschmidt Vodka campaign for his son Edgar. A tough father, he passed off what he considered a frivolous whiskey category to keep his son busy. My ads of talking bottles and oranges and tomatoes and onions was a big hit, and the booze world took notice, helping launch his son into becoming a powerful business leader. Proving him wrong about vodka, I couldn't help feeling Massa Sam was gunning for me. One day one of Seagram's brand managers asked me if I would do him a favor and take a look at some new labels for Leroux Cordials. I thought they were a mess, so he asked me to do him another favor and design new labels. He loved them. "Let's show these beauties to Massa Sam," he said. (My nickname was catching on.) Off we went to the sixth floor of the Seagram Building, and before I realized I was walking into a snake pit, the ad manager said, "Mr. Sam, here are some new Leroux label designs that Lois *insisted* he do for us." I showed Bronfman my designs, but in a flash I realized that he himself had supervised the design of the old labels and they were his babies. Bronfman peered up at the brand manager and asked for *his* opinion. "Well, Mr. Sam," he said, "I think I agree with the agency on this." Bronfman leaned forward and drilled the ad manager with his eyes. "Who do you work for," he growled, "*me*...or this pig-fucking agency?" I fell to the floor, doubled over with laughter. "Why are you laughing?" Bronfman asked me as I rolled on his Bokhara carpet at the foot of a massive Rodin sculpture of Balzac, guffawing uncontrollably. "Lois, I just insulted you." But the lovable old tyrant enjoyed my slapstick groveling. "Oh, Massa Sam," was all I could mumble. The mighty Bronfman looked confused, then he leaned toward me and said, "*You* I like." Not long after that encounter, the labels that were supervised by my Massa were replaced by the new designs from his pig-fucking agency.

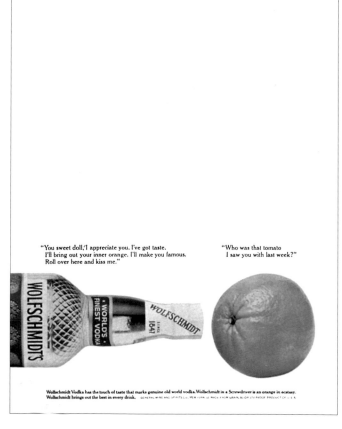

פסח

MY MOST MEMORABLE CLIENTS
4. NATHANIEL GOODMAN
"YOU MAKE THE MATZOS, I'LL MAKE THE ADS!"

In 1959, a year before I started the second creative agency in America, I worked
for the first creative agency in America, Doyle Dane Bernbach. My first assignment was to
create a subway poster, for Passover, for Goodman's Matzos. I hand-lettered a headline
in Hebrew with two universally understood words (at least in New York),
even to a Greek gentile: *Kosher for Passover*. The poster was a stopper, but the account
man came back and told me to do another one because the client didn't buy it–
so I went to my boss, Bill Bernbach, to get justice. He told me to hop a subway to Long Island
City and sell it myself, and he made an appointment for me to see Goodman's boss,
an Old Testament, bushy-eyebrowed tyrant, a master kvetch. His office was a glass sanctuary
that looked out at a network of glass cubicles–not for architectural effect, but for purposes
of surveillance. His staff surrounded him at his imperial desk. He leaned back and yawned as I
opened with a passionate pitch. When I unfurled the poster, he muttered, "I dun like it."
I disregarded him and pressed forward, selling my guts out. "I *love* it," I said. "It's a fresh, fast,
clear, provocative way to say that Goodman's is *the* matzos for Passover." The tyrant
tapped the desk for silence as one, then two, then three of his staff registered support for the
powerful Hebrew headline. "No, no," he said, "I dun like it!" I had to make a final move–
so I walked up to an open casement window. As I began to climb through the open window
he shouted after me, "You're going someplace?" As I stepped through the window,
I shouted back, "I'm leaving." They gasped at me as though I were some kind of *meshugener*,
poised on the outer ledge three floors above the pavement like a window washer. I gripped
the vertical window support with my left hand and waved the poster with my free hand,
and screamed from the ledge at the top of my lungs: *"You make the matzos, I'll make the ads!"*
"Stop, stop," said the old man. "Ve'll run it, ve'll run it. You made your point already.
Come in, come in, *please!"* I climbed back into the room and thanked the patriarch for the nice
way he received my work. As I was leaving, he shouted after me, "Young man, if you ever
qvit advertising, you got yourself ah job as ah matzos salesmen!" My heart was still thumping
as I stepped off the elevator back at the agency. Casually I walked to my office.
"What happened?" came voices. Account executives surrounded me. "We had a quiet chat
and he bought it," I said coolly, chucking the tube holding my poster onto a taboret
in my room. "He's a very sweet, reasonable gentleman."

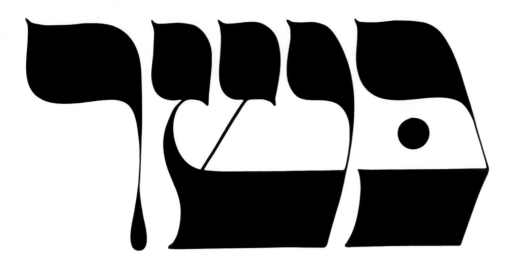

MY MOST MEMORABLE CLIENTS
5. ED HORRIGAN
BARBARIAN AT THE GATE.

In the midst of my successful *Don't give up the ship!* campaign for Cutty Sark,
Ed Horrigan was brought in by Dick Strudel and Ben Heineman (who were big fans of
the ad campaign) to run the company. But when Horrigan became captain
of the ship, he immediately, almost arbitrarily, torpedoed our campaign. Ed Horrigan,
of R.J. Reynolds Nabisco fame, had made a name for himself for his greed-filled
involvement in the wild Wall Street LBO days of the '80s, brought to an almost comedic
level in the book and TV movie, *Barbarians at the Gate*. His "Smokeless Cigarette"
was the butt of many a joke when he and his boss, Ross Johnson, shamelessly tried
to jack up the value of their "cookies and cigarette empire." But all was not lost
when I convinced Horrigan to let me create the Ali/Frazier III fight program with Cutty Sark
as the sponsor (see 116, Favorite Celebs 1). The Carter case was attracting
famous names so he was happy as a clam. But after helping Rubin Carter get a new
trial in 1976, the Hurricane was stiffed once more, and the press blindsided
me and my gallant gang of celebs who had worked so hard to publicize the case.
(A front-page article in *The New York Times* actually implied that Ali, Bob Dylan
and I were foraging for personal publicity.) Despite this second conviction, my
faith in Carter's innocence was unshaken. When *The New York Times* got on my case,
Horrigan called me into his office, and without a greeting, he barked,
"Stop working for the nigger or I'll fire you." I didn't blink. I told him I still believed in
Carter's innocence and could not turn my back on him. Horrigan, red-faced,
stomped to the door of his sprawling office, opened it, and gave me an ultimatum:
"Last chance, Lois, yes or no! Give me a one-word answer."
I said, "No." The next day he gave us the gate.

MY MOST MEMORABLE CLIENTS
6. WARREN MAGNUSON
THE FINGER-POINTING SENATOR.

As Ron Holland, Jim Callaway and I were leaving Senator Warren Magnuson's
apartment at the Shoreham Hotel after our first meeting with him in 1968,
his negligee-clad, ex–burlesque dancer wife strutted, in her high-heeled mules,
to a phone sitting on a low table in their foyer and dramatically pointed to it.
"Do you see that phone? Well that phone, that *very* phone, would
ring 10 at night, 11, 12, sometimes 2 o'clock in the *morning*!" exclaimed
the stacked Mrs. Magnuson. She continued, "Jack...the *President*...
wanting to talk to Maggie about the problems of the day, needing his advice."
Standing 10 feet behind his wife, still dressed in a bathrobe and
slippers in the early afternoon, Maggie caught my eye and poked the middle
finger of his right hand in and out of a circle formed by the thumb
and index finger of his left hand, ribaldly describing, through sign language,
that our Commander in Chief was ordering Senator Magnuson to deliver
a female companion to his quarters in the White House!
A month later, after premiering our TV campaign for his re-election, wherever
Maggie went in the state of Washington, people pointed a finger to
their heads, mimicking the Senator in *our* version of his finger-pointing
(see 59), calling out affectionately, "Hey, Maggie! You still got it up here!"
Early one morning we went with Magnuson to a Boeing
aerospace plant. He was greeted by thousands of hard hats
at the front gate, most of them pointing to their heads.
He was marvelous, pressing the flesh and hugging the
workers–until one said to him, "We love you like
a brother, Maggie, but there ain't a single guy at Boeing
who's not nuts about hunting. How could you possibly
vote for *gun control?*" "Why don't you go fuck yourself,"
Maggie replied. From Boeing we went to a women's
breakfast, where the senator was trying to win more votes.
One of the ladies, a Magnuson partisan, asked him in
a friendly way, "Senator, could you tell us in your own words
why the people of Washington should re-elect you?"
Menacingly pointing at her, he barked, "If you don't like me, *don't vote for me!*"
Maggie was shooting himself in the foot at every turn, his vision clouded
by booze. A few days later his aides sent Maggie on a sabbatical,
out of state and out of range of any television cameras, and he was returned
to the Senate with an overwhelming 65% of the vote.

MY MOST MEMORABLE CLIENTS
7. J. DAN BROCK
MY $4,000,000 PHONE CALL ON NOV. 22,1963.

At first, dynamic CEO Bud Maytag called the shots on
National Airlines advertising, but he quickly got caught up in
other duties. The decisions on our new client's campaign passed on
to his No. 2 man, J. Dan Brock, a tall, drawling southerner.
Maytag was thrilled with our ad campaign, *Is this any way to run an airline?
You bet it is!* (see 127), but Brock never pulled the cork from champagne
bottles over our work. Good ol' boy Dan Brock was transplanted to Miami from Texas,
and his tough young boss had saddled him with an offbeat Noo Yawk ad agency.
Suddenly he's stuck with a Jewish writer (Julian Koenig) and a Greek art director who sounds
more Jewish than most Jews (yours truly). We once suggested that National
serve matzos on their New York–Miami flights during Passover. *"Maatzos?"* drawled Brock
incredulously. We suggested a *Gambling* Flight, 15 miles beyond the offshore
limits. Gut the plane's interior and install gaming tables. Fuhgedaboutit! And he continually
pronounced Julian, *"Jewww lian."* To announce new routes in a catchy style, we used
TV in our New York, wise-guy way. One of several Papert, Koenig, Lois commercials in that
genre ran in the fall of 1963, around November. To promote a new National route
from Miami to Dallas we had a cowboy shoot off his revolver, blow the smoke off its barrel
and tell the public, "Anyone who doesn't want to go to Dallas got to be plumb loco."
It was running on TV at the precise time John F. Kennedy's open car was moving in front
of the Book Depository building! As soon as we got over the initial shock after hearing
the first horrific reports from Dallas, we called each of our dozen or so PKL clients to cancel
their TV advertising, pronto. The president's condition was still unclear and the
networks hadn't yet slapped a moratorium on advertising, but obviously, this was no time
for business as usual. Our biggest account, National Airlines, was called by our
account supervisor to get his okay, and he reported to me that Brock told him they would
talk about it down there in Miami, whatever that meant. I got on the phone and
said to Brock, "I'm sorry Dan, I guess you haven't heard, but the president's been *shot!*"
"I know he's been shot," said Brock. "He's *dead.*" "Well look, Dan," I said,
"we think it would be in *terrible* taste to run those spots now." Now what do you say to
a $4 million client on November 22, 1963, when he tells you in a taunting drawwwl,
"I think you boys in New York are blowing this out of proportion. Hell–we're *celebrating!*"
Thunderstruck, I shouted at him, "Hey, Dan, kiss my New York ass!
We're pulling all your stuff off the air and we don't give a damn *what* you think!"
The next day (surprise, surprise) J. Dan Brock fired us.
Six months later, with apologies, Bud Maytag rehired us.

MY MOST MEMORABLE CLIENTS
8. THE REISE BROTHERS
THE BIGGEST GONIFFS IN TOWN.

One day in 1978 I received a call from the greatest restauranteur of our time,
Joe Baum, informing me that somebody wanted to work with me.
"Really?" I said, "That's terrific. Who?" "The Reise brothers," he said.
"The Reise brothers?! I shouted. "You gotta be kidding, Joe. Those guys are
the biggest goniffs in town." "George, George," Baum persisted.
"They're the best marketing guys in New York!" In our Manhattan argot, the great
Joe Baum was telling me the Reises were plenty smart and considerably
more than colorful bandits. Thus, among my most picturesque clients, did I run into
the Runyonesque brothers Irving and Murray Reise, the Manhattan
restaurant/real estate moguls who owned a restaurant (and property) on damn near
every block in midtown Manhattan. As New York originals, they felt at ease with
a Bronx boy whose accent was worse than theirs, and who could appreciate their
comic banality. Murray once reminisced about his early days in the restaurant
business as the owner of a coffee shop near Grand Central Station. To save money
on garbage disposal, they would surreptitiously stash their mighty load
each day on the Twentieth Century Limited. "We kept New York *clean*," he boasted.
"All our garbage was unloaded in *Chicago!*" One of Murray's vital aphorisms:
"I'm gonna let that guy chase me until I catch him!" At our meetings at their tiny,
shabby office (despite their extensive real-estate holdings), Murray,
the younger Reise, played prosecutor and defense attorney. Irving, older and
statesmanlike, played the avuncular judge who would step in before
Murray overkilled. Murray once told me, "George, people you really like and work
with, you *fire*"–eloquently expressing the Reise philosophy that nobody
who ever worked for them must ever be made to feel secure.
Recognizing the totality of his younger sibling's remark, Irving interrupted,
"Not necessarily all the time. George, we like *you*, and love your names and logos
and advertising campaigns, but we wanted to talk to you about that markup
on what you call 'production.' How come it has to be 17.65% that you agency people
always charge? Why can't we round it down to 10%?" Then came the punch line:
"Why do we need it at *all*?" added Murray.
Every meeting with the funniest brother duo since Groucho and Harpo
was material for a raconteur, and I will always look back fondly at the Reises,
who paid some of their bills some of the time.

MY MOST MEMORABLE CLIENTS
9. ALAN MacDONALD
HOW STOUFFERS GOT FAT ON LEAN CUISINE.

In 1977, at a dinner at The Four Seasons celebrating the acquisition of the Stouffer's account, I asked the top guns at Stouffer's when they intended to market a frozen gourmet fitness line. Savoring a shrimp dipped in mustard fruits, their chairman said, "A *delicious* frozen diet product would require expensive ingredients and would eke out low profit margins." Perplexed, a few days later I sent him a name in logo form (for a product category he wanted no part of). He opened the 18 x 24 FedEx package and saw... Lean Cuisine! He immediately summoned his marketing and production staffs into his office and told them to create and market a frozen diet gourmet food line, case closed. Lean Cuisine became one of the great food brands in American marketing history within a year, and *the* power brand in a healthy new marketing category. Here are a few other marketing mavens that recognized a Big Idea, pulled the trigger and hit the bull's-eye. I presented a thousand ads to Joe Baum and he said, "Run the shit"–999 times. Paul Screvane saw our N.Y. Bets logo (see 42) and said "Bingo." When Tommy Hilfiger first saw his intro campaign, he had many sleepless nights, but he gritted his teeth and grabbed his chance to be famous, fast. Pauline Trigère was warned by Bill Blass not to run my "Dear John" letter, but she called me and said, "Fuck it" in French (see 111). I showed John Hay Whitney, the owner of The Herald Tribune, a comp of a new supplement for his Sunday Trib that I named *New York*, and he went to town. Thrillingly, my list of the great clients is long and keeps growing. I've always joked that my smartest clients just say "Yes" and let me do my thing. It may sound vain and incorrigible, but that's what I think, take it or leave it.

Jiffy Lube is a famous brand name today, but when I started to work for Jim Hindman and his pioneering quick-oil-change company in 1982, it was unknown, with a handful of locations in a sprinkling of states. In my first meeting with the rough 'n tough he-man founder, Jim Hindman introduced me to his marketing team, a gang of young studs whom he had mentored as their college football coach! As a prelude to creating an ad campaign that I was convinced would make them famous, I insisted that they needed a new logo and design program. I told them they could be the McDonald's of the '80s, but they needed a logo and look that drove their image. They had recently produced signage for their 18 units at $25,000 a pop, so they balked plenty. Until I showed them my "action logo," a circular "J" in the form of a directional sign, a striking curved red arrow that almost forced you to make a turn off the road into the Jiffy Lube driveway. The Jiffy Lube team listened to my pep talk attentively, and before long I reeled his linemen in, then his backfield, and finally, and dramatically, Coach Hindman grabbed a Magic Marker and scrawled a facsimile of the logo on a large drawing pad as if he were diagramming a play, as his gladiators started to chant like a football team chomping to tear out of their locker room and take on the world. But then their legal counsel timidly raised his hand, stood up and said haltingly, and very seriously, "George...don't you think your design... with that curved arrow...has a kind of *phallic symbolism*?"
The room was stunned. "Well, sir," I said, "I don't know what *your* peepee is shaped like, but *my* peepee don't look like that." The room howled, Jim Hindman became a real pal, and I went on to quarterback the Jiffy Lube team to a great business success story– the incredible saga of a tiny company that grew to over 1,600 locations, and changed the way America changed its oil.

11. HARDING LAWRENCE
THE HAWAIIAN ROUTE FOR BRANIFF WAS IN THE BAG.

When it came to understanding an idea that would fly, Harding Lawrence is at the top of my list.
When his constipated operating committee vociferously rejected my *When you got it–flaunt it*
campaign, he overruled them and subsequently proved them wrong (see 50).
During the last days of President Lyndon Johnson's reign, Harding Lawrence
was a man possessed, committed with all his being to carrying Braniff to the corners
of the earth. I was told the coveted Hawaiian route was "just about in the bag,"
and my partners Ron Holland, Jim Callaway and I were given the assignment to announce
this momentous news that would firmly establish Braniff as a big-league airline.
The painted planes by Alexander Calder, lush leather interiors, dazzling terminals–
and the edible food–prompted me to show Lawrence a campaign with the slogan
Braniff and Hawaii. A marriage made in heaven. The devilishly handsome, bushy-browed,
gunslinging Texan (he actually *was* a quick-draw champion), notorious for his rough
and tough ways with his staff, plainly and simply lost his cookies! He raved at me with
a frightening incoherence, his fierce eyes became burning coals as froth actually
began to bubble out of the corner of his mouth. "Sheeet, Lois! Don't you New York faggots
understand how the world works?!" He was a man accustomed to wounding with words,
and he did. Then he screamed at one of his lieutenants, "Go get the goddamn bag."
I was dumbstruck, with no idea what he was talking about. His VP bag man swaggered
across the room and brought a heavy black canvas gym bag to his boss, who
slammed it down ferociously in front of Lois, Holland and Callaway. "Open the fucking bag
and get an education!" he scowled. I unzipped the bag...and stared at stacks of
hundred-dollar bills, headed the next day, I was told, to our good ol' cowboy Commander
in Chief, as a "gift" for his "help" in obtaining the lucrative Hawaiian route
(after expansion to Latin America a few years before). The Dallas slicker screamed
"Get it Lois? 'A marriage made in heaven' *admits* to the Civil Aeronautics Board,
and that left-wing goddamn *New York Times*, that I'm in cahoots with Lyndon. Don't you
understand sheet?!" And this big-city hick, finally, "got it." My dazed partners
and I, all FDR Democrats, flew back to New York City that night on Braniff Airlines,
not sure if Harding Lawrence's Hawaiian war dance was the *funniest* meeting of our lives–
or the saddest.

FIVE YEARS AFTER THIS BRANIFF AD RAN,
THE AIRLINE WAS NAILED FOR FAILING
TO REPORT A $40,000 CONTRIBUTION TO THE
1972 RE-ELECTION CAMPAIGN OF
REPUBLICAN PRESIDENT RICHARD NIXON,
SPREADING THE WEALTH TO WHATEVER
BOZO SAT IN THE OVAL OFFICE.

MY MOST MEMORABLE CLIENTS
12. DR. HANS NORDHOFF
SELLING A NAZI CAR IN A JEWISH TOWN.

When Volkswagen chose Doyle Dane Bernbach as its agency in 1959, I refused to be on the creative team.
It was hard to forget that Hitler himself had been directly involved in creating the Volkswagen. Even
though Der Führer was helped by the Austrian car engineer Dr. Ferdinand Porsche, the VW in 1959 reminded
the world of the ovens. The very week my boss Bill Bernbach was trying to persuade me to take an
orientation junket to Germany, West Germany sold a fleet of jets to Israel, and I gave up and flew Lufthansa
to visit their Wolfsburg factory. I wasn't the most polite guest of our German client, "Herr Docktor" Nordhoff.
On a walk through their picturesque factory town early one evening, I asked, "Would you please
point out the ovens?" Around the bend we came to a handsome church spire with scaffolding surrounding it.
I commented to Herr Nordhoff that it looked remarkably like a V-2 rocket launching pad. VW's head
man visibly exhaled. Our DDB group had heard about a mysterious room where VW prototypes were stored.
We bugged the VW staff and reluctantly they led us to a cavernous basement room and peeled the
tarpaulin off the earliest Porsche version and other historic models, including the millionth VW,

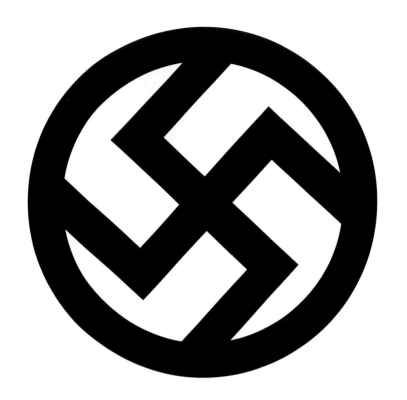

AS FAR AS I WAS CONCERNED, IN 1959, DR. NORDHOFF'S VOLKSWAGEN PLANT STILL REEKED OF THE STENCH OF THE HISTORY OF THE THIRD REICH. FOR MY AMUSEMENT (OR POSSIBLY AS AN ACT OF ATONEMENT FOR SUCCUMBING TO HELPING SELL HITLER'S "PEOPLE'S CAR"), WHEN I RETURNED FROM GERMANY I SPENT A MORNING DESIGNING A FOUR-INCH-SQUARE FLIP BOOK: 24 PAGES WHERE THE VOLKSWAGEN LOGO MAGICALLY TRANSFORMS INTO THE DREADED NAZI SWASTIKA, OR, FLIPPING BACKWARDS, THE FORBIDDING SYMBOL TURNS INTO THE VW LOGO. A FUNNY, BUT TOTALLY DEVASTATING VISUAL ACCUSATION. WHEN BILL BERNBACH, MY BOSS AT DDB, SAW MY SOCIAL COMMENTARY, HE FLIPPED. "VERY CREATIVE," HE SAID. "NOW BURN IT!"

a gold-plated museum piece. I slipped away to search for war vehicles I assumed they had preserved and stashed somewhere. I peeled off a suspiciously shaped tarpaulin and Bingo!–a Nazi jeep, swastikas intact, with a mounted machine gun! I leapt into the vehicle, trained the machine gun on our group 50 feet away, and in a chilling imitation, broke the quiet conversation with an "ach-ach-ach-ach," swinging the empty weapon on its swivel mount, then adding mein zinger: "Und ve almost *did!*" When I got back to the States I ran into Bernbach in the hallway and excitedly said, "Bill, Bill, I got the marketing problem solved– we have to sell a Nazi car in a Jewish town!" He was not amused. Before VW chose DDB, they had spent many deutsche marks with a major New York agency and sold three cars. A few weeks later, when Bill Bernbach unveiled *Think small,* Julian Koenig's first DDB ad for VW, the "Beetle" was brilliantly positioned as a breakthrough idea in America: a small car! It ultimately ran, of course (and is arguably the most famous print ad in advertising history), but Dr. Nordhoff's initial, immediate, Teutonic response to Bernbach on viewing the ad was, "Nein, nein. You people don't seem to undershtand. Ve at *Volkswagen*...think *big!*"

MY (NEW YORK ART DIRECTORS CLUB)
HALL OF FAME BOSSES:
THE FAB FIVE

MY FIVE HALL OF FAME BOSSES
1. REBA SOCHIS
THERE IS NOTHING LIKE A DAME.

Before I started my own agency in 1960, I worked for five all-time creative giants who changed the world of advertising and were inducted into the New York Art Directors Club Hall of Fame, the most coveted worldwide award for advertising and design creativity. My first big break, in 1950, was when my teacher at Pratt Institute, Herschel Levit, insisted I was ready to attack the hackneyed world of advertising, and sent this 19-year-old to a job interview at a female-owned design studio, unique in those days. The greatest day of my professional life was when I met my first boss, Reba Sochis Hayett–a great designer, a great dame, a great curser. Reba kept a barrage of expletives going when the spirit moved her, berating the witch-hunting House Un-American Activities Committee, tricky Dick Nixon, McCarthyism, or merely lamenting a bad hair day. The loveliest lady ever in the world of design had a nose more crooked than mine. What a kisser! When I cashed my first pay check of $45, I couldn't believe I was actually being paid to refine my craft in her queendom of perfectionism. In 1980 she was only the second woman voted into The A.D. Hall of Fame. Amazingly, her atelier produced four designers she mentored who received the same prestigious honor. My wife Rosie (who Reba drafted to replace me when I went to Korea) and I buried Reba and her husband Will Hayett on a hillside near our family plot. On the sacred days we visit the graves of my parents, my big sister Paraskeve and her husband Bill, and my beloved son Harry, we always lay a rose on a Lois-designed tombstone, in loving memory and appreciation of her great influence on our lives.

MY FIVE HALL OF FAME BOSSES
2. BILL GOLDEN
THE CBS EYE AND ME.

After I returned from Korea, Reba Sochis sent me to CBS, the most elite atelier of brilliant design talent in the world. Bill Golden, a totally fearless, uncompromising perfectionist, was my boss.
Golden was the father of the corporate image symbolized by the CBS eye. To a young designer like me (I was 22, already married two years) he was an icon of integrity, taste and courage. Breaking the ice with Golden was another story. The first day on the job I went to his office and asked his secretary if he had a minute to OK my first ad—for a new television series called *Gunsmoke*. She looked up at me from behind a massive dictionary and smiled nervously. Golden was at work at the far end of a long corner office. I walked to within four feet of his drawing table and waited for him to look up, but he continued working. I began to feel like a fool, standing there without being acknowledged. After almost 30 seconds—an eternity to a supplicant—I cleared my throat, but the gangly Peter O'Toole look-alike continued ignoring me. I leaned forward and held my layout almost in front of my knees to catch his eyes, but he kept working, his left shoulder jerking with a slight tic. I looked back at his secretary of 20 years, and the smirk on her face confirmed that the great Golden was busting my balls. I returned to his secretary, lifted the massive dictionary from her desk, and went back to the drawing table. I held the dictionary chest-high and opened my hands. It fell to the floor with an earsplitting bo-o-o-om. The pencil flew from Bill Golden's hand and his face jerked up.
"Oh, George—can I help you?" he asked. His tic had stopped. "Uh, yes. I'd like to show you an ad for *Gunsmoke*." I handed him my layout of the back of James Arness going for his gun, a bad guy seen between his legs a distance off, and Golden fixed his eyes on it. "Good. *Very* good,"
was all he said. From that day on, when I showed Bill Golden my work, he snapped to attention, proving, to get anything done in life, *first* you gotta get their attention.

MY FIVE HALL OF FAME BOSSES
3. HERB LUBALIN
THE GREATEST LEFT-HANDED,
COLOR-BLIND ART DIRECTOR
WHO EVER LIVED.

Leaving Bill Golden's atelier was wrenching, but I knew working alongside Herb Lubalin was
a step to stardom. Herbie was a meteor in the graphic arts field. His pages glistened, his type talked,
his ideas moved. And his graphic influence throughout the entire world was enormous.
(His color choices in his ads and promotion pieces were always unexpected and handsomely unusual.
Then I found out he was *color-blind*.) Lubalin made his reputation in the pharmaceutical
field, with his humor and rascality feeding his ouevre. He wrote the majority of his headlines.
I once asked Herbie what he considered his all-time *best* headline.
"Kiss Your Hemorrhoids Goodbye," he answered. I loved the man and I loved his work.

MY FIVE HALL OF FAME BOSSES
4. BILL BERNBACH
THE GOD OF CREATIVITY
IN THE AD WORLD.

Bill Bernbach was the greatest force for good in an industry that is still regarded by too many
as an evil preoccupation. Decades ago, Frederic Wakeman wrote *The Hucksters*, Sloan Wilson wrote
The Man in the Grey Flannel Suit and Vance Packard wrote *The Hidden Persuaders*. They
effectively convinced America that the ad agency world was full of fake-out artists who sell their souls
while manipulating society's values. When Brooklyn-born Bill Bernbach emerged on the scene
in 1948 (the year he founded Doyle Dane Bernbach), he was the loneliest of voices in a wilderness that
did resemble the unsavory vision of Wakeman, Wilson and Packard. Bernbach precipitated what the
marketing world now accepts as the Creative Revolution. Bernbach is to advertising what Freud was
to psychoanalysis. In the pre-Bernbach dark age of advertising, *businessmen* rather than artists,
working primarily with writers, actually *created* America's ads and TV commercials. Predictably, 99%
of their labors were dreadful. His contribution reduced the deplorable level of advertising from
99% to 85%–a Herculean feat, because out of Bernbach's vision came the Creative Agency, where the
emphasis was shifted from the cut of account executives' suits and the reams of their statistics–
to *advertising,* to intelligent work that was crafted by gifted art directors thinking with inspired writers.
Bill Bernbach was the first person in the ad game who truly understood the power of imagery–
vivid verbal themes and/or powerful visual symbols. He clearly understood the distinction between
imagery that would shock for shock's sake–and imagery that was *seemingly* outrageous,
imagery that could attract and hold attention because of an intrusive and meaningful message.
After an action-packed and award-winning year at DDB, I left Bernbach to start the second
creative ad agency in the world, hoping to emulate him.

MY FIVE HALL OF FAME BOSSES
5. BOB GAGE
THE FIRST MODERN ART DIRECTOR.

Doyle Dane Bernbach got its initial creative reputation from the graphic power of Bob Gage's immensely warm and humane advertising. In the early '50s, Bob Gage tackled the printed page and it hasn't been the same since. He made it jump. He made it talk. He made it look simple. Gage has had as great an influence on the printed advertising message as Toulouse-Lautrec. He started an era of art directors who used their talents unashamedly and enthusiastically to *sell* products. The four greatest advertising art directors of all time (in my unashamed opinion) were Bob Gage, Bill Taubin, Helmut Krone and yours truly, and in the late '50s, the four of us worked in successive rooms at DDB. We were thrilled to be amongst each other, but competed with a frightening passion. But Bob Gage was the first.

TIMELINE

1931   Born June 26 in Manhattan, the son of immigrant Greek parents, Vasilike Thanasoulis and Haralampos Lois.
(Lois is not an anglicized name. Logios, meaning "orator," has been traced back to the time of Alexander the Great.)

1932   Haralampos opens the Columbia Florist at 231st Street and Broadway, where George and older sisters
Paraskeve and Hariclea are raised in the Irish Catholic section of the upper Bronx.

1945   George divides his boyhood between delivering flowers, schoolwork, sports and drawing, drawing, drawing.
Ida Engel, his art teacher at P.S. 7, sends her student to the High School of Music and Art
("the greatest school of learning since Alexander studied at the feet of Aristotle," Lois has said).

1949   His heroes are Franklin Delano Roosevelt, Joe DiMaggio, "Maestro" Arturo Toscanini, the Romanian sculptor Constantin Brancusi,
the modernist painter Stuart Davis, and the trailblazing designer Paul Rand. Lois graduates, his father expecting
him to devote his life to the family florist. But he enters Pratt Institute in Brooklyn, tuition paid with years of delivery tips.
He meets Rosemary Lewandowski and it's love at first sight.

1951   Herschel Levit, Lois' design teacher in his second year at Pratt, tells him he is too advanced for what Pratt
could offer, and sends him to Reba Sochis, the owner of a stylish design studio, where he becomes her protégé.

1951   Underage, and without the consent of his parents, George and Rosie elope.

1952   Lois' career is interrupted by Army service in the Korean War.

1953   Newly returned from Korea, mentor Lou Dorfsman sends him to Bill Golden at CBS Television.
He is a multi-award winner at The Art Directors Club and AIGA award shows.

1955   Lois leaves CBS to enter the roughhouse world of advertising with the Lennen & Newell ad agency.
His career there is brief and explosive.

1956   He escapes to Sudler & Hennessey, working alongside the supremely talented Herb Lubalin, winning dozens of design awards.

1958   Intervening once again, Lou Dorfsman sends Lois to Bill Bernbach and Bob Gage at
Doyle Dane Bernbach ("the only creative agency in the world"). He becomes a driving force
in the Creative Revolution by winning three gold medals at the New York Art
Directors Club show for his work on Volkswagen, Chemstrand and Goodman's Matzos.

1958   His dream year comes to a climax with the birth of his first son, Harry Joe.

1960   At age 28, George Lois and Julian Koenig leave DDB to found Papert, Koenig, Lois. Lois is the first
art director in history on the masthead of an important ad agency. After a few short months, PKL is referred to as
"the second creative agency in the world."

1962   Lois' first iconic Esquire cover hits the newsstands in October.

1962   Luke George Lois, George and Rosie's second son, is born.

1963   Papert, Koenig, Lois becomes the first publicly held ad agency in history.

1963   Lois is named Art Director of the Year by the prestigious New York Art Directors Club.

1965   "Go home to Greece, where it all began." George takes Rosie and his father home to Kastania,
high in the mountains of Greece, where his "Papa" had grown up as a shepherd boy, playing his flute
among the cypress trees, dreaming of new horizons in America.

1967   The restive Lois leaves PKL to start all over again. Papert, Koenig, Lois, he feels, had grown too fat and comfortable
for his taste, and becoming a public corporation had altered the soul of his agency.
With new partners Ron Holland and Jim Callaway, Lois, Holland, Callaway soon repeats the rapid success of PKL.

1967   Rosemary (Lewandowski-Lois), has her first one-woman show, with a glowing review from *The New York Times*.

1971   Elected President of the New York Art Directors Club, Lois founds the Art Directors Hall of Fame
lifetime achievement award in advertising and design creativity.

1972   The publication of Lois' first book, *George, Be Careful*, receives rave reviews. *The New York Times* says,
"George Lois may be nearly as great a genius of mass communications as he acclaims himself to be."

1974	*The Seven Year Itch*, a retrospective show at New York's TGI Gallery, exhibiting seven years of the work at Lois, Holland, Callaway, packs 'em in.
1975	Lois initiates a passionate battle to exonerate Rubin Hurricane Carter. He draws bolts of criticism from the conservative press, the advertising press, and finally, some important clients. (Undaunted, he is vindicated in 1988 when Carter is freed by the United States Supreme Court.)
1976	His book, *The Art of Advertising,* is published by Harry N. Abrams, Inc.
1977	Lois stuns Madison Avenue–again. He quits LHC to become president of an industrial/corporate agency, Creamer FSR. During a whirlwind 15 months the obscure agency (with the name changed to Creamer, Lois) becomes one of the hottest creative agencies in America.
1978	Citing a profound dispute over business practices, Lois departs Creamer. He starts a fourth agency to bear his name, Lois, Pitts, Gershon. His great friend, marketing pro Bill Pitts, and media guru Dick Gershon become his partners. Once again Lois' agency is instantly successful, remaining intact (eventually called Lois/USA) until his "retirement" in 1999.
1978	The sudden, tragic death of his beloved, gifted 20-year-old son, Harry, mourned forever by the Lois family.
1978	Lois becomes the youngest inductee in the Art Directors Hall of Fame. His friend Senator Bill Bradley makes the emotional presentation, soon after the death of George's son.
1982	Lois receives an honorary Doctor of Fine Arts degree from Pratt Institute for his "trend-setting career in the advertising business," giving an inspirational keynote address, the first by an advertising art director in Pratt's history.
1984	The One Club adds art directors to their "Copywriters Hall of Fame." The newly named "Creative Hall of Fame" inducts George Lois as one of their first art directors.
1985	A two-man retrospective, *Paul Rand and George Lois, The Great Communicators,* inaugurates the new Pratt Institute Gallery, to honor its "two most illustrious alumni."
1987	Another Lewandowski-Lois retrospective.
1989	George and Rosie's first grandson, George Harry Lois, is born to Luke and Diane Lois.
1990	*The Wall Street Journal* names the 10 Best Marketing/Advertising breakthrough successes of the previous decade. Three out of 10 are from the Lois agency (MTV, Jiffy Lube and Tommy Hilfiger).
1991	His third book, *What's the Big Idea?,* becomes a primer for advertising and marketing schools throughout the world.
1992	A second grandson, Alexander Luke Lois, is born.
1993	*Art & Antiques* magazine names Rosemary & George Lois one of America's Top Art Collectors for the eighth year in a row.
1994	Lois receives the coveted SVA (School of Visual Arts) Master Series lifetime achievement award, and is the subject of a comprehensive lifetime retrospective exhibit.
1995	*The Wall Street Journal* honors George Lois as a "Creative Leader."
1995	With the retirement of partners Bill Pitts and Dick Gershon, one-time client Ted Veru becomes a partner. Veru's vision of national expansion brings great growth to Lois/USA, with agencies in Chicago, LA and Houston.
1996	*Covering the '60s, The Esquire Era,* is published.
1996	The American Institute of Graphic Arts (AIGA) awards Lois their lifetime achievement Special Medal Award for being "the century's most accomplished progenitor of Big Idea advertising."
1998	The Hellenic Medical Society presents Lois the Distinguished Helene Award, calling him "The Golden Greek of Advertising." George observes, "Golden Greek is redundant."
1999	*Advertising Age* names Lois "one of the most important men of advertising in the Twentieth Century."
2000	Lois begins a new career as an entrepreneur, creating new business concepts and products for the marketplace.
2001	George and Rosemary celebrate their 50th wedding anniversary, more in love than ever.

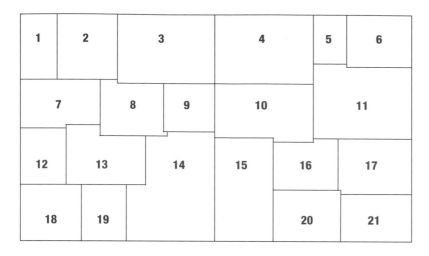

1. MAMA VASILIKE THANASOULIS LOIS (1925)
2. JOE NAMATH, ROSEMARY LOIS, MICKEY MANTLE (1972)
3. FRED PAPERT, JULIAN KOENIG, GEORGE LOIS (PKL,1962)
4. GEORGE LOIS, RON HOLLAND, JIM CALLAWAY (LHC,1970)
5. GEORGE LOIS (DDB, 1959)
6. SUSAN ANTON, GEORGE LOIS, MARVIN HAGLER (1975)
7. STEVE BERKENFELD, GEORGE, LUKE AND HARRY LOIS (N.Y. KNICKS GAME, 1971)
8. GEORGE LOIS, US 51161237 (R & R IN TOKYO,1952)
9. ROSEMARY LEWANDOWSKI LOIS (1966)
10. BILL BRADLEY (ROASTING LOIS AT THE U.N.,1974)
11. ROSIE AND GEORGE LOIS (CELEBRATING NIXON RESIGNATION,1974)
12. GEORGE LOIS (LHC,1972)
13. MALCOLM BRICKLIN, JIM CALLAWAY, GEORGE LOIS, PAUL NEWMAN (1973 BRICKLIN AUTO LAUNCH)
14. GEORGE LOIS (AT LOIS, PITTS, GERSHON,1982)
15. PAPA HARALAMPOS LOIS (GREEK EVZONE,1918)
16. GEORGE LOIS, DON KING (1992)
17. ROSIE AND GEORGE LOIS (WEDDING DAY,1951)
18. LUKE LOIS, MUHAMMAD ALI, HARRY LOIS (1975)
19. SID CAESAR, GEORGE LOIS (1966)
20. ALEXANDER LOIS, LUKE LOIS, GEORGE LOIS (1992)
21. TOM COURTOS, DENNIS MAZZELLA, GEORGE LOIS, KURT WEIHS (LOIS/USA,1990)

IN THIS PRAGMATIC AND COMMERCIAL WORLD, WHERE MONEY TALKS AND BULLSHIT WALKS,
I'VE ALWAYS DEPENDED ON CLIENTS WHO TRULY DIG WHAT I'M DOING AND SHOW THEIR BELIEF—
BY NOT MESSING WITH THE BIG IDEA.

EXTRAVAGANT APPRECIATION TO A CONSTELLATION OF $ELLEBRITIES WHO WILLINGLY (OR UNWILLINGLY)
WERE MNEMONIC IMAGES IN MY WORK: ED SULLIVAN FOR WIGGING OUT, WARHOL FOR SPOILING THE SOUP,
ALI FOR POSING AS AN INFIDEL CHRISTIAN, ZSA ZSA FOR GOING HOME TO GREECE, THE MICK
FOR BAWLING ON TV, GOVERNOR ANN RICHARDS FOR FLASHING HER LEGS, JOE LOUIS FOR DRAGGING
SONNY LISTON AWAY FROM THE CRAP TABLES. CHICAGO MAYOR JANE BYRNE FOR SINGING (BADLY),
AND TOMMY HILFIGER AND PAULINE TRIGÈRE FOR NOT CHICKENING OUT. FOR THOSE WHO TURNED ME
DOWN, I FORGIVE YOU. YOU WERE PROBABLY RIGHT. (BUT LOOK AT ALL THE FUN YOU MISSED.)

THE PASSION, TALENT AND TECHNIQUES OF GREAT PHOTOGRAPHERS ARE ESSENTIAL TO NAILING DOWN
MY IDEAS, CLEARLY, SIMPLY, AND POWERFULLY. MY LOVE, THANKS AND GRATITUDE TO ALL OF THEM.
THE FOUR I HAVE JOYOUSLY WORKED WITH OVER THE YEARS HAVE BEEN CARL FISCHER, TIMOTHY GALFAS,
THE LATE TOM WEIHS, AND LUKE LOIS. AND MY GUNG-HO SON LUKE DOUBLES AS A PLUPERFECT
COMPUTER ARTIST, WHO DESIGNED THIS BOOK WITH ME, PAGE BY PAGE, AT HIS NEW YORK ATELIER,
GOOD KARMA CREATIVE.

MY LAST WORD ON CELEBRITY.

To promote the sports section of the newly published USA Today,
I produced dozens of ads, each with a wacky, ribald or
poignant quote from assorted athletes and sports aficionados.
Toots Shor, once a speakeasy bouncer, was a garrulous, big-mouth
proprietor of a nationally famous saloon on West 51st Street.
Jocks, Broadway stars, Hollywood ingenues, crumb-bums, guys and dolls,
and gaping tourists went there to rub elbows with the rich and famous.
Mel Ott was a slugging New York Giant (a 16-year-old Boy Wonder in 1925)
unfortunately known for cheapo 260-foot pop-fly home runs
that dropped into the short right-field cheap seats at the Polo Grounds.
This ad was a satirical commentary on the absurd perception
of the relative accomplishments of celebrities in our star-struck culture.
Not happy with my ad, Toots phoned me and called me a bum
(which I contend was a bum rap).

TOOTS SHOR
TO SIR ALEXANDER FLEMING,
THE DISCOVERER OF PENICILLIN,
AS HE SAW MEL OTT
COMING THROUGH THE DOOR
OF HIS RESTAURANT:

"Excuse me—somebody important just came in."

INDEX

TO ROSIE & LUKE

Phaidon Press Limited
Regent's Wharf
All Saints Street
London N1 9PA

Phaidon Press, Inc.
180 Varick Street
New York, NY 10014

www.phaidon.com

First published 2003
© 2003 Phaidon Press Limited

ISBN 0 7148 4284 2

A CIP catalogue record for this book is available from the British Library.

Designed by George Lois & Luke Lois
Printed in China

All photographs and illustrations in this publication are courtesy George Lois.